COUNTERCULTURE KALEIDOSCOPE

COUNTERCULTURE KALEIDOSCOPE

Musical
and Cultural
Perspectives on Late Sixties
San Francisco

Nadya Zimmerman

THE UNIVERSITY OF MICHIGAN PRESS   Ann Arbor

Copyright © by the University of Michigan 2008
All rights reserved
Published in the United States of America by
The University of Michigan Press
Manufactured in the United States of America
⊚ Printed on acid-free paper

2011   2010   2009   2008·   4   3   2   1

A CIP catalog record for this book is available from the British Library.

Library of Congress Cataloging-in-Publication Data

Zimmerman, Nadya, 1973–
     Counterculture kaleidoscope : musical and cultural perspectives on
late sixties San Francisco / by Nadya Zimmerman.
        p.   cm.
     Includes bibliographical references and index.
     ISBN-13: 978-0-472-11558-7 (cloth : alk. paper)
     ISBN-10: 0-472-11558-8 (cloth : alk. paper)
        1. Haight-Ashbury (San Francisco, Calif.)—Social life and
customs—20th century.   2. San Francisco (Calif.)—Social life and
customs—20th century.   3. Haight-Ashbury (San Francisco, Calif.)—
Intellectual life—20th century.   4. San Francisco (Calif.)—
Intellectual life—20th century.   5. Counterculture—California—San
Francisco—History—20th century.   6. Rock music—California—San
Francisco—History and criticism.   7. Rock musicians—California—
San Francisco—History—20th century.   8. Youth—California—San
Francisco—Social life and customs—20th century.   9. Social change—
California—San Francisco—History—20th century.   I. Title.

F869.S36H357   2008
979.4'61054—dc22   2007045197

Jacket photo and frontispiece: "1967 Bus and People at Be-In,"
© Lisa Law 1967.

For my mother, Louise

Contents

Chapter One

Refusing to Play, Pluralism, and Anything Goes

Defining the Counterculture

In the American popular imagination, the sixties are remembered as a time of widespread political upheaval and social unrest, fueled by both fervency and idealism. The torchbearer of these mythologized sixties was an emergent youth culture, actively rebelling against fifties social norms that had seeped into every corner of human activity. Indeed, there were major progressive movements in the sixties, and many of them politically driven and goal-oriented. Martin Luther King Jr., the best-known leader of the civil rights movement of the fifties and sixties, spoke repeatedly about the movement's goal—"justice and equality" for people of all races and creeds—while guiding campaigns throughout the country to end racist practices in everything from voter registration to interstate bus travel.[1] Similarly, supporters of the antiwar movement of the late sixties and early seventies participated in protests, marches, and acts of civil disobedience specifically aimed at ending the war in Vietnam. Leaders like Tom Hayden (author of the Port Huron Statement) of Students for a Democratic Society (SDS) helped to rally thousands of youth, encouraging their participation in politics and eliciting their support for core democratic causes such as freedom of speech.

In retrospect, it is possible to outline the putative goals of key political causes like the free speech movement, the antiwar movement, or the civil rights movement, ask what each accomplished, and assess degrees of success or failure. Yet however politically savvy and directly involved in sociopolitical movements many young people were at the time, it is a romanticized myth (encouraged by both liberal and conservative histories) that *everyone* during the sixties was actively seeking to change the world. Equally mythical is the idea that *everything* during the era was driven by oppositional forces.

The work of renowned historian Todd Gitlin reflects a common thread in much politically liberal sixties scholarship, implying that the era as a whole was defined by laudable attempts at progressive social change in the face of a dominant, oppressive system.[2] Many American historians—Howard Zinn, Doug Rossinow, Gerald Howard, David Halberstam, to name a few—share Gitlin's historical and political perspective. They considered the sixties to be a formative time in their own lives and history, and they converse, at times nostalgically, about the sixties in relation to the current sociopolitical climate.[3] As parallels emerge between the Vietnam War and America's current war on and occupation of Iraq, nostalgia leads to liberal laments over our current corporate society, which is compared invidiously to a conscientious sixties that triumphed over social oppression and moral repression.

Not surprisingly, conservative interpretations of the sixties provide fuel for contrasting polemical fires. Among the era's prominent critics on the right is columnist George Will, whose diatribes against the evils of "hippie radicalism" echo the sentiments of former Speaker of the House Newt Gingrich, who, in 1994, argued in front of Congress that sixties' radicals were "taught self-indulgent, aristocratic values" that catered to "the indulgences of an elite few." By crafting an image of the sixties as maniacally radical, and then using the image to denounce current liberal policy and policymakers, Gingrich attempted, among other things, to discredit President Bill Clinton by associating him with the sixties "counterculture."[4]

Often lost in this mythologizing of the sixties is the decade's complexity. Like any other, it was populated by varied, heterogeneous groups, many of whom had nothing to do with one another, even within the smaller circles of the budding youth culture. Specifically, as this book will show, many elements of what we now refer to as the sixties "counterculture" have had ascribed to them political and social platforms that they never embraced. Unlike the civil rights movement, for example, large portions of the "counterculture" were far from being an organized sociopolitical community: they were not oppositional in orientation, not bound by specific agendas, and not determined to bring about major changes in the system.[5] In fact, many parts of this sixties "counterculture" were not, as the name implies, *counter* to anything. Yet these very parts often assume the largest share in our collective memory of the "counterculture" because they spawned the defining cultural products—the music and the lifestyle—that came to be associated with an entire era. It is with this part of the sixties counterculture that this book is concerned—in particular with the geographical hub in the Haight-Ashbury district of San Francisco. In the chapters that follow, I will seek to untangle this segment of the counterculture from the historical myth that has grown up around it, distinguishing it and its members from the political actors and agents of change, the goal-oriented movements and utopian communities that set out to remake the world around an image of peace and love— or at the very least are so credited.

In his seminal 1969 work *The Making of a Counter Culture*, social critic and historian Theodore Roszak defined counterculture as "a culture so radically disaffiliated from the mainstream assumptions of our society that it scarcely looks to many as a culture at all, but takes on the alarming appearance of a barbaric intrusion."[6] As if wary of giving the counterculture no tangible shape at all, Roszak went on to argue that the counterculture could be perceived as a loose grouping of those disaffiliated, in any number of ways, with mainstream society. This attempt to give the counterculture a defined shape has proven problematic in historical interpretations. And although the understanding of counterculture developed throughout this book doesn't directly oppose Roszak's definition, it does differ from it in several ways.

The first main difference is a matter of focus. Following Roszak's notion of a loose grouping, history has made it easy for the sixties counterculture to be associated with different antimainstream and antiestablishment threads in various geographical locations, from the 1968 Paris demonstrations and general strike, to Abbie Hoffman and Paul Krassner's political Youth International Party of Yippies, to the anti–Vietnam War efforts organized by the Students for a Democratic Society, to the so-called hippie lifestyle in San Francisco. Rather than systematically assigning the counterculture label to specific antiestablishment groups, activities, and locations (a task that has already been performed by many historians), this book investigates the development and disintegration of the countercultural sensibility in San Francisco's Haight-Ashbury district. Focusing on the music, participants, culture, and aesthetics of the late sixties in a specific geographical location and referring to these phenomena collectively as "the counterculture" is not to imply that "the counterculture" or elements that might be deemed "countercultural activity" in areas other than the geographical center of San Francisco's Haight-Ashbury district were inauthentic. Rather, because the burgeoning counterculture of the Haight in late 1965 to 1967 was a nucleus of the countercultural sensibility, it is used here as scaffolding for a study of how the countercultural sensibility coalesced and then became distorted, commercialized, and corrupted as it spread out by the end of the decade.

The second main difference is in what cultural evidence will be examined and how it will be analyzed. The sounds and lyrics of the San Francisco counterculture's music (along with other markers of the era) have been left to rot on oldies radio stations as relics of a long-gone liberalism or been disfigured to serve a conservative political agenda. But this book argues that an entirely different set of stories can be heard in those sounds and cultural symbols. The music of San Francisco bands such as the Grateful Dead, Big Brother and the Holding Company, the Charlatans, Country Joe and the Fish, and Jefferson Airplane reveals that the countercultural sensibility was pluralistic, not oppositional; it embodied an anything-goes mind-set, not an antiestablishment stance; it attracted people who sought, on the whole, to disengage from mainstream society, not to transform it. The countercultural phenomenon in the Haight-Ashbury district rapidly deteriorated in 1967 and was appropriated by other cultural and social forces by the end of the decade. This book will develop and give detail to the growth of the San Francisco counterculture, examine how it perceived itself in relation to the "outside" world and what tools it used to define itself, trace the evidence and reasons for the counterculture's deterioration, and show that it was only after the 1967 Summer of Love that history began to define the premises of the countercultural sensibility not as tools of disengagement but as tools of protest, not pluralistic opportunities but agendas to be followed. This book investigates what happened inside the Haight and out, in its music and its incubating culture, to enable this transformation of the meaning of counterculture in history.

One possibility for the transformation is that when a central tenet of the countercultural sensibility—to live without conventional social restrictions—was advertised and popularized across the nation in psychedelic music, it was quickly misinterpreted as a means to protest mainstream repressive values through indulgence. Another possibility is that the countercultural sensibility was co-opted wholesale by mainstream consumer culture and sold back to the public as an antiestablishment ideology. Both of these accounts bear some truth; as we will discover, the nondialectical aspect of the countercultural sensibility was seething with potential for distortion, exploitation, and violence from the very beginning. The San Francisco counterculture in the Haight-Ashbury district collapsed by the end of the decade because, in part, it falsely believed that it could drop out of the system when, in reality, it relied on and mirrored aspects of the system to sustain itself. The countercultural sensibility, so neatly encapsulated in the lyrics and melodies and riffs of the San Francisco sound, became an ethos of rebellion when it spread on the airwaves to the rest of the country.

The remainder of this chapter and the chapters to come present studies of the San Francisco counterculture, using musical and cultural analysis to offer a new approach to understanding the countercultural sensibility as pluralistic rather than oppositional. The intertwining facets and faces of four prominent countercultural identities or personas will be examined—the outlaw, exotic, natural, and new age—while building a picture of the cultural cocoon of the counterculture in the Haight-Ashbury district and moving toward an understanding of the evolution (or devolution) of the San Francisco counterculture as a whole by the end of the decade. Ultimately, the book's aim is twofold: first, to understand what placing value on pluralism implies about the role of the countercultural sensibility in the American imagination and, second, to develop a detailed portrait of the sociocultural complexities of late sixties America that can be used to address comparable complexities in our own time.

To introduce some of the themes, personas, and features of the countercultural lifestyle and sensibility that will be examined throughout this book, let's consider the details of a major cultural event, called the Human Be-In, which occurred on January 14, 1967, in San Francisco's Golden Gate Park near the Haight-Ashbury district. The estimated twenty-five thousand people in attendance spent an extended afternoon listening to readings by Beat poets, speeches by countercultural "celebrities," and performances by several local rock bands, including the Grateful Dead, Country Joe and the Fish, and Jefferson Airplane. The phrase *human be-in* plays on the notion of "human being," a concept that resembled the impetus behind other "in" events of the era. Like a sit in, love-in, bed-in (or even laugh-in), organizers asked participants to *be in*, to be present in the moment, to be involved, to be individual now. But unlike other "in" events associated with particular actions or agendas, the Be-In asked its participants to simply *be*. This notion was reinforced by countercultural figures in attendance. Richard Alpert (known as Ram Dass by 1969) would soon articulate his "Be here now" philosophy. And it was here that one of the best-known figures on the outdoor Be-In stage, Timothy Leary—who was on his first trip to California—uttered his now-famous mantra—"Tune in, turn on, drop out."

Even more loosely defined than the aim, or goalless goal, of the Be-In was the audience at which the event was aimed: the poster announcing the Be-In casts a wide net, incorporating a motley array of images and symbols, from the banner announcing the event as "POW-WOW: A Gathering of the Tribes," to a four-fingered claw grasping two lightning bolts, to a central image of a Native American man on a horse, to a list of iconic names written in flared script. Cultural theorist Philip Deloria has argued that representations of and allusions to

"Indians," particularly ones as obvious as those connected to the Be-In, are often means by which white Americans "have their cake and eat it too." "Indians" signal spiritual and environmental purity. They are "antimodern primitives" yet also "fundamentally American."[7] So, for a predominantly white counterculture, Native Americana could easily represent a distinctly nonmainstream, nonmodern ideal of original wisdom carried by other cultures. To adopt symbols of those Others was to assimilate the Others' wisdom into the modern world, lending character and depth to the counterculture. Absent from the poster are any images of high-rise buildings or Ford Thunderbirds, names of government leaders or war heroes, or representations of official society. No one image reveals, in itself, who is and isn't countercultural, yet taken together, they lay claim to a shared sense of nonconformity.

The counterculture represented by the Be-In appears free of the trappings of mainstream daily existence. Yet at the same time, the counterculture managed to remain contiguous with age-old traditions. This quality of simultaneous disengagement and historical continuity shows itself strongly in the music of the counterculture period, as it did, for example, in the equally groundbreaking work of literary artists in the early twentieth century. We can look at how this quality has been theorized before with respect to James Joyce's landmark novel *Ulysses*.[8] Literary theorist Franco Moretti argues that the main character of *Ulysses*, Leopold Bloom, is restricted from traditional character development because he is confined to the flow of his inner stream of consciousness. At the same time, however, he is bestowed with openness and variety such that whatever memory, thought, or emotion his imagination can touch is available to his interior world. Because of Bloom's ability, *Ulysses*, as a whole, accumulates the old in the present, becoming a stylistic melting-pot of techniques, forms, and historical references. In a sense, then, *Ulysses* is like Bloom's Be-In: instead of a goal toward which the novel is directed, there is just an intense presence in the moment. As Moretti explains, Bloom's character does not, in fact "produce anything in the strict sense," but allows for, instead, "an innocent passivity: one that sees the wealth of the Western metropolis as a *given*, for which it bears no responsibility."[9]

Moretti's notion of abundant pluralism without responsibility, everything available without allegiance to any one thing, is one that also helps describe and make vivid the sensibility manifested by the various strands of the countercultural lifestyle. It becomes clear from the sundry facets of the outlaw persona examined in chapter 2, for example, that the counterculture was more interested in detachment from, rather than reform of or revolt against, the mainstream system and its values.[10] In its indirect address to social struggles for equal rights by the residents of the Haight's neighboring black Fillmore district, its indiscriminate use of racially charged musical styles to craft its own appearance of self-sufficiency, and its cunning exploitation of social referents (such as the Black Panthers and Hell's Angels), the counterculture crafted its outlaw individualism out of detachment from any one cause or style.

On the Be-In poster, detachment from, rather than opposition to, the mainstream system is apparent in the way music is represented. In the hands of the poster's central figure, the Native American rider, is an unplugged electric guitar. At first glance, the combination of images seems contradictory, the instrument exemplifying the progressive drive of modern technology, the seeming antithesis of Native American spirituality and naturalness and environmentalism. Yet the guitar is "unplugged" and drawn into the Native American fold so that the electric guitar-centered music—the very music that was heard all day in San Francisco's Golden Gate Park on January 14, 1967—is authenticated as the conveyor of past cultural significance. Close examination of the natural persona in chapter 4 reveals similar paradoxes, exploring the ways in which the counterculture not only failed to exorcise the modern world of technology and materialism but, rather, deliberately naturalized it. Indeed, modern technology was crucial to creating the San Francisco counterculture's unique sound and atmosphere. The musical and cultural details of work by the Grateful Dead show the complications of crafting a unique, free, nonmainstream, and noncommercial countercultural identity reliant on commercial and cutting-edge musical technology.

Over and over again, the counterculture celebrates its distance from modernity, while simultaneously enjoying its

benefits.[11] To achieve this distance, we see in the counterculture a repeated ethic of disassociation from people, actions,
and value systems perceived as mainstream. For example, the
staff at the *San Francisco Oracle*—the de facto newspaper of the
Haight-Ashbury culture from September 1966 through January
1968—claimed no overt political program for itself, but, as its
editor Allen Cohen recalls, found a safe retreat in the Haight-
Ashbury district and scorned "the powers that ruled the world
[that] were decadent, corrupt, and calcified."[12] In chapter 3's
examination of the exotic persona, we discover how pervasive
this disassociation was and how intensely the counterculture
attempted to distance itself, in particular, from the dominant
American sociopolitical address to the world through capitalism and neocolonialism. From the music of Jefferson Airplane
to the shops lining the streets of the Haight-Ashbury district,
the exploration of the Otherworldly—from exotic sounds of
sitars to hallucinogenic drugs—was one of the counterculture's main means to disassociate from Cold War politics and
a system fueled by violence, war, and hatred. The more the
mainstream grew to fear Otherness, the more the counterculture embraced it. While technocratic society relied on rationality, scientific forms of knowledge, and technological innovation—including heinous weapons of mass destruction like
napalm and radar-guided missiles—to generate an atomized
society, the counterculture shrouded itself in adopted forms of
spirituality from esoteric and religious traditions like Chinese
astrology, Zen Buddhism, and Sufism.

Surprisingly, countercultural voices didn't particularly advocate for actively combating or protesting the mainstream
system, with its rigid structures and repressive values. On the
contrary, in a February 1967 dialogue among four countercultural figures—LSD guru Timothy Leary, philosopher Alan
Watts, and Beat poets Alan Ginsberg and Gary Snyder—the
notion of disengagement was grounded in a negation of anything associated with the mainstream, including social ac-

tivism. Watts, for instance, was not dismissed out of hand by the other three participants when he argued that "nobody can be more emotionally bound and intolerant . . . and working on the basis of moral violence" than a "pacifist." Nor did Watts's examples of such morally violent pacifists—Mario Savio and Gandhi—seem to faze the other participants. Leary, instead, chimed in with support, arguing that such moral pacifist violence fuels mass movements and "I want no part of mass movements. I think this is the error that the leftist activists are making."[13]

Certainly, it's not helpful to take these examples as reflective of everything and everyone associated with the counterculture. And, needless to say, there are examples of countercultural participants who did take part in mass protests and countercultural musicians who did write songs openly (or even subtly) opposing the Vietnam War and making other political interventions. Buffalo Springfield's "For What It's Worth" and Country Joe and the Fish's "I Feel Like I'm Fixin' to Die Rag," for example, were two songs popular with the counterculture that raised questions about the war relatively early on in its escalation (1967). What's noteworthy about these examples is that they illustrate trends. Antiwar songs were rare listening fare for the San Francisco counterculture in its formative stages of late 1965 to early 1967. But by the end of 1967, things had begun to change. In May 1968 the Doors' "Unknown Soldier" hit the charts, with Eric Burdon and the Animals' "Sky Pilot" coming out a month later. The following year Credence Clearwater Revival's "Fortunate Son" and Steppenwolf's "Draft Resister" came out. The frequency of antiwar sentiments and songs increased as the decade came to a close and, notably, as the anything-goes sensibility of the counterculture diffused into the larger American culture.

Early on, the shapers of the countercultural sensibility went so far as to discredit those they labeled pacifists because of their link, even as opponents, to mainstream politics, illustrating one of the ways that the countercultural sensibility was about appearing to be outside the system. As journalist Jerry Hopkins, in the April 1967 issue of the underground Haight-Ashbury leaflet *Communication Company,* advised: "Why should we trade one establishment for another establishment? Do your thing. Be what you are. If you don't know what you are, find out. Fuck leaders."[14] Perhaps countercultural participants genuinely aimed to negate association with the mainstream, to exist outside the system. It's not that people associated with the counterculture were unaware of politics or inequalities or unmoved by the horrors of war. But by refusing allegiance to sociopolitical struggles and showing scorn for traditional political activism aimed at institutional reform within the existing system, the counterculture showed that it didn't want to play the game at all. Many perceived that the only way to avoid playing it was to reject the system in its entirety.[15]

Historian Richard King has speculated that the impulse of the counterculture was "to promiscuously create a new religion, out of nothing or out of everything."[16] At first glance, King's statement seems to contradict itself. A religion or ideology or new culture can't be made of nothing or, alternatively, everything. But perhaps there is a more subtle idea to be drawn from his statement, namely, that the counterculture negated its association with any single cultural thread by pursuing pluralism, by adopting everything. In the case of the San Francisco music scene, a key way to develop and promote an image of a unique and detached community distinct from the norm was to embrace multiple and divergent styles and genres. For example, Bill Graham, impresario of the Haight-Ashbury's Fillmore Auditorium, explained: "When we began . . . we could prepare a bill like a well-rounded meal. Along with the rock headliner, we'd put a side order of blues or jazz on the menu— a B. B. King or Roland Kirk or Howlin' Wolf. Or we'd co-bill the Grateful Dead with Miles Davis. It was a righteous thing to do."[17] Popular music critic Martha Bayles lends support to the idea that countercultural music was simultaneously everything and nothing, not minimalist, empty, or ahistorical, but emerging from a countercultural image culled out of disassociation with any one stance. "The counterculture was really rooted in the assumptions . . . that the 'system' was rotten; that happiness within it was illusory; that compromise would yield a living death; and that the only hope lay in negation."[18]

So while it could be argued that countercultural participants who listened to psychedelic rock music, smoked pot, dropped acid, read non-Western spiritual texts, and had multipartner sexual relationships thought that mainstream society was their enemy and that they were fighting against repression, it could prove more useful to see such formulations as examples of the multiple ways that history has wrongly forced the all-embracing, anything-goes countercultural sensibility into an oppositional mold. The countercultural notion of "rejecting" the system has been morphed into narratives of "resistance" and "revolt" such that history asks, "What did the counterculture accomplish?" and then assesses its success or failure.[19] But let's consider a different set of possibilities—that the countercultural sensibility wasn't about changing the world. It was more concerned with negation than opposition, with the moment than with future goals, with disassociation than with alignment or allegiance to sociopolitical causes.

The San Francisco counterculture discovered LSD, in part, because of its popularization by Timothy Leary. An unwavering advocate for the possibility of spiritual growth through LSD, Leary started his League for Spiritual Discovery in 1966. The League was one of several official, group-oriented, psychedelic/sexual/spiritual endeavors Leary forged in the sixties—including his consciousness-raising workshops in Mexico, replete with LSD, orgies, and East Indian musicians, his quasi-church named International Federation of Internal Freedom, the thirty-member Castalia Foundation at Millbrook (funded by millionaire stockbroker William Hitchcock), and his journal, *Psychedelic Review.* Leary proselytized to youthful audiences, trying to secure their participation in his League and convince them to adopt his life mission. Leary was not the only countercultural figure to fixate on a pluralistic interwoven matrix of drugs, rock music, spiritualism, and sex. Chapter 5 examines how the intersection of sex and unacknowledged sexism, spirituality and non-Western philosophies, dropping out and dropping acid, and unexamined gender roles developed in Haight-Ashbury and why its promise of pleasure in the *now* over the prospect of delayed gratification was a signal of the counterculture's impending disintegration. What is seldom mentioned about the matrix of elements in this new-age countercultural identity, and almost never examined, is that the decaying undertow was present in the counterculture from the beginning. Ultimately, the ways in which the concoction of elements comprising the countercultural sensibility played out were never as innocent as history often makes them out to be.

One of the most telling illustrations of the visible and hidden qualities of the countercultural lifestyle and sensibility is in the dynamics of the first Monterey Pop Festival. A landmark event in sixties history, the festival took place from June 16 to June 18, 1967, and in many ways mimicked the kind of concert-hall shows that were being put on in Haight-Ashbury. Though the festival attracted an estimated fifty thousand people, its setting in the quiet town of Monterey managed to keep much of the mass media away. Several "San Francisco" organizers and promoters arranged the event, and the Haight-Ashbury's own LSD "whiz kid," Augustus Owsley III, handed out hundreds of his special acid tabs, named for the occasion "Monterey Purple." The major San Francisco bands—the Grateful Dead, Jefferson Airplane, Quicksilver Messenger Service, and Big Brother and the Holding Company—were all there. And psychedelic lighting was provided by Jerry Abrams (one of the men who lit up the San Francisco concert halls).

Not everything at the festival, however, was idyllic, unique, and lovingly San Franciscan. The weekend included guitarist Pete Townsend and drummer Keith Moon of the British band the Who smashing their instruments to pieces on stage following, ironically, a performance of "My Generation." Eric Burdon and the Animals, also British, concluded their set with a foreboding performance of the Rolling Stones's "Paint It Black." And, of course, there was Jimi Hendrix—an American expatriate of sorts, returning from London to make a name for himself in his home country. The Jimi Hendrix Experience was the second-to-last act to play at the festival and gave one of the most famous rock performances in history, captured for posterity on D. A. Pennebaker's film *Monterey Pop*. After humping the amplifier, Hendrix finished the last chorus of "Wild Thing" and dropped to his knees. As if performing some kind of obscure religious ritual, he put his guitar on the stage, sprayed lighter fluid on it, kissed it good-bye, and ignited it, throwing its burning shards into the audience.

Along with the unprecedented guitar immolation, Hendrix's highly stylized sexual antics dazzled audiences and critics alike. By playing his guitar between his legs, as if masturbating, and tonguing the neck, as if performing oral sex, Hendrix made crudely explicit a long-standing link between rock and roll and sex. He deliberately manipulated this link by transforming the electric guitar into a high-tech musical/sexual limb. One consequence was that songs like "Purple Haze" came to embody a unique fusion of LSD, the blues, sex, and theatrical display. Reviewing the Monterey Pop Festival, rock critic Robert Christgau harshly dismissed Hendrix as a "psychedelic Uncle Tom," focusing on Hendrix's flamboyant sexual image as a reflection of what his white audience wanted, or expected, rather than as something of his own design. Christgau's presumption was that a black man with an integrated band (drummer Mitch Mitchell and bassist Noel Redding were both white) who appealed almost exclusively to a white audience must embody racist stereotypes of superstud blackness to please the white counterculture. Although Christgau was well enough versed in black musical traditions to realize that many of Hendrix's musical techniques were rooted in the blues, his comments allowed Hendrix no ties to that history. On the contrary, he "proved" his point by describing Hendrix's act "as a consistently vulgar parody of rock theatrics."[20]

It would appear that Christgau, conscious or not, was uncomfortable with Hendrix's image and his popularity with the white countercultural audience. Hendrix wasn't "dignified" like a veteran blues musician. He failed to fit the "noncommercial" image that the San Francisco bands had. And his "vulgar" sexual theatrics were threatening because of their marketability and appeal to the masses. Christgau, and other white critics, seemed compelled to paint a picture of Hendrix as a hypersexual black outsider. But with what objective? With Hendrix as an entertainer of the counterculture rather than one of its representatives, his commercial appeal and aggressive sexual performance at Monterey Pop wouldn't be taken as reflective of the countercultural sensibility. The counterculture might still be preserved in its unique, detached, utopian cocoon. But Christgau was too late. Representatives from the major record labels were scattered throughout the audience and had been courting bands for three days behind the scenes. Jefferson Airplane, Country Joe and the Fish, Big Brother and the Holding Company, and, eventually, the Grateful Dead willingly signed contracts with major record labels. They would soon advertise the countercultural sensibility in sound to the rest of the country, tempting media attention from beyond the borders of the Haight-Ashbury district.

One might be inclined to ask whether the San Francisco counterculture, before Monterey Pop, was successful in its attempt to disengage from the mainstream. But questions of assessment—"Did it work?"—are not the most fruitful for examining the counterculture. This book asks a more nuanced question about the fundamental nature of the relationship between the counterculture and the mainstream, with the hope that from it a new understanding of the types of cultural and social dynamics that have abounded since the sixties can emerge.

Consumer capitalism—the driving force of technocratic culture—relies on reproduction, mass distribution, materialistic desires, and mass consumption, all of which, it would appear on the surface, were anathema to the image of detached uniqueness that the counterculture sought to shape for itself. The following chapters show how the counterculture, whether intentionally or not, revealed signs of—and indeed relied on— the trappings of capitalist consumer culture underneath its ideological and stylistic dismissal of mainstream materialism and values. The counterculture showed affinity for "natural" materials, handmade items, noncommercial ideas, and home-grown music and musicians. Countercultural participants bought silver jewelry, hand-crafted leather sandals, used Levis, Hindu texts, LSD, and tantric yoga sessions. Examined together, these items seem to symbolize a rejection of mainstream American values. The problem is that all these associations didn't put enough distance between the counterculture and the technocratic foundation of its home in the heart of one of the most recognized industrialized cities in the world. The counterculture was engaged in consumerism—buying and selling—the main mode of action in a capitalist system.[21]

A few cultural historians and critics, including Thomas Frank, David Brooks, Joseph Heath, and Andrew Potter, have asked whether there ever was any tension between the countercultural sensibility and the ideological underpinnings of the capitalist system.[22] The first part of their argument is that because "everything"—the mainstream, sociopolitical movements, the counterculture, revolutions—is part of the larger system, "everything" requires buying into the system and dealing in consumer capitalism. The counterculture was one of many social lifestyles and cultural alternatives within the system and, hence, was as invested in capitalism and consumerist values as any other alternative. The second part of their argument is based on the assumption that the counterculture *opposed* or *fought against* or *aimed to change* the prevailing system through cultural rebellion. From these two parts, the authors conclude that because the counterculture wanted to change the system by rebelling against it, it was unsuccessful, its ideology failed, and it changed nothing. Why? Because the counterculture was part of the system from the beginning.

Thomas Frank takes this one step further by arguing that countercultural rebellion posed no threat to the consumer capitalist system in the first place. "The counterculture may be more accurately understood as a stage in the development of values of the American middle-class, a colorful installment in the twentieth century drama of consumer activity."[23] In a bold statement, Frank concludes that the countercultural sensibility was a mirror of the capitalist mentality. As brand-conscious consumers of the products that symbolized their lifestyle, participants in the counterculture sold individuality, newness, and uniqueness much as the Pepsi-Cola Company sold soft drinks.

One of the most popular arguments against a formulation like Frank's is the notion that the counterculture was commercialized by the media and then co-opted by the mainstream. The argument is as follows: If the market absorbed the countercultural sensibility and sold it back to the people, then the onus of responsibility for the failure of the counterculture was not on the counterculture itself. Mass culture always takes over the new and the different, guiding the progress on the path between innovation and passive mass consumption. And when the mainstream co-opted a counterculture that was, at its most basic, about not being mainstream, then the counter-cultural sensibility was forced, through no fault of its own, to be grist for the capitalist mill.

The above arguments miss a crucial point, one that this book examines in detail with particular focus on what the music, the great beacon of this sensibility, reveals. The principal shapers of the San Francisco counterculture in the Haight-Ashbury district in 1966 and 1967 wanted to promote an image of a unique, detached, and free community that was distinct *from* the mainstream, not *against* it. By valuing nonalignment, negation, disassociation, and pluralism, the counterculture appeared, at the time and decades later, to be nonmainstream, natural, color-blind, open-minded, sexually free, and unmediated by commercialism. For Frank and others, the counterculture was unsuccessful either because it was a mirror of middle-class consumer values all along or because it opposed the mainstream and failed to change it. The main thesis of this book is that neither of those reasons is why the counterculture eventually fell apart. The counterculture dissolved because it falsely believed, from the beginning, that it could drop out of system when in reality, it negated association with any one category while simultaneously mirroring various aspects of the capitalist system to sustain itself. The countercultural lifestyle and image needed both the semblance of autonomy and access to the system for its unique image to be realized. Having grasped its vulnerability, the system transformed it into an ethos of antiestablishment dissent that was purportedly opposed to the mainstream. The media, along with daily tour buses and an influx of young teenagers from across the United States, took over the Haight-Ashbury district during the 1967 Summer of Love and people flocked in to get a piece of counterculturalness to make themselves unique. The newly transformed countercultural ethos was cast as a fixed ideology, a way to question authority, an illusion of possessing freedom from conformity, a cultural formula—all transformations heralding the loss of whatever all-embracing vibrancy that might have been present at the beginning.

The chapters ahead throw into question the narrative that sees the psychedelic rock music of the counterculture as proof that "hippies" meant to transform mainstream capitalist society and its institutionalized materialism. They show that the counterculture's literary, philosophical, cultural, and spiritual influences (from Henry Miller to Herbert Marcuse to Aldous Huxley) were as cobbled together, disjointed, and intertwined with mainstream values as the music of Jefferson Airplane and the Grateful Dead. They explore the contrasts of utopian and decaying qualities in the sounds and scenes from the Haight-Ashbury district in late 1965–67 through to the crises of the Manson murders and the Altamont Festival at the end of the decade. And they open up a new route for understanding the reverberations of the countercultural sensibility in history and what that might mean for today.

Chapter Two

The Outlaw Persona

Joplin, Big Brother, and Pluralism in Black and White

From Henry David Thoreau to John Brown, James Dean to Malcolm X, the outlaw-rebel persona has been prominent in America's cultural memory. It played a part in literary movements and western expansion and, for the counterculture, ignited the early flames of its development in the Haight-Ashbury district. A band named the Charlatans, often referred to as the first psychedelic San Francisco band, was one of the first to test the appeal of the outlaw persona. The band had never performed in public before getting its first gig to play the entire summer of 1965 as the quasi house band at the Red Dog Saloon in Virginia City, Nevada. According to historian Alice Echols, the Charlatans had cultivated their Wild-West-outlaw-meets-young-white-rebel look well before they worked on making music or cultivating "their sound." The band members held regular meetings to discuss the group's image, "posing as rockers" with "more publicity pictures than licks."[1]

This odd fact about the value of image to the Charlatans reveals an important clue to understanding the burgeoning San Francisco counterculture. Groups like the Charlatans were vigilant about maintaining their outlaw image. Living together in a large Victorian house in the Fillmore district of San Francisco, all of the band members had been or still were students at San Francisco State University in 1965. When the band finally got the summer gig at the Red Dog Saloon, they quickly put together and rehearsed their playlist, matching their eclectic look of long hair, wide-brim hats, string ties, three-piece suits dating from the 1890s, and guns, with songs like "Wabash Cannonball" that juxtaposed country music twang, clunky dance-hall motives, and R & B rhythms. They glorified the image and lifestyle of Wild West outlaw Americana but didn't snatch their look out of thin air. San Francisco was one of the West's oldest cities, and abundant antique stores allowed for cheap access to its history. In addition, the old Fox Theatre went out of business in 1965 and sold off stacks of costumes, velvety period clothing, and decorations to the growing youth culture.

The Red Dog Saloon was another outpost of outlaw imagery. With a busy highway of music, musicians, coordinators, artists, props, decorations, foodstuffs, supplies, and clothing styles traveling back and forth between the Red Dog Saloon and San Francisco in the summer of 1965, the Red Dog became the prototype for the San Francisco dance halls that would start up in the fall of that year and soon become a fixture of the counterculture. At first glance, the Red Dog Saloon, like the Charlatans, was an almost faultless re-creation of the Wild West—as portrayed in the television series *Gunsmoke,* spaghetti Westerns, and John Wayne movies that the baby boomer generation (counterculture included) had been raised on. The saloon had been in Virginia City for decades, but, over time, had been abandoned and left in shambles. Its transformation in 1965 was a concerted, successful, and miraculous effort. Every detail of the saloon's appearance, as well as the appearance of its guests and employees, was crafted to create the desired ambiance—"hookers" with low-cut sateen and velvet dresses, vigilantes with guns, whiskey and shot glasses, beer barrels, a huge hardwood bar, and a barn-red paint job with white trim.

The details of the saloon were so meticulously attended to that the line between truth and fiction that human beings so often rely on for gauging their sanity became blurred. Real guns, for example, were commonplace in the Red Dog. They were emblems of outlaw Americana, prized for their symbolic significance, but the owners of the saloon also used them as a real form of payment to musicians, bartenders, and staff. Quicksilver Messenger Service, another San Francisco band with a Western look, came to the Red Dog Saloon in the summer of 1965 to be part of the excitement. Quicksilver actually carried pistols and shotguns, not only in the Wild West world of Virginia City that summer, but in San Francisco when they got back home. Next to the guns and live ammo, the huge, muscular, Native American door bouncer was a relatively unthreatening feature of the Red Dog Saloon.

There were certain things at the Red Dog that could never have existed in the Wild West or in the spaghetti Western—bikers with guns, synthetic psychedelic drugs, and a San Franciscan named Bill Ham, along with his light box invention. Ham positioned his light box at the back of the performance area, behind whichever band was playing. The sound-operated machine, with three frequencies and an electric motor, moved amorphous liquid shapes based on the musical tones being played and then projected those shapes onto a screen. Ham had built the box in San Francisco and rushed it to the Red Dog for the grand opening. At the end of the summer in Virginia City, Ham and his light box, along with the Charlatans, Quicksilver Messenger Service, and several Red Dog participant-organizers headed back to San Francisco. With them they carried the ambiance and culture of the Red Dog—a fun-all-the-time place free from the rules of the establishment, a geographical cocoon where people felt that they were able to do anything without restriction. Only months later back in San Francisco, they had created the Family Dog—an organization that would put on dances and party events with liquid light displays and local San Francisco bands. The first show—called "a Tribute to Dr. Strange"—was at Longshoreman's Hall on October 16, 1965, featuring, among others, the Charlatans.[2]

The outlaw persona—shaped, in part, by the Red Dog experience—was integral to the newly developing counterculture in San Francisco, not so much for its *actual* manifestations of aggression, but for its *potential* for disregarding or breaking the law. Famous outlaws like Jesse James and Billy the Kid were certainly violent, but that violence had emerged out of their ability to reject mainstream culture and, at the same time, appear to remain above the law. Countercultural music seethed with this outlaw potential. A blistering Jimi Hendrix guitar solo, an unstructured Grateful Dead jam session, or a glass-shattering Janis Joplin scream were outside musical laws, outside the boundaries of traditional social behavior. At the same time, such musical gestures reveled in the present moment rather than getting caught up in the past. These were the aspects that drew the counterculture. The outlaw figure refused to be told what to do, and a conceptual and occasional real alliance with the outlaw granted the counterculture permission to go its own way, to step out of the rule-bound world of the establishment and instead create an insulated space away from the traditional society of work. For the counterculture, the outlaw persona was particularly and intimately intertwined with race, beginning with its very geographical location.

The outlaw's home was like a country within a country. Like Christiania, which was for thirty-five years a partially autonomous country within the Danish capital of Copenhagen, the Haight-Ashbury district within San Francisco had its own economy and values, where the potential for unfettered freedom and pleasure reigned. The Haight, however, had not always existed as a place of outlaw freedom. In much the same way as the Beats, a generation before, had shaped the North Beach district of San Francisco into their own cultural neighborhood, the counterculture co-opted the southwest portion of the existing Fillmore district and out of it crafted the Haight-Ashbury. The Fillmore had risen to prominence following the 1906 earthquake. With thousands of people displaced, the Fillmore grew with old Victorians-turned-boardinghouses, increased commerce, theaters, and a servant-class Japantown. By the twenties, a mix of low- and middle-income Jewish, Japanese, African American, and Mexican immigrants and workers claimed the Fillmore as home. But with increased immigration came increased political conservatism. The National Origins Act of 1924, directed mainly at people of Japanese and Chinese descent, aimed to curb immigration. And in the early forties Japanese Americans were interned in camps along the West Coast, leaving something of a worker vacuum in the Fillmore district. African American industrial workers flooded to San Francisco for wartime work at the port, becoming, by 1945, the majority group residing in the Fillmore.[3]

Immigrant and minority groups had made their homes in the Fillmore because laws prohibiting ownership and rental to such groups did not apply there. Yet, as urban renewal programs aimed at developing city centers to attract wealthier (usually white) citizens took hold in a conservative, post–World War II America, the status of the Fillmore was repeatedly challenged. Like other government-sponsored organizations across the country, the San Francisco Redevelopment Agency promoted urban renewal at the expense of the poor and racially disenfranchised in the hope of luring wealthier whites back to the city. Throughout the fifties, residents in the predominantly black Fillmore district fought for their housing rights, but by the sixties their struggle was not only with the city government but with a growing group of students and ex-students who saw the Fillmore as a potentially cheap home for a burgeoning youth culture. While the longtime residents of the neighborhood had struggled for years to prevent urban renewal and to keep housing affordable, the youthful, educated, white, middle-class counterculture came in and took advantage of the large Victorian homes at cheap rental rates. And though the counterculture wasn't working for the Redevelopment Agency and would never have openly allied itself with such a mainstream organization, it ended up helping the "cause" of urban renewal by being the first stage in the familiar story of gentrification.

The history of the Majestic Ballroom also encapsulates the changes in the Fillmore's dynamic cultural geography. A large beige brick building at the corner of Fillmore and Geary in the heart of the Fillmore district, the Majestic was built in 1911. In the fifties and early sixties, an African American man named Charles Sullivan leased the ballroom and became one of the best-known promoters of black music. He scheduled big-name R & B acts like Ray Charles and the Temptations and sold a majority of the concert tickets to African American residents from the Fillmore district.

In 1965, Sullivan gave up his lease on what was, by then, the Fillmore Auditorium, to a promoter named Bill Graham. Graham's first concert in the auditorium on December 10, 1965, featured Jefferson Airplane, the Great Society, Mystery Trend, and the Warlocks (soon to become the Grateful Dead). Few African American residents of the Fillmore district showed up for the concert, or for subsequent ones. The only concert promoted by Graham that proved to have strong appeal among African American Fillmore residents was when Otis Redding headlined. This same concert had a significantly reduced number of counterculture members in attendance. But this wasn't so surprising: Graham successfully promoted the Fillmore as a unique new venue for a unique new culture, and it might have undermined that agenda to schedule headlining acts that were too popular or mainstream.[4]

Strangely enough, traditional historical narratives that address San Francisco's counterculture make little mention of the importance of race and racialized elements to the outlaw-rebel persona. The reasons for this omission include both national and local geography. On a national scale, Martin Luther King had led a movement that, though challenging and subtle in its aim to respect the humanity in black and white alike and refrain from a competitive game of "which race is morally superior," at the same time laid bare the racial and economic atrocities at the root of American capitalist society. A movement of this nature made the most impact in the southern part of the United States because of the Jim Crow racism and segregation there. More difficult to confront was the typically northern anonymous, distant, and often hypocritical brand of racism that seethed below the surface. The West, and California in particular, though not as wedded economically to racist policies, was also fluent in hypocrisy—a brand of racism that recoiled at open acknowledgment of any racial tensions.

In terms of local geography, the city of San Francisco lies between the Pacific Ocean to the West and the San Francisco Bay to the East. You can travel north from the city to Marin County (via the Golden Gate Bridge) or south along the coast to Pacifica, Monterey, and further to Big Sur; within an hour's drive were many of the counterculture's more rural, communal getaway spots. Yet even closer than the Grateful Dead's Rancho Olompali in Marin County or Big Nig's roadhouse in the South Bay (the site of Ken Kesey's first Acid Test) was the East Bay. A fifteen-minute drive across the Bay Bridge separated San Francisco from Berkeley and Oakland. Yet despite the geographical proximity of these cities, cultural apartheid appeared to reign throughout the Bay Area in the sixties. Berkeley was home to a mostly white student population focused on free speech activism, racial integration, and, later, antiwar activity. Oakland housed a population of mostly poor and working-class black people and provided the fertile ground out of which the Black Panther Party grew. In the southern part of San Francisco, students and faculty (mainly white) connected with San Francisco State University protested for sexual and civil rights throughout the sixties. And, as discussed earlier, the majority black Fillmore district experienced various grassroots struggles, in particular against the city's systematic attempts to undermine equal housing rights. However, day-to-day life on the commercial streets of the Haight-Ashbury district and on the residential streets of the outlying parts of the Fillmore district, on the whole, lacked interracial interaction.

The main thrust of Bay Area activism up until 1967 was for equal rights in various forms (young and old, black and white, gay and straight), and the counterculture appeared to have little to do with this intensifying landscape. Organized protests for civil rights and racial integration were rarely staged in the Haight-Ashbury district. With the notable exception of African American activist-comedian Dick Gregory, the speakers and performers at the Human Be-In were white. Counterculture participants, for the most part, were neither members of, nor active contributors to, the black power movement. And throughout the late sixties, the headlining acts at the Fillmore Auditorium (and at the Avalon Ballroom—the counterculture's other main musical venue) consisted predominantly of white performers, with a few significant exceptions like Jimi Hendrix, Otis Redding, and Ritchie Havens.

Racial politics required people to pick sides (for example, an active integrationist agenda or a deliberate call for racial exclusivity/separatism), asking for the very commitment and alignment that an outlaw culture, outside of traditional boundaries, would resist association with. To avoid alignment meant avoiding direct engagement with racial issues, and the counterculture's mode of avoidance was pluralism. The counterculture made everything equally available in the now, detaching itself from any single goal-oriented agenda, and, most importantly, detaching itself from the mainstream. Racialized elements were thrown in the pluralistic mix of signifiers that underscored the counterculture's cultural landscape, allowing the counterculture to deal *implicitly* and indirectly with racial politics without being pinned to a particular cause or *explicit* racial agenda. So while the thrust of Bay Area activism and participatory politics appeared, on the whole, to be integrationist, the counterculture seemed more interested in distance. It crafted its own bohemia in the run-down Victorians and dirty streets of the Haight-Ashbury, isolated in the belly of San Francisco, surrounded by the longtime black Fillmore residents. Historians Peter Braunstein and Michael William Doyle depict this counterculture as one that deliberately "fashioned" a "hippie fantasy ghetto."[5] Though the term "fantasy" may place too much value on the assessment of legitimacy—who is "truly" down and out and who is merely pretending—Braunstein and Doyle's depiction helps open up a new perspective on the counterculture. Legitimacy aside, the counterculture conceived of itself as a risk-taking outlaw culture, and it shaped that self-image by trading upon symbols of racially charged "outlaw" cultures in the Bay Area—namely, the Black Panthers and the Hell's Angels.

In the late sixties, Huey Newton and Bobby Seale organized the Black Panther Party for Self Defense and Justice in Oakland. There, the black population was policed by a white force, something Newton likened to an occupying army in a foreign land. The party encouraged black Oakland residents to take up arms and police the police. So with guns, raised fists (at the 1968 Mexico City Olympics, for example), and eloquent orators calling for revolution, the Panthers advertised their movement for black solidarity. Drawing on such thinkers as Karl Marx and Frantz Fanon, the Panthers ideologically sought to organize the downtrodden black man on the street into an independent and powerful voice.[6] Initially Seale and Newton conceived of the Panthers as an organization that would be local and community-oriented, concerned with, as their name stated, self-defense. And though party chapters sprung up around the country and the organization became national, their initial conception of local and communal efforts remained. What is seldom noted, however, is that the number of members was noticeably low. Relatively speaking, few African Americans heeded the Panthers' call for racial separation and community isolation. Yet counterculture members took up the call like newly converted religious zealots.

The standard radicalizing narrative of the sixties claims that people across America saw the 1965 Watts riots and 1967 Detroit riots as extensions of the civil rights movement. African American people, following Martin Luther King, had exhausted all avenues of nonviolent protest, and significant change wasn't forthcoming. So then, as the story goes, they turned to people like Bobby Seale and Stokely Carmichael (who himself had undergone a similar transition), protesting violently to illustrate their outrage at poverty and discrimination. While this interpretation of the sixties, as social historian Michael Eric Dyson points out, has been canonized across the political spectrum in history textbooks, ultraconservative radio talk shows, New Left histories, and mainstream newspapers, the problem is that the riots never did correspond with a shift among African American people toward black nationalism. Dyson remarks that the stances adopted by Bobby Seale, Huey Newton, and even an early Malcolm X *always* appealed more to white counterculturalists and white political radicals than to black people. "Always" is strong language, but one reason that whites were more drawn to black nationalism was that they had more leeway to experiment with their lives. America had consistently provided a safety net of privilege, however minimal, for white people, whereas black people who experimented were gambling with their survival.[7] Some white cultures felt drawn to the black power rhetoric and agenda because it spoke to the separatism and potential for being outside the law that they too wanted. Someone like Eldridge

Cleaver was the perfect outlaw role model for the counterculture. In the early sixties he was a heavy pot smoker who had also been an editor at the hip leftist magazine *Ramparts* before helping to found the Panthers. As the Panthers' minister of information in 1966–67, Cleaver was outspoken, drawing on the cachet of his early years in prison. His reputation for being above the law became more and more exaggerated when he was caught in a shootout with Oakland police, jumped bail, fled to Algeria, and lived in exile there and in Paris until his return in 1975.

The Black Panthers' militancy and drama appealed to the counterculture and so did the party's separatist mentality and masculinist metaphors, images, and symbols of liberation. While Martin Luther King argued that a person's internal and external conditions could not change if he responded to his oppressor with identical tones of hatred, the Black Panthers called for matching violence with violence and insult with insult in a bid for people to claim power after having been denied it, to define themselves after having been molded by others. Here the counterculture felt a resonance: they also perceived themselves as throwing off the shackles of others who had defined them—in their case, the fifties parental generation. But because countercultural groups, for the most part, did not directly participate in black power groups, they found a unique way of positioning themselves with respect to the concept of black power. The anonymous Haight-Ashbury theatrical and social activist group called the Diggers, for example, included a full-page poster-style collage tribute to the Black Panthers in their free pamphlet, along with a proclamation of the counterculture's allegiance, not to the Panthers themselves, but to the Panthers' "outlaw" philosophy. "What's necessary is active imagination, active Black Power, Digger Autonomy—active manifestation of the understanding, manifestation, active things, not sitting around on your ass."[8] And in one of many manifestos from the late sixties that invoked the model of black power, counterculture participant Joseph Berke suggested ways of living outside of traditionally responsible parameters. In *Counter Culture* Berke argued that the only way to face the "monolith" of "mainstream conformist normative America" was to engage in activities that neither relied on nor participated in the official system.

> Survival is at stake . . . all the developments we describe are part of a convulsive disassociation of people from contemporary society. . . . This is what is to be done. . . . Subvert the social-economic-political roles prescribed by advanced bourgeois society for itself . . . this work has already begun. . . . It is rooted in innumerable projects of social erosion and practical self-survival which are decentralized, heterogeneous, self-supporting, and non-participatory in the parent system . . . it is exemplified by the rapidly emerging political consciousness of the black people in the US, as expressed in the Black Power movement.[9]

The expressions of the Diggers and Joseph Berke exemplify how the counterculture appropriated the antiofficial, outlaw sensibility of the Panthers, while remaining one step removed from participatory racial politics. On the one hand, the actual *blackness* in black power appears to be fairly irrelevant in their statements. Historian Todd Gitlin has argued that in the eyes of the counterculture, the black power leaders—or "intelligent brothers in black leather jackets"—were merely icons, "James Dean and Frantz Fanon rolled into one, the very image of indigenous [revolutionaries]."[10] Huey Newton and Bobby Seale, then, become representatives of the deracinated outlaw. "The political consciousness of black people" in the black power movement illustrated a way to live, rather than being heard as a call to fight alongside people who had been discriminated against for hundreds of years. But on the other hand, by indiscriminately grouping such things as "Black Power," "Digger

Autonomy," "self-survival," and "non-participation in the parent system," the counterculture drew upon an array of signifiers to distance itself from what it perceived as the established order. And in this sense, race *is* a significant element of the counterculture's outlaw pluralism—in its minimizing (or overlooking at best) of racism for the crafting of its own self-image.

Like the "intelligent brothers in leather jackets," the Hell's Angels crafted an outlaw image. In one respect, we could describe both the Panthers and Angels as behavioral models for the counterculture, exemplars of self-reliant, nonparticipatory community. Yet, in a practical sense, the counterculture cultivated a very different relationship with the Angels than with the Panthers. The white biker gang became the vigilante protectors of the San Francisco counterculture, while the black revolutionary Panthers remained at arm's length as idealized images in the underground media. Before authoring his countercultural best seller, *Fear and Loathing in Las Vegas,* journalist-novelist Hunter S. Thompson wrote a documentary-style nonfiction novel about his year with the Oakland chapter of the Hell's Angels.[11] Thompson demonstrates that while the Angels were predominantly violent, white men—often racist—who appeared to make their own rules, the counterculture developed a relationship with them because of the "bargaining" power they seemed to possess. The counterculture walked a fine line by choosing such outlaws as their unofficial police. The Angels satisfied many practical needs for the maintenance of life in the Haight-Ashbury district, but, at the same time, the counterculture had to risk their potential for (and real outbursts of) violence. The Angels provided security at concerts in the San Francisco ballrooms, distributed and maintained much of the electronic equipment for the San Francisco rock bands, and trafficked marijuana and speed onto the streets of the Haight-Ashbury district. It appears that the counterculture's indirect negotiation of racial politics made it possible for a white, often racist, outlaw group to be a real presence on the streets, a black hyperracial outlaw group to be lauded in imagery, and somewhere in between, a seemingly peace-loving, nonracist, nonparticipatory counterculture to thrive.

Cultural theorist George Lipsitz has examined the multiple ways that white people and white cultures (like the counterculture) rely on racial stereotypes (both black and white) to shape their own identities. In particular, Lipsitz notes that "the frequent invocation of people of color as sources of inspiration or forgiveness for whites, and the white fascination with certain notions of primitive authenticity among communities of color, all testify to the white investment in images that whites themselves have created about people of color."[12] Much like exoticism, racialized cultural and musical codes reveal information not so much about the people and traditions being evoked but about how a culture perceives race in relation to itself. When a predominantly white culture strives to appear disconnected from real-life racial tensions, the racial stereotypes embedded within that culture's aesthetic works often meet with little resistance and are left unexamined.

In the late sixties, rock critics noted this racial obfuscation in the relationship between the counterculture's musical tastes and its cultural sensibility. Renowned critic Greil Marcus, for example, remarked, "If the Jefferson Airplane had little to say to blacks, the fact that they and bands like them brought a white audience into the Fillmore ghetto every weekend seemed unimportant, even if racial tensions were beginning to emerge in the Haight. No one knew what to say about that, so no one said anything, except that they sure dug spades."[13] To present-day eyes and ears, the transformation of a racist slur ("spade") into a term of praise is, at the very least, a deeply patronizing gesture when coming from a white audience. At the time though, when the counterculture was first crafting its unique persona in a geographical cocoon carved out of the

Fillmore district, the reaction likely had additional meaning and purpose. Marcus's argument is that the counterculture was sheltered behind a veil of racial naïveté, afraid to acknowledge anything but unadulterated adoration for "spades."[14] This veneer of racial naïveté allowed the counterculture to appropriate the marginality and rebelliousness that white culture typically associated with black culture to help craft its own image, and at the same time, to avoid racial tensions by not dealing with the sociopolitical reasons for that marginality.

Critic Dave Marsh gave a contrasting explanation for the counterculture's ties to racialized elements. The emergence of Sly Stone, the black San Franciscan DJ and producer turned musician, was a signal, in Marsh's view, of racial reconciliation between white countercultural psychedelia and black culture. Sly "expressed as well as anything the sentiments of the Haight and the hopes of the ghetto. For a time, it seemed Sly's approach could heal all wounds; offer black kids a model for something other than slick, Copacabana-level success; give whites a fairly wholesome black star; produce for both a meeting ground where they could work out their mistrust."[15] The problem is that Sly didn't enter the San Francisco scene as a musician until 1968, years after events like the Red Dog Saloon summer and Fillmore protests for fair housing practices had shaped and helped solidify the counterculture's relationship with the racialized outlaw. Marsh implies that Sly represented the counterculture's interest in, or at least awareness of, the possibility of racial integration. But he does not ask whether the counterculture was even musically interested in a racial "meeting ground" (allegorical or real) or whether extreme racialized outlaw images (like the gun-toting Wild West fugitive, the Hell's Angel, or the militant Black Panther) would be translated into equally marginal and extreme musical language.

One way that the outlaw counterculture musically crafted its particular racial playing field was through metaphorical and tangible connections to the blues. In August 1967 the musical schedule at the Fillmore Auditorium was as follows:

August 1–6: Muddy Waters, Buffalo Springfield, Richie Havens
August 8–13: Electric Flag, Moby Grape, Steve Miller Blues Band
August 15–17: Chuck Berry, Steve Miller Blues Band, Charles Lloyd Quartet
August 18–19: Young Rascals and Charles Lloyd Quartet
August 20–21: Count Basie Orchestra and Charles Lloyd Quartet
August 22–27: Paul Butterfield Blues Band and Cream
August 29–31: Cream, Electric Flag, Gary Burton

This schedule represents a trend. By 1967, veteran blues musicians often played at the Fillmore and Avalon ballrooms, while hundreds of white kids danced to their music. Typically scheduled as opening acts, artists like Little Walter or Muddy Waters (listed above) warmed up the crowds for the headlining San Francisco bands.[16] Hugely popular with the counterculture, these blues musicians were also regularly featured in the underground media. *Crawdaddy,* the counterculture's music magazine, for example, included full-page advertisements for recordings of blues artists. One advertisement, drawn with characteristic psychedelic lettering, touted Bo Diddley, Muddy Waters, and Little Walter as the "original cast" of the blues, promoting "super togetherness" as they "join forces" on a single record for the countercultural listener's pleasure.[17]

At first glance, it might seem a strange combination of musical traditions and musicians that came together on the stages of the San Francisco ballrooms in the late sixties. But the history of the blues musicians resonated in a number of ways for psychedelic bands and their countercultural audience. The African American blues musicians that saw the stages of the Fillmore and Avalon in the sixties had moved north decades before from places like the Mississippi Delta during the Great Migration, quickly making Chicago and Detroit centers of a new kind of electrified blues. Muddy Waters, Howlin' Wolf, and John Lee Hooker were just some of the big-name musicians who, though not playing solo acoustic blues for the most part, kept their groups small—usually comprised of a lead singer, electric guitar, bass, piano, sometimes harmonica, and drums—while developing a gritty, pulsating, rhythmically driving, amplified sound that became associated with an urban environment. Not only could the counterculture hear these key features of Chicago blues as reflective of its own unique, urban situation that was similarly developing on new fertile ground (just as the Chicago bluesmen had done upon migrating), but the bluesmen themselves could be seen as symbols of mobility and innovation outside traditional geographic and cultural boundaries.

In addition to possessing mobility and uniqueness, these blues musicians were touted as being noncommercial and "original" artists rather than entertainers, allowing countercultural music, by association, to appear free of mainstream mediation. Some of the counterculture's white blues-rockers realized the value of such metaphorical associations with the bluesmen and, on occasion, expressed surprise when the bluesmen did not see the same significance in their association. Sam Andrew, guitarist for Big Brother and the Holding Company recalls the following incident. "I asked Muddy Waters' guitarist in 1966 what chord he was using to close one very intriguing tune and he refused to tell me. This was the first time I encountered such a proprietary attitude about the elements of the blues and he wasn't smiling."[18] Andrew apparently believed (before his rebuff) that musical styles should be freely exchanged with no cultural strings attached. That would explain his shock at Muddy Waters's guitarist's reluctance to give away trade secrets. Equally revealing is the reaction of Waters's guitarist. Perhaps he knew better than Andrew that musical styles *are* culturally loaded and, hence, there is no such thing as free exchange. Jerry Garcia, lead guitarist of the Grateful Dead, in a 1967 interview conducted by rock critic Ralph Gleason, also grappled with the implications that musical exchange had for the image of uniqueness. Asked whether he "got any heat on the racial question" for playing the blues, Garcia remarked: "The ideas that I've pulled from blues musicians and from listening to blues are from *my* affection for the blues which is like since I was a kid."[19] Rather than naive surprise at fellow musicians not wanting to share, Garcia was remarkably defensive. In his view, the blues weren't to share in the first place. His musical influences were always his own.

Whether openly claiming influences or not, the counterculture's connection to the blues was economically lucrative—at least at home in San Francisco. Alice Echols discovered that white countercultural musicians, such as members of Quicksilver Messenger Service, the Grateful Dead, and Jefferson Airplane, enjoyed economic success for their performances at the ballrooms, while the older blues artists were meagerly compensated by comparison. It was a "bittersweet experience . . . that young kids who'd learned their licks from older black players could parlay their music into a level of fame and fortune the originals could never have."[20] What Echols conjectures is that unless veteran blues musicians were ready to create more mainstream popular rhythm-and-blues songs in a mold that had proved to have huge crossover appeal, their blues would either be poorly remunerated as opening material or be taken and filtered into the music of white blues-based bands to the counterculture's own cultural and economic profit.

The August 1967 schedule for the Fillmore Auditorium lends support to Echols's theory. There was enormous popularity with the countercultural audience of white quasi-psychedelic bands—like Steve Miller Blues Band, Paul Butterfield Blues Band, and Canned Heat—that were trained in the blues and fashioned themselves (down to their very names, in some cases) with blues imagery. Such bands were popular over a year before the 1967 Summer of Love. In what turned out to be a major event with two thousand people in attendance the first night, the Paul Butterfield Blues Band played at the Fillmore Auditorium in March 1966. The members of the band were schooled in many traditions: the rhythm section had previously backed Chicago blues legend Howlin' Wolf, guitarist Mike Bloomfield had already been featured on Dylan's electrified "Like a Rolling Stone," and together, the band had backed Dylan at the controversial 1965 Newport Folk Festival. In contrast, the homegrown San Francisco bands, for the most part, had a different musical schooling. They consisted of players trained in folk music traditions, with some jazz thrown in, who were groping for a new electric rock music sound. Most of the San Francisco bands saw in Paul Butterfield and Steve Miller the enormous positive cultural and economic possibilities of adopting basic and recognizable musical features of the twelve-bar blues, such as the I–IV–V–I chord structure and AAB lyrical structure.

From the Grateful Dead's "Viola Lee Blues" to Sopwith Camel's "Anthropomorphic Misidentification Blues," many of the San Francisco bands started to incorporate explicitly blues-based pieces in their repertoires. It's important to be wary of seeing this musical incorporation in essentialist racial terms (i.e., psychedelic rock, or "white music," arrogantly stole the blues, or "black music," to entertain countercultural audiences). As musicologist Philip Tagg warns, relying on such oppositional terms, or "dualisms of alterity," such as *black* and *white* to label different kinds of "musical production" turns them into stamps of assessment rather than tools for critical inquiry.[21] The question here is why countercultural bands saw incorporating elements of the blues as valuable; the reason, in part, had to do with the counterculture's white, middle-class audience. As the San Francisco bands developed their sound, they introduced and made hugely successful a psychedelic version of a blues persona that white male British bands, including the Yardbirds, the Animals, the Who, and the Rolling Stones, had tapped into with their masculine, guitar-centered blues since 1962.[22] British rockers had already set a precedent of drawing together the outlaw and the blues. The Rolling Stones, for example, crafted their image as working-class, law-breaking ruffians, in part, by elevating blues artists into iconic symbols, imitating and covering Chicago blues, and celebrating their alliance with musicians like Muddy Waters.

One difference, however, between counterculture bands and the British Invasion set was that the British also openly claimed musical ties to Motown, while the counterculture bands hid the connection beneath the surface. If anything, this was also a matter of audience appeal. A rare article on Motown titled "The Whiter Shade of Black" in the October 1967 issue of *Crawdaddy* informed its countercultural readership that Motown's music, negatively coded as "white," was not unique enough because of its mainstream popularity and commercialism in the United States.[23] For the American counterculture, Motown artists weren't musical outlaws willing to break the rules. So while British bands covered girl group songs (such as "Please Mr. Postman"), countercultural bands appeared disconnected from the music that was in heavy rotation on AM radio stations in their own country.

In one sense, the counterculture didn't discard everything associated with Motown. Girl groups, typically comprised of four African American girls or young women, were the most recognizable face of Motown, with their stylized vocals and choreographed moves. Certainly the counterculture showed little allegiance to the seemingly manufactured and popular Motown appearance, but women and girls could present themselves in many ways. Into a predominantly masculine-oriented countercultural environment that lauded the white male guitar-driven blues persona made popular by male

British bands entered a person who, in many ways, came to epitomize the outlaw quality of the counterculture. A woman, not a man, singing, and even screaming the blues, but not strumming them—Janis Joplin was the quintessential outsider drawing on a tradition crafted by African American female blues vocalists who were similarly outside the mainstream and outlaws in their own time.[24]

Joplin came to San Francisco from Austin, Texas, in 1963 with a man named Chet Helms (soon to become one of the founders of the Family Dog and promoter at the Avalon ballroom—lit up by Bill Ham's light box). At the time she had been attending the University of Austin and singing in folk clubs. On her trip to San Francisco, she began to change her folksinger image and closely study various African American singers. She went back to Texas and then returned to San Francisco, where she joined Big Brother and the Holding Company in the spring of 1966.[25] Joplin's first large-scale show with Big Brother was at the June 1967 Monterey Pop Festival, where she gained near-instantaneous fame for her performance. Representatives from record labels were at the festival, and like several of the other bands that performed, Big Brother and the Holding Company began negotiations for a record deal with a major label. Though the group had tied themselves up in a contract with the Mainstream label that had put out their first album, *Big Brother and the Holding Company,* Columbia Records agreed to produce the *Cheap Thrills* album.

For over a year leading up to the festival, Joplin honed and refined the musical persona that thousands would hear in June 1967. One of Joplin's idols was Otis Redding, the African American singer from Georgia, and in December 1966 Bill Graham convinced Redding to come play for the San Francisco crowd at the Fillmore Auditorium. For Joplin, Redding's show was the key to opening the door of a new musical world in which she wanted to live. As if she had been detailing his every move, intonation, and gesture during the performance,

Joplin embraced Redding both metaphorically and as a teacher who provided the definitive lesson on how to induce euphoric states in an audience. Joplin was transforming her more laid-back folk music style into something like a dramatic musical stance, and Redding and renowned female African American blues singers were her role models.

The classic African American blues queens from the early part of the twentieth century—Ma Rainey, Bessie Smith, Ethel Waters, and Ida Cox—had often worked in traveling carnivals and vaudeville shows, giving them a kind of gypsy status with the power of freedom and mobility that most women had never known.[26] As historian Hazel Carby explains, because the blues women were travelers, they could take the stereotypes of black female sexuality that had been confined to an oppressive private sphere and transform them in the "public sphere."[27] By celebrating the music and legacy of these women, singing some of the same blues standards they had, and openly crediting her musical models (she praised Etta James and Big Mama Thornton on stage and paid for half of a headstone for Bessie Smith's grave), Joplin, in part, applauded the "marginalized black woman" and reclaimed a black female sexuality as her idols had done.[28]

Of course Joplin reclaimed and embodied her own understanding of black female sexuality, and not all critics and historians have viewed this musical persona of Joplin's as affirming. Historian Brian Ward, for instance, asserts that Joplin's idolization of the blues queens pigeonholed black womanhood instead of recovering its powerful subjectivity. Joplin's "exaggerated" blues persona reinforced stereotypes about black women's "hyper-sexuality" and "stoicism."[29] And indeed, many critics, historians, and even personal associates of Joplin derided her as a racial impersonator, for "trying to be black."[30] Joplin's relationship with Big Mama Thornton's famous song "Ball and Chain" encapsulates this double-edged sword of Joplin's affirmation/impersonation persona. In November 1966, soon after Redding performed at the Fillmore Auditorium, Joplin and Big Brother's guitarist Jim Gurley went to see Big Mama Thornton perform. Impressed with Thornton's "Ball and Chain," they went backstage after the performance to ask Thornton's permission to use the song. Thornton agreed and in Big Brother's version, Thornton is openly acknowledged. But the spirit of someone who had become one of Joplin's biggest idols is obscured and strangely exaggerated. Thornton's version uses the major mode and a strong, mellifluous, vocal production that together create an uplifting and affirming blues. Joplin transforms the potential for affirmation that the song clearly embodied in Thornton's voice and instead sings it in a minor mode at a much slower pace. Joplin hangs on notes that desperately long for resolution and hammers away at others that might easily have gone unnoticed. Joplin's "Ball and Chain" becomes angst-ridden, with undue moments of tension, like a daytime television soap opera.[31]

Certainly not all the San Francisco bands packaged the blues in such a dramatic and seemingly stereotypically tragic way as Joplin did. What was important for the counterculture as a whole was that musical influences, in the hands of any of the San Francisco bands, appeared new and original, unique without being too obscure not to be recognized as unique. So while Ward criticizes Joplin for failing "to show any real comprehension of the racial stereotypes she was inadvertently helping to perpetuate with her fervent minstrelsy," perhaps Joplin didn't care how much critical baggage she would accumulate. Like Jerry Garcia claiming his musical influences as his own, Joplin appeared content to use certain people and certain musics in order to appear to do her own thing.[32] And it was the resulting qualities of unbounded, eclectic uniqueness and individuality that the outlaw counterculture attached significance to.

The complex workings of this outlaw culture were tellingly revealed in the skewed mixing in the San Francisco scene of singer, band, visual image, cultural symbol, critical review, and musical signifier. The cover art for Big Brother and the Holding Company's second album *Cheap Thrills,* for example, came about after countercultural artist Robert Crumb (of *Zap Comix* fame) watched the band perform one night and designed an outlandish cartoon collage. His sixteen caricatured impressions of the band members, the album's songs, and scenes in the Haight made it to the front of the album along with an invitation for listeners to experience "all live material recorded at Bill Graham's Fillmore Auditorium."[33] And as if to verify the quality of the material contained in the album, Joplin herself insisted that Crumb include a cartooned insignia reading "Approved by Hell's Angels Frisco."

As it turns out, it wasn't "all live material," and every track on *Cheap Thrills,* except for "Ball and Chain," was recorded in the studio with manufactured live-audience sound effects.[34] But the impression of "live" was important because it implied a quality of less manufacturing, less orchestration, and more reaction in the moment. Live meant outlaw potential and some rock critics made sure that it was a quality associated with the counterculture. Robert Christgau, for example, described "spontaneity" as "the subject of Janis's art. Again and again she acted out what it might be like to experience a feeling as an impulse and move according to that impulse."[35] Christgau was responding to a report by critic Myra Freidman (who was not so much of a countercultural insider as Christgau) claiming that Janis Joplin largely "preconceived" every melisma and vocal nuance before performing. Freidman's implication is that Joplin was something of a fake, presenting less than the real thing by preparing ahead of time. In response, Christgau positions "spontaneity" as the "subject" of Joplin's art to get past assessments of genuineness and get to the kinds of feeling that might have been evoked in the listener. Though it's likely that Friedman was correct in that Joplin rehearsed her vocal gestures off stage and then recreated them in performance, where those gestures came from and what they evoked are equally important to address.[36] Drawing from improvisatory aspects of musics she had most closely studied—blues and folk—Joplin used the interconnected techniques of reemphasizing a particular word or phrase, pitch bending, and delay. Reemphasis, or troping, in particular was a technique for her to mold, manipulate, and transform pitch and tone quality in the moment, as well as control temporal flow regardless of a metrical push toward resolution.[37]

Joplin's troping and extreme blues persona was not only a metaphorical source of tension, but a tangible one in the dynamic between her and the other members of Big Brother and the Holding Company. Along with "Ball and Chain" the *Cheap Thrills* album boasted the song "Summertime," a familiar jazz standard that Joplin and Big Brother catapulted into the psychedelic rock scene and made hugely popular with the counterculture audience. "Summertime" was composed by George Gershwin (lyrics by DuBose Heyward and Ira Gershwin) as part of his 1933 "folk opera" *Porgy and Bess*. In the opera, it is ostensibly meant to lull a baby to sleep, and as a lullaby, it serves as a soothing mechanism to ameliorate upheaval. Metaphorical threats to social order, such as a hurricane, the "happy dust" of the drug dealer Sporting Life, the dismal conditions of black life on Catfish Row (South Carolina), and Bess's female sexuality are tamed by and contained in "Summertime." Since its first appearance in 1933, Gershwin's lullaby has been covered hundreds of times by jazz and blues artists and, as if mimicking its jazz predecessors, Big Brother's version begins with a quiet ride cymbal and bass drum underscoring an arching electric guitar melody (played by Sam Andrew) with subdued timbres.[38]

Even with James Gurley's backup, finger-picking, amplified, electric guitar line reminiscent of a gospel-style Hammond organ, the overall impression oozes a laid-back jazz style.[39] Classical music influences are also heard in Big Brother's opening, as the rhythm section is subtly overlaid by the lead guitar line that is ostensibly the Prelude in C Minor from Bach's *The Well-Tempered Clavier* slowed down to become almost ostinato-like.[40] With Big Brother's understated allusion to Bach, attempts at classical counterpoint, and opening Baroque era texture, a feeling of *refined* cool jazz sets in that countercultural participants would certainly have been familiar with growing up when it was piped out of their parents' record players.[41]

The most jarring thing about Big Brother's version of "Summertime" is the distance and tension between Joplin's extreme bluesy sound and Big Brother's cool backup musical signifiers, and the relationship of both to Gershwin's original version. While overall Gershwin's "Summertime" is simple, starkly modern in the minor mode, and even impressionistic with colorful chords, Big Brother's version is a clichéd minor blues with cool jazz and classical music signifiers woven in at every turn.[42] For Joplin's part, she revises Gershwin's lyrics, stretching and squeezing his original lines as she wishes, accenting what, in spoken language, would be unaccented syllables, and producing slippery pitches that are often indecipherable as she bends and twists away from a tonal center.

Joplin, for example, follows Gershwin's formal structure where each line of lyrics spans four musical bars so that each stanza lasts for sixteen bars. But although the two versions follow this same formal structure, when Joplin begins the song's first stanza in a very slow 4/4 meter, as opposed to Gershwin's original mild foxtrot pace, the similarities between the two versions quickly disappear. The meter Joplin chooses gives her the flexibility to elongate one line or truncate the next as she pleases. The opening line in Gershwin's original, for instance—"Summertime, an' the livin' is easy"—becomes for Joplin, "Summertime, time, time, chiiiild, the living's easy." In addition to the obvious use of troping (reemphasis of certain words), Joplin toys with the phrasing and temporal movement of the line in her own characteristic manner. In spoken language, the word "summertime" has its natural accents on the first and third syllables. A typical rendering of the song following Gershwin's normative text-setting would feature a vocalist singing the three-syllable word "sum-mer-time" with "sum-mer" leading up to an emphasized arrival or downbeat on the syllable "time." Joplin, however, squeezes "summer" into the end of the bar, as an upbeat, then holds onto the second syllable across the barline for an unpredictable length of time, leaving the expected resolution on "time" unfulfilled.

Musical and performative differences influence the impressions of race that are portrayed in each of the versions. Gershwin's original "Summertime" never stages a breakthrough to a happy or upbeat major mode, never leaves the "easy life" of the "soft" minor mode. Impressionistic washes of chords that, for Claude Debussy and other turn-of-the-century French impressionists, represented the staticity of the Orient, are used by Gershwin to create a modernist construction of white America's perception of black America.[43] Gershwin assembles a static black utopia, while Joplin simulates a burlesque, even stereotyped, African American blues queen, and her bandmates languish in a cool jazz style associated with whiteness. While Big Brother seems to intellectualize Gershwin (as the cool jazzers had done)—either in an attempt to honor him or appropriate his cultural capital—Joplin tries to shape Gershwin's work in the mold of a much blacker tradition. The fact that Joplin and Big Brother offer no stability or meeting ground in their version of "Summertime"—and no consensus on their relationship to Gershwin—parallels the counterculture's implicit engagement with race without explicit engagement in racial politics.

On the cover of *Cheap Thrills,* the most outrageous image Crumb created is for "Summertime." Joplin is grotesquely depicted as a stereotyped black, Aunt Jemima "mammy" with huge gold-loop earrings, big lips, and bulging eyes, holding a white baby. However grotesque, perhaps Crumb's depiction of "Summertime" captured something of the racial dynamics going on in the counterculture. The last line of Gershwin's version of the song explains that nothing can harm us when "daddy and mammy" are "standin' by," but Joplin refuses the protection of traditional authority figures. "Nothing going to harm you now. No no no, no no no, no no no, no don't you cry." She replaces "daddy and mammy" with her own consoling words, implying that if the counterculture's refusal of the parental culture meant "outlaw" independence from the outside world, then Joplin herself (with the Hell's Angels' approval) exemplified this doctrine of self-sufficiency. Throughout "Summertime" Joplin appears almost oblivious, not only of Gershwin's original, but to the backup music of the other musicians. She goes at her own pace, in her own time, effectively corralling the rest of the band in her meter by the sheer force of her powerful persona. In *Porgy and Bess*, "Summertime" is a lullaby that a black woman sings to her own black baby. In Joplin's version, "Summertime" is her lullaby to the culture of which she was a member. "Don't you cry"—the outlaw culture in the Haight-Ashbury district needed no other "Mammy" but Joplin.

It's certainly within the realm of possibility that when Marshall McLuhan, sixties philosopher and culture critic, remarked that for the counterculture "the blues sound like caressing nursery lullabies," he had heard Joplin's rendition of "Summertime."[44] McLuhan's statement is noteworthy, not because the blues had ever lacked the capacity to soothe or console, but because however innocent it may seem on the surface, underlying the statement is the implication that the counterculture was childish. Like an infant who finds an object and claims it as his own for his own pleasure, the counterculture used the blues for its own entertainment, enjoying the recognizable musical features and cultural cache of the blues without explicitly engaging with its history or intricacies or potential expression of racial oppression. The strange web of racial dynamics in Big Brother's "Summertime" seems to bolster McLuhan's observation even further. Joplin's blues persona, an extreme bluesy sound, Crumb's image on the album's cover, cool jazz, the Hell's Angels, live recording, and Gershwin's black utopia— these elements are melded in Big Brother's "Summertime," exemplifying an outlaw identity that was forged and indulged in by a culture clearly enlivened by pluralism yet motivated by the image of self-sufficiency and detachment.

George Lipsitz maintains that in the sixties, "white youths could not or would not embrace black culture and politics directly; for the most part they preferred to fashion alternative cultures and communities that spoke more to the alienations of middle-class life than they did to the racial and class inequities of American society."[45] In songs like "Summertime," "Ball and Chain," and even the Charlatans' "Wabash Canonball," there is very little direct address to the horrific social ills and racial discrimination of late sixties America. In part, this is because the remedying of social problems endemic to mainstream America was, for the most part, not an explicit aim of the counterculture. Arguably, if this had been a major aim, then the counterculture would more likely have adopted the symbols of the civil rights movement rather than those of black power, assimilation rather than separation, racial integration rather than black nationalism.

Although many historians and cultural commentators have grouped together the counterculture, the civil rights movement, and the New Left as all vaguely leftist, the counterculture is misplaced in the collection. History has indiscriminately grouped together everything nonmainstream, but clearly the reconciliatory quality of Martin Luther King, the Freedom Riders, and black spirituals was different from the rebellious quality of Eldridge Cleaver, the Hell's Angels, and psychedelic rock. The counterculture equated outlaw potential with being unbounded by the system, being above the law. So anything that limited freedom, anything that was not do-your-own-thing, didn't fit comfortably in this equation. By adopting plurality, remaining culturally and geographically at arm's length from racial politics, and appropriating racially charged musical styles without addressing their sociopolitical implications, the counterculture appeared to live out Abbie Hoffman's notion: cultural revolution breeds outlaws.

Chapter Three

The Exotic Persona

Absorbing the Postcolonial Political Pill

On September 2, 1945, Ho Chi Minh proclaimed Vietnam independent from its French colonizers. The French had ruled Indochina—including Vietnam, Cambodia, Laos, and the colonies of Tonkin, Annam, and Cochin China—for over fifty years, and, despite their ostensible agreement with the concept of freedom, the French were loathe to relinquish the ideological and practical fruits of colonialism. The French, however, were not alone in having a stake in the Indochinese peninsula. Historian George Herring explains that as one of the world's main producers of natural rubber, oil, tin, tungsten, and rice, and as a home to numerous American naval bases, Southeast Asia, with Vietnam at its center, was a strategic linchpin in America's economically driven policies as a growing superpower. So when French troops returned to Vietnam in 1950 in an effort to suppress Ho Chi Minh and the Vietminh's nationalistic revolution, the United States supported France's efforts, albeit quietly.[1]

America faced something of a bind: even in the midforties, President Roosevelt had realized that any overt allegiance to colonialism would imperil economic power pursuits among colonized countries seeking independence through nationalistic movements. The difficulty with supporting nationalism in Vietnam, though, was the element of Communism. Ho Chi Minh's Marxist ideology, Mao Tse-tung's overthrow of Chiang Kai-shek in China in 1949, the increasing power of Joseph Stalin in the Soviet Union following World War II, and the possibility of control of Southeast Asia's precious commodities shifting into non-Western, noncapitalist, and hence non-"democratic" hands, were clearly out of line with U.S. interests and political rhetoric.

Few political historians deny that the anti-Communist mind-set in America had escalated to the point of serving as justification for demonizing any potential threats to America's economic and political interests at home and abroad. Renowned Cold War historian John Lewis Gaddis, in a fairly noncontroversial history of American strategies for "containing" the Communist threat, explains that both conservative and liberal political administrations used this ability broadly to put down threats in the name of national security.[2]

Until June 1954, when the French granted independence to Vietnam, the United States covertly bore a significant portion of France's war costs against the Vietminh while overtly supporting the new and tenuously U.S.-friendly South Vietnamese government with economic and technical assistance. After the French left, the United States took hold of the reins and spread Western propaganda across South Vietnam and pumped millions of dollars into South Vietnam's economy (and American corporations) through imports of Western goods. Militarily, the United States also stepped up its influence by awarding huge weapons contracts and military budgets to increase the presence of American military supplies, advisors, and eventually soldiers in an increasingly resistant South Vietnam. In the early sixties, President John F. Kennedy was so forthright in his anti-Communist agenda and desire to appear tough to the world that his foreign policy openly declared that the "walls of freedom" be patrolled and protected by actively containing Communism rather than waiting for it to come to American shores. At the very least, this preemptive stance translated into a massive buildup of nuclear weapons and missile technology and unparalleled amounts of money designated for nation-building in countries inclined toward capitalist-style democracy.[3]

The containment policy, which, as Gaddis points out, every president from Roosevelt to Reagan subscribed to in one way or another, was built on a disturbing ideological chassis born out of racism, arrogance, and ignorance. In Vietnam, containment not only underscored a new brand of imperialism that authorized America to do such things as indiscriminately decimate the Vietnamese countryside with herbicides and defoliants produced by American corporations like Dow Chemical, but it also ushered in a new brand of colonialism that ultimately sanctioned the murder of millions through a failure to distinguish between Vietcong and civilians.[4] Being allied with a neoimperialist and neocolonialist approach to dealing with foreign countries, the containment policy also had implications that shaped the political, social, and cultural atmosphere of America. In general, anti-Communism mobilized the American populace against a shared enemy and upheld the primacy of the status quo over anything deemed "radical."[5] It was one side of a two-sided phenomenon, and that dialectic was built up as an unbreachable fortress. With issues framed in extremely dichotomized terms of Communist or anti-Communist, black or white, radical or patriot, the dialectic tried to force allegiance to one side or the other.[6]

In this polarized, us-versus-them atmosphere, the counterculture's own ideological underpinnings were unavoidably tested. The counterculture was wary of taking sides, guarded against pledging allegiance to causes, and distrustful of the rules of the mainstream's political games. Somehow the counterculture would have to exist in this dialectical world but simultaneously disengage from it. The issue for the counterculture, however, was not so much about creating modes of disengagement. Individualism, libertarianism, self-reliance, and isolationism were already core to the countercultural lifestyle and the scene in San Francisco's Haight-Ashbury district. The issue was crafting the cultural clues, the telling symbols, and the coded flavors of the countercultural disengagement package. Just like a "Jesus Lives" bumper sticker or a Raiders baseball cap articulates the owner's sense of identity and places him or her as an insider in the community that shares that same identification, these elements would have to speak a shared language to those in the know, binding them together as countercultural constituents with a shared value of disengagement.

As the first San Francisco rock group to sign with a major record label, Jefferson Airplane soared into prominence across the country on the FM airwaves with their 1967 RCA debut album, *Surrealistic Pillow*.[7] In addition to the strangely postmodern and sexualized "Plastic Fantastic Lover" and the chart-topping single "Somebody to Love," the album featured "White Rabbit," a song that, at least on the surface, describes a journey into Alice's Wonderland. Traveling down a rabbit hole, listening to a caterpillar, playing life-size chess with human pieces—"White Rabbit" discards any semblance of traditional verse-and-chorus form to venture into a magical world of discovery. Precisely because of the song's symbolic through-composed, chorus-free narrative structure, it would have taken little effort for countercultural listeners to decipher at least one other kind of trip that hid behind the veil of Lewis Carroll's children's story—the experience of hallucinogenic drugs.

In 1951 Disney released the animated movie *Alice in Wonderland,* contributing to the growing appeal of the story in the mainstream American cultural imagination. In December 1966, Indian sitar player Ravi Shankar composed and performed music for a British television production of the story, adding a non-Western layer to Wonderland's intrigue. And by the late sixties, the allegorical underpinnings and lurid associations of Alice's Wonderland began to attract a new underground audience. For the San Francisco counterculture in particular, the interest signaled not only adolescent indulgence, but also a culture invested in fantastical Other worlds seemingly disconnected from the political divisiveness of mainstream American reality.

In addition to the ubiquitous references to non-Western religions (which will be addressed shortly), drug references were among many signifiers pointing to the stereotypical sixties love affair with the Otherworldly, and musicians, in particular, provided a wealth of evidence attesting to their unique Other-fascination. David Crosby, guitarist and founding member of the Byrds and later Crosby, Stills, and Nash, shared these same interests. In an interview with the *Southern California Oracle* newspaper (an offshoot of the counterculture's alternative newspaper, the *San Francisco Oracle*), Crosby was asked what made him "high." He replied: "I get high a lotta different ways . . . on music, a lot on making love . . . [on] Buddha and Christ and Shiva and Krishna and Mohammed and everybody. . . . I get high and I think it's a groove. I'm not trying to blow your mind or fuck with you or inflict it on you. I'm not telling you to get high, but I'm stoned."[8] Obviously there is no way of knowing, definitively, whether Crosby was indeed high on drugs during the interview. But his omnivorous response makes the question moot. Drugs, music, sex, non-Western spiritual figures, and free-flowing spirituality, all indiscriminately thrown in the mix, provide access to the "high" life.

Since, as music historian Barney Hoskyns explains, Crosby was the Los Angeles rock star "who most fervently embraced the San Francisco ethos," his meandering and seemingly carefree "high" could be (and often was) dismissed as countercultural posing.[9] By late 1967, Crosby and a host of other musicians *had* probably bought into the countercultural hype and were acting out the exaggerated and commercialized roles that the media had created of them. The Steve Miller Blues Band, for one, revolved around hardened white blues musician Steve Miller. He had grown up with the likes of T-Bone Walker and trained in Chicago nightclubs with veteran blues musicians such as Muddy Waters and Howlin' Wolf. After reaching the Bay Area in late 1966, the newly formed Steve Miller Blues Band played edgy blues. Following a gig on the UC Berkeley campus in November 1966, the band was quickly folded into the San Francisco scene, and their image soon changed. They headlined at the Avalon Ballroom, got booked for the Fillmore Auditorium, played at the Monterey Pop Festival, signed a record contract with Capital Records, quickly dropped the "blues" from their name, and by late 1967 the Steve Miller Band would be heard playing Indian ragalike inventions with Miller himself seated cross-legged on stage wearing an East Indian tunic.

Such Otherworldly poses that musicians like Steve Miller adopted were not only well crafted but were well-tested places of refuge that those on the fringes could inhabit and identify with. Crosby's florid response, for example, didn't spring out of thin air. He had been influenced by his long stays up in Marin County, enjoying parties with the Grateful Dead and Jefferson Airplane. And indeed, Crosby's rhetoric showed remarkable similarities to the coded language thriving in the San Francisco scene. In an interview with the Grateful Dead's bassist, Phil Lesh, a few years after the Human Be-In, the interviewer asked for Lesh's analysis, in retrospect, of the event. "We were seeking a return of this once voluptuous country, attempting to regain the forests and great herds by chanting mantras, the songs of the Hindu Buddhists, and by focusing on the magic center of energy that was forming there in the backyard of the Haight Ashbury."[10] Lesh's description almost completely failed to mention specifics of the event—such as the Zen Buddhist meditating on stage all day or Beat poet Allen Ginsberg leading a group chant to the god Shiva or Joe MacDonald of Country Joe and the Fish leaping around the crowd with pseudo–Native American war paint streaked across his face. Instead, Lesh had a more ideological and nebulous reunion with the event. The jumble of disparate images and impressions—"magic," a "return" to an idealized past, the "great herds," even "Hindu Buddhists" (whoever they may be)—became conflated such that mysticism, mythology, natural origins, non-Western spirituality, insular community, and fantasy were constituent elements of one presumably coherent Otherworldly package.

The exotically tinged flavor of the Haight exemplified, as Theodore Roszak said, everything that a Judeo-Christian-based technocracy was not. From "ancient" astrology charts to Indian textiles, hash pipes to Celtic jewelry, Native American attire to Kamasutra-inspired sex—an exotic technicolor cloak enveloped Lesh's "backyard." Everyday activities, such as drug-taking, listening to music, dancing, and sex, were transformed into "mystical" quests, secular experiences into sacred adventures.[11] This druggy, exotic sacralization of the secular was integral to the development of the San Francisco counterculture from its early days following the summer at the Red Dog Saloon in 1965. Including returnees from the Red Dog, promoter Chet Helms and several other people living at the Pine Street Commune formed the Family Dog and put on rock concerts in spacious venues where attendees were encouraged to dance freely. The first Family Dog show (on October 16, 1965) included the Charlatans and also featured Jefferson Airplane and the Great Society (including Grace Slick). The show was so successful that the rock-dance event featuring local bands became a signature activity of the burgeoning counterculture. In addition to the 1966 Acid Tests, staged by Ken Kesey and musical hosts the Grateful Dead, and free live-music gatherings in Golden Gate Park, such as the psychedelic

Love Pageant Rally to "honor" LSD becoming federal contraband, Family Dog's shows began to get local media attention and pique interest in homegrown radio stations.

For most of the sixties, AM radio had been the key American pop music medium. It played everything from Motown hits to folk ballads, the Beatles to Aretha Franklin. Countercultural "rock" music, however, was played, for the most part, on the FM band, which had, until then, been far less popular, and thus more available for alternative programming. Historian David Szatmary has noted that it was not only the type of music played that distinguished AM from FM, but the format of the programming.[12] Former Top 40 DJ Tom Donahue, for example, took over San Francisco's FM station KMPX and broke the AM mold. He often played entire albums of San Francisco rock music, in addition to its non-Western and non-mainstream musical influences—including long cuts of Indian ragas and experimental jazz.

Because of their initial obscurity and new programming and formatting practices, FM stations were not associated with the popular and hence "commercial" AM stations in the countercultural mind.[13] Music promoters in San Francisco seized on this image, touting the musical counterculture as "serious" and insular. At the Avalon and Fillmore dance halls, promoters Chet Helms and Bill Graham advertised San Francisco's musical experience as community art. They put on performances, seemingly "thrown together," where the San Francisco bands were integral headlining acts in an eclectic artistic experience. *Billboard* magazine reported, "[Graham] has dramatically broken the rock music mold by booking rhythm and blues acts, jazz performers, a Russian poet and several other nonraucous presentations as the second half of his bills."[14] John Rocco, one of several biographers of the Grateful Dead, recalls the San Francisco music scene as a communal whole, greater than the sum of its exotic parts. "San Francisco's secret was not the dancing, the lightshows, the posters, the long sets, or the complete lack of a stage act, but the idea that all of them together were the creation and recreation of a community."[15] And Grace Slick of the Great Society and then Jefferson Airplane remembers the dance-hall shows as providing coherency to an otherwise cultural eclecticism: "As you walk onto the dance floor, you have the feeling you've just entered seven different centuries all thrown together in one room. . . . Electronics and Indians, disco balls and medieval flutes, Day-Glo space colors and Botticelli sprites, the howl of an amplifier and the tinkling of ankle bracelets. . . . This is the American dream."[16]

The San Francisco counterculture, according to reporter Richard Goldstein of New York's *Village Voice,* seemed completely immersed in what he called "pop mysticism." Outside of San Francisco, the rest of the country heard this "pop mysticism" piped over the airwaves in psychedelic sounds and the message was loud and clear—here is a taste of our own unique, untouchable, Otherworldly reality.[17] The counterculture appeared to be the perfect Other alternative to the neocolonialist realities of global Cold War politics and the Vietnam War. But not all critics were similarly impressed by the Haight-Ashbury counterculture, and they questioned how special its ambiance was. Rock critic Lester Bangs acerbically called Jefferson Airplane, in particular, "radical dilettante capitalist pigs." Ripe with colloquial double-edged sarcasm, Bangs's verdict was that the counterculture was less disengaged from mainstream reality than it first appeared.[18] Musical exoticism, on the surface, allowed listeners the freedom to retreat from mainstream reality to the comfort of their insular community. But while this experience encapsulated, in Slick's terms, "the American dream," it also meant that the counterculture was to some degree complicit in the dialectical, neocolonialist policies that were making that dream possible.

In 1956 Hermann Hesse's *Journey to the East* was translated into English, and the short novel enjoyed huge countercultural appeal a decade later.

> Our goal was not only the East, or rather the East was not
> only a country and something geographical, but it was
> the home and youth of the soul, it was everywhere and
> nowhere, it was the union of all times.[19]

In this passage Hesse absorbs "the East" by deconstructing its physical boundaries. The East no longer represents locations on the map, but symbolizes a mutable and ephemeral state of mind (or "soul"). About one hundred years prior to *Journey to the East,* in the American Northeast a group of writers—including Thoreau, Emerson, Hawthorne, and Melville—had tested this same literary technique, delving into untamed mystical worlds, shaped, in part, by their experiences and impressions of that which was non-Western. Their immersion in these Other boundary-less worlds was so comprehensive that their own culture came to be seen as Other to the mainstream American norm. Historian Gary Valentine Lachman conjectures that it was this facility for immersion, this particular technique of pluralistic "cultural meshing," that reverberated with the counterculture.[20] And indeed, the counterculture reveled in a Hessian "East" of its own design, a boundless existential state that seemed free of the mainstream's racial and religious prejudices. But the story doesn't end there, especially when the Hessian "East" of the counterculture thrived within a larger dialectical, neocolonialist system.

Edward Said seminally argued that the Orient or Other (or "East" in this case), as portrayed in Western art and culture, is neither an imagined entity nor an accurate re-creation of another culture. What he dubbed Orientalism necessarily springs from politically imperialist cultures, where the colonizer constructs the colonized exotic object as radically foreign, radically different from the norm.[21] This allows the essential difference between West and non-West, colonizer and colonized, or "self and Other," to be most apparent. Western constructions of Others are means by which Europeans and Americans spotlight difference in order to view themselves with respect to the rest of the world. Exoticism deals with political realities by transforming them into the aesthetic.

The motivations behind exoticism, of course, vary a great deal. They can assuage guilt or feelings of lack, vilify or demean a potential enemy, satisfy a culture's desire for an "edenic experience" or "for return to [an] ostensibly uncomplicated yet essentially mythical primitivism."[22] When one's own sociopolitical system is oppressive and imperialist, then freedom, escape, and alternative realities can seem possible by immersion in radically different constructions of radically different cultures. When the veterans of World War II who had fought in the Pacific returned to the United States, for example, they typically said little about the realities of the gruesome warfare they had had to endure and the violent side of their encounters with Others. Instead, stories abounded about the exotic locales, locals, styles, sounds, and cultural rituals that they had experienced. By the fifties, things Polynesian, Hawaiian, and South Pacific were all the rage in the United States—from hula skirts to Tiki lounges, mai tais to Martin Denny's brand of music termed "exotica."

Confronting, dealing with, or even throwing off the chains of the Western technocracy by adopting the cultural habits, dress, and beliefs of others is laden with potential problems. Namely, such transference onto others can easily lead to an unexamined romanticization of anything that is different. As bell hooks explains: "Contemporary longing for the 'primitive' is expressed by the projection onto the Other of a sense of plenty, bounty, a field of dreams."[23] A fantasy world is built where the Western culture grafts its own desires onto Other cultures, constructing the Other as a reflection and affirmation of its own ideology. In this regard, the counterculture's use of the Other directly paralleled the normative political use of the Other. Both constructed it as an emblem of change sought by the West.

A handful of musicologists have elaborated upon this formulation of exoticism in popular music in the late sixties. Jonathan Bellman looks at how British Invasion rock bands evoked non-Western sounds to provide a substitute for disenchanting aspects of Euro-American culture. He cites the Kinks' use of Indian musical influences as a way to allude to "deviant" sexual matters—because, among other things, "homoeroticism was too dangerous for the [Western] world of mid-1960s popular music."[24] And Susan Fast describes Led Zeppelin's use of exoticism as an evocation, in part, of untainted spiritual experience beyond the bounds of modern Western civilization.[25] Both musicological assessments argue that the Other is cast, to varying degrees, as a utopian object, offering the very qualities that dominant Western civilization appears to lack Both Bellman and Fast focus on the sociological and spiritual issues that late sixties musical exoticism raises, but don't take the crucial next step of relating their arguments to questions of politics and nationalism.

Clearly countercultural music didn't quote Vietnamese sounds or explicitly deal with America's dialectical policies by producing an aural representation of Southeast Asia. Rarely is exoticism so direct. America was (and is) a colonialist power, of sorts, but it was not a "traditional" one. The containment policy and its driving ideology of "You're either with us or against us" were so pervasive throughout the sixties, not only in political, but social and cultural realms, that the counterculture shaped its own position within that ideology by crafting a unique relationship with the Other. In 1968, jazz and rock critic Frank Kofsky observed, "The current 'generation' of young people, less explicitly political than the last, looks elsewhere for salvation: its members put on headbands and feathers and become white Indians; or get involved in Eastern philosophies, religion, meditation techniques, and try to transform themselves into Hindu or Zen mystics."[26] American policy did not perceive Vietnam in a traditional sense as a colony, and its representation in the American exotic imagination was nontraditional. Kofsky's list of exotic means of "salvation" could, in some way, be understood as the counterculture's stand-in for Vietnam.

The United States officially introduced ground troops into Vietnam in 1965, claiming that America was unbeatable and would quickly secure "victory." By late 1967 America had nearly five hundred thousand troops in Vietnam and had suffered over 13,500 casualties. It had implemented the draft, already dropped more bombs on Vietnam than in all of World War II, and was spending more than two billion dollars a month on war and military expenses. While the North Vietnamese had an estimated thirty thousand miles of tunnels, population groups shifting to the countryside, viable industries concealed in caves, vehicles and modern weaponry like fighter planes, surface-to-air missiles, and tanks provided by Russia, and raw materials, food supplies, and small arms provided by China, the United States still touted itself as the superior and more sophisticated war machine. The United States had radar units that could pick up the smell of urine, IBM computer technology that predicted likely times and places of attack, chemical herbicides like Agent Orange that destroyed ground cover, and gunships that could fire eighteen thousand rounds a minute.[27] This dazzling technology did not, to say the least, mask America's neoimperialist agenda. A massive influx of American goods destroyed South Vietnam's few native industries and made the economy dependent on continued American aid, the flow of American consumer goods, and a workforce of Vietnamese providing services to the American occupiers.

Such conceptualizing of American empire is further complicated when we remember the neocolonial connection between France and the United States on the Indochinese peninsula. In a sense, Vietnam was the last colonial battle for the French empire, one that America not only entered, but adopted wholesale as its own fight.[28] In this situation, the counterculture's musical exoticism addressed the politics of U.S.-Vietnamese relations and Cold War politics in two quite different ways—first, by appropriating and reshaping a standard Orientalist narrative associated with a traditional colonial power; and second, by evoking non-Western (but not Southeast Asian) musics of countries recognizably outside the Communism/democracy dialectic. What follows are two case studies examining how the Haight-Ashbury sound moved from the last gasp of colonialism to the Cold War perils of nonalignment, outlining a countercultural chronology of increasing marginality, from the political center to the periphery.

Jefferson Airplane's hit song "White Rabbit" will serve as the first case study. In 1965 Marty Balin set out to create a rock band. After finding four other members, Balin and the newly created Jefferson Airplane moved into a house together. By March 1966, Bill Graham had obtained a three-year lease on the Fillmore Auditorium and hired Jefferson Airplane as the house band. They quickly rose to fame through the underground and mainstream media. Ralph Gleason, the jazz columnist for the *San Francisco Chronicle* and one-time editor of *Down Beat* magazine, had a reputation of unshakable integrity. He saw the Airplane perform at a small pizza place–turned–music club called The Matrix and remarked, "It's not really a rock and roll group. Few are any longer. It's a contemporary-popular music-folk-rock unit and we have no less cumbersome phrase so far. They sing everything from Bob Dylan to the blues, from Burl Ives to Miriam Makeba, from Lightnin' Hopkins and Jimmy Reed to 'Midnight Hour.'"[29] Gleason's review tipped off the record industry, and company representatives came out to hear the band perform.

Grace Slick joined the group soon after the Airplane's lead singer decided to leave. Slick's own band, Great Society, was disbanding because, as she put it, "they were enthralled with the sounds of tablas and sitars [and] considering going to India so they could be near the source and study with the masters."[30] The members of the Great Society—including Grace Slick, her husband Jerry Slick, and Darby Slick, his brother—had grown up next door to each other in privileged Palo Alto. Grace and Jerry got married, went to college, and formed their band. As bassist Darby Slick took classes from Ali Akbar Khan and got more involved in Indian classical music, the band went its separate ways. Notably, Slick herself did not strive to be "near the source," choosing instead the East of Hesse over the real thing.

Songs such as Jefferson Airplane's "Somebody to Love" and "White Rabbit" reveal why many in the San Francisco counterculture made the same decision as Grace Slick, staying at home to enjoy a pluralistic, countercultural construction of the East.[31] Even the opening of "White Rabbit" is a strangely mixed exotic bag. It begins with the bass repeating a military-style bolero motive that, far from being aggressive, is calm, as if heard from a distance. There is something eerily portentous about it, though, as it gets louder and more charged with the addition of the snare drum and the creeping upward motion of the bass harmony by a half step. These two elements create the expectation of continued intensification, yet this is quickly thwarted. No new layer enters and the bolero motive is left to repeat itself while the bass ceases its ascent up the harmonic ladder and starts again on its original pitch.[32]

For the countercultural listener, the ominous and engaging opening of "White Rabbit" had some familiar elements. By 1967, Maurice Ravel's *Bolero* had become standard listening fare as light classical music on AM radio stations and in movie soundtracks such as Fellini's *8½* (1963). As critic Sandy Pearlman noted in her review of the song in the April 1967 issue of *Crawdaddy,* "White Rabbit, Lewis Carroll and then Ravel's *Bolero,* clichéing the cliché."[33] Incorporating an already clichéd piece of classical music and an equally clichéd Victorian drug allegory allowed the FM listener to be "in the know" with respect to shared Western cultural symbols. "White Rabbit" gave audiences an East—an Orientalist discourse—with which they were already familiar.

On first examination it might seem inappropriate to describe as "Eastern" a countercultural song that tropes a piece by a French impressionist composer who was himself exoticizing Spain. But strangely enough, Grace Slick herself connected the bolero trope with an Eastern, hallucinogenic exoticism. Concerning the musical influences on "White Rabbit," she explained: "During an acid trip . . . I realized I had an almost eerie affinity for anything Spanish. In fact, I discovered that I could jam in the *Eastern* flamenco tradition easier than I could sing in the Western twelve-tone scale . . . the music, dance, architecture, and culture of Renaissance Spain is still burned into my psyche as if I had actually lived there. . . . Out of this same influence came the song 'White Rabbit.' The music is a *bolero* (Spanish) rip-off."[34] Indeed, the opening of "White Rabbit," in the use of the half step and the bolero pattern, is, as Slick suggests, somewhat characteristic of the musical practice of flamenco. But the difference between traditional flamenco and Jefferson Airplane's "*Eastern* flamenco" is also striking. The song *ascends* up by half step (rather than a traditional flamenco descent), thereby immediately highlighting flamenco's harmonic signature by turning it upside down.[35] From the outset, "White Rabbit" blatantly shows off its exoticism, not only in the inverted movement of the harmony, but in the more general association it creates with "Spanish" music.

The opening gestures of "White Rabbit" bear the "Spanish tinge" that had been heard in American popular musics for over two decades—challenging Slick's one-to-one psychic connection with "Renaissance Spain." Dizzy Gillespie's 1946 "A Night in Tunisia," for example, rocks back and forth on two chords, a half step apart, evoking a Spanish influence in much the same fashion as "White Rabbit." By the midforties, Havana-born Machito had made Afro-Cuban jazz well known in the United States. Miles Davis and Gil Evans, in their 1959–60 *Sketches of Spain,* had further popularized an exotic Latin sound, including on the album an arrangement of classical composer Rodrigo's *Concierto de Aranjuez.* And by the sixties, performers such as Herb Alpert and the Tijuana Brass, Xavier Cugat, and Yma Sumac (at different times playing the Inca, Spanish, or Peruvian princess) enjoyed success across the country.[36]

Given the extent of Spanish influences in American culture (and particularly in California, which knew centuries of typically violent interaction with Mexico), it is not surprising that Spanish-sounding musical tropes surfaced in other psychedelic popular music in the late sixties. Particularly in Los Angeles, the group Love, fronted by Arthur Lee, made it onto the music scene in 1966. Lee, an African American, had played with Chicano musicians in the midsixties before forming the interracial Love and being signed by Jac Holzman from Elektra records. The bossa-nova style arrangements on Love's first album, *Love,* hinted at the Latin-influenced innovations to come on their January 1967 *Da Capo* and November 1967 *Forever Changes.* Although Elektra released *Forever Changes* in November 1967, Love recorded the album early that year and, for months before the recording sessions, played up and down the Sunset Strip refining the album's songs on stage. Coincidentally, Jefferson Airplane was in Los Angeles intermittently through October and November of 1966 recording *Surrealistic Pillow* at the RCA studios in Hollywood.[37]

Love has been described as "exciting," "aggressive," "schizophrenic," and "apocalyptic," and Barney Hoskyns argues that their album *Forever Changes,* in particular, embodied all their descriptive energy.[38] Presumably Jefferson Airplane knew of Love, and even a superficial knowledge of their work would have given the Airplane a sense of a potential palette of

Latin influences and what those influences could allude to. The Airplane did not credit Love as one of the influences on *Surrealistic Pillow* or "White Rabbit" in particular, but there are some similarities worth noting.[39] The first track on *Forever Changes*, entitled "Alone Again Or," recognizably tropes rhythmic and harmonic features of flamenco (including an ascending half step) and marks them, in an Orientalist fashion, as menacing. Arguably, the bolero motive in "White Rabbit" could also be described as menacing, as in "Alone Again Or," especially taking into consideration its development over the course of the song and its qualitative associations with flamenco.

According to ethnomusicologist Peter Manuel, flamenco carried with it symbols of Andalusian *gitanismo*, or "gypsy ethos." The Andalusian part of Spain, when under Moorish rule centuries ago, enjoyed a relatively peaceful cosmopolitan life that embraced Arab, Christian, Gypsy, and Jew.[40] Following the Reconquista and Inquisition, however, Andalusians were persecuted and their cosmopolitan identity stigmatized. Flamenco emerged out of this sociopolitical matrix of cultural ferment and historical oppression and its *gitanismo* incorporated such themes as oppression, sorrow, machismo, pride, and persecution. During the twentieth century, the cultural dimensions of Spanish flamenco expanded. In some instances, twentieth-century flamenco claimed an overtly politicized ground. With the inclusion of "sophisticated" lyrics by well-known poets such as García Lorca and performances by renowned flamenco singers, it voiced protest against Franco's Fascist policies. Yet around the same time a branch of flamenco arose that de-emphasized political themes and accentuated flamenco's sexual tension and bottled sensuality.[41]

As in Bizet's *Carmen* and Ravel's *Bolero*, the evocation of flamenco in "White Rabbit" opens a door for the listener into an exoticized engagement with both the cultural and politicized dynamics of Spanish history and the changing quality of flamenco's *gitanismo*. To the twentieth-century listener, Spain was more than just another European country. Musicologist Susan McClary asserts that, because of its Arab- and Gypsy-influenced history, Spain became musically coded by the rest of Europe as part of the Orient.[42] Consequently, Europe heard Spain, and flamenco, as conforming to its own image of exotic difference. In a Western Orientalist narrative, flamenco signaled political pride and machismo while simultaneously reinforcing notions of the Iberian Other as dangerously seductive.

"White Rabbit" draws on these meanings to drive its own coded geopolitical narrative agenda. As the bass slips back to repeating the bolero motive, a melody in the guitar glides and wanders above it, melismatic and ornamented.[43] While the bolero motive can be heard as the proud, macho, even stoic flamenco identity, the guitar solo appears as flamenco's alter ego—desiring, seductive, intoxicating, even uncontrollable. Into the mix enters Grace Slick, whose vocal production and melodic line mimic the wandering guitar. Her voice twists and turns, rolls R's at the front of her mouth, pierces and recedes dynamically—playing with the beat and undulating around the ever-present and intensifying bolero rhythm. "One pill makes you larger and one pill makes you small / and the ones that mother gives you don't do anything at all. Go ask Alice."

On first hearing, Slick's emphatic message seems to have nothing to do with the exoticism encapsulated by flamenco, but is just about taking drugs. The pills (experiences) that we try will transform us, yet the ones that mother (the parental generation) gives us offer nothing worthwhile. If we are unsure about entering this new, youthful, hallucinogenic world, Slick suggests we "go ask Alice." In other words, don't believe the mainstream, but instead trust Alice, someone who has been on that fantastical druggy ride for herself. What gives Alice her authority though, is the underlying flamenco idiom. With its repetition and insistence, the bolero motive is hypnotically appealing and, when combined with Slick's exotic vocal ornamentation, the ever-rising tension of flamenco's *gitanismo* is alluring. The song constructs an exotic musical character with whom the listener can identify, even though there is no sense of where its accelerated movement will end up.

Like many in the counterculture, the members of Jefferson Airplane grew up in middle-class homes, raised on children's classics such as *Alice in Wonderland, The Wizard of Oz, Snow White and the Seven Dwarves,* and *Peter Pan.* Slick remarks that the lyrics of "White Rabbit" mean to point out the "hypocrisy of the older generation . . . to remind our parents (who were sipping on highballs while they badgered us about the new drugs) that *they* were the ones who read all these 'fun with chemical' children's books to us when we were small."[44] Certainly, many of these stories either intentionally allegorize drugs, or could easily have had that subtext read into them. So Slick's comment highlights an important imperative associated with the counterculture—adopt things Otherworldly (in this case, the childlike transgression of Wonderland underscored by the exotic flamenco world) as a means to negate, or disengage from, the mainstream parental generation. Of course "White Rabbit," at the time, was youth music, and it would never serve to "remind parents" of anything because "parents" were not the ones listening to it. So rather than a reminder, the song was more significant as an expression, agreed to among peers, of anger and dissatisfaction with an older generation.

Dissatisfaction was only part of what was being expressed, though. Coded allusions to hallucinogenic drugs in a child's fantasy-world fill the song lyrics, yet the music itself is decidedly not blissful. The Beatles' "Lucy in the Sky with Diamonds," for instance, evokes no exotic Other so it can easily be heard as a "good trip," an idyllic escape into a psychedelic child's fantasy. But by grafting the exotic onto a drug narrative, "White Rabbit" constructs a frightening subtext that is hauntingly palpable when heard next to the Beatles' song. The LSD "trip" of "White Rabbit" intensifies and gets more forceful over its duration, and the listener is drawn to the repetition, almost hypnotized by its increasing forcefulness.

After Slick's vocal introduction to Alice's Wonderland, the bass line momentarily breaks out of its half-step cycle, only to fall back into the bolero pattern with a new level of instrumental density. Tension mounts and a more and more forceful repetition of the alluring pattern strains to relieve the tension and reach a new place in the musical narrative. This comes only as Slick takes narrative control of the progress of the story. She confidently sings longer sentences and pierces through the ever-persistent rhythmic backdrop, and then suddenly, the half-step harmony is conquered (or abandoned, at best) in favor of Western harmony.[45] "When men on the chessboard get up and tell you where to go / and you've just had some kind of mushroom, and your mind is moving slow." On the one hand, the listener is immersed in the exotic world that Slick describes. She sings directly to us, out of her personal knowledge of Alice's world and to our desire for her experience. Yet this world feels comfortable *particularly* when the climactic moment is reinforced by Western harmony.

As the rhythmic part of the bolero pattern gains intensity over the course of the song, so does Slick's vocal insistence. The rhythmic pattern mounts, repeated ever more loudly with added percussive layers, and Slick's range reaches higher and higher when "the white knight is talking backwards and the red queen's off her head." Strained against the density of instrumental noise behind her, her final vocal line ("Feed your head, Feed your head") hammers away in a harmonic realm that could never be mistaken for anything but Western tonality.[46] Together, at the song's ending, they have reached a climax. But without a denouement in what feels like a truncated song (it is only 2:30 long), this final moment gives no clarification, no final outcome that has been achieved. As the high point of tension, the ending could either be a doorway to a new world or the step before a tragic end. One thrills to the freedom and transformation offered in Alice's world, and in this sense, the exotic Other that Slick vocalizes signals individual discovery. Yet there is also danger that has increased to an intense magnification. The persistence of the instrumental backup demands we relinquish control to the group.

In sociopolitical terms, the relation between the exotic Other of flamenco and Western tonal practices in this signature counterculture song bears remarkable similarities to a traditional Orientalist narrative: "*We* shape and use *them* for *our* needs as the dominant group." Said argued that Orientalism is a way for imperialist cultures to transform political reality into the aesthetic. As we know, throughout the sixties, America increased its military presence in Vietnam, and preoccupation with the war filtered into every aspect of American life. A moral stance against Communism, in Southeast Asia in particular, was a support for the democratic "freedoms" that those in the West enjoyed on a daily basis. With mainstream television and radio stations depicting the North Vietnamese as both ruthless and godless, America conceived the Other (Vietnam, Communism) as nothing short of a threat to everything the West stood for. And although Vietnam, like Korea, was marked by Cold War politics and imperialist-style regional control, it was more than a battle between the Soviet Union and the United States fought on Asian soil. American and Vietnamese histories and memoirs alike remember how strong the French subtext was in Vietnam, especially in the South, where the French language and a Francophile lifestyle were prominently displayed by the ruling class.[47] Because the political actions of the United States propped up a former French colony, those actions preserved the political relevance of decadent Orientalist tropes associated with France.

This neocolonial situation is embedded in the lyrical and tonal narrative of songs like "White Rabbit." Though Jefferson Airplane may not have crafted the subtext so specifically or intentionally, it is well within the realm of possibility to hear

"White Rabbit" as telling the story of Vietnam by appropriating a decadent Orientalist discourse associated with an ailing colonial French empire (which included North Africa and encompassed Spanish/Moorish cultural influences and sounds). Even the origins of *Alice in Wonderland* reinforce this convoluted narrative. The story's lavish, late-nineteenth-century exotic setting reappears in the Airplane's "White Rabbit" with Lewis Carroll's same Orientalist images, including the "hooka," the "white knight," and the "red queen." Such images help position Slick and the character Alice as femmes fatales, exotic women who are seductive and intoxicating, but also dangerous. The more enticing they become, the more of a threat they pose because the propeller that drives them (the bolero pattern) mounts without finding resolution, and ultimately they are caught in a cliffhanger.

Slick's vocal production becomes even more imperative as she reaches the end of the song, indicating that she is either driving toward an unrevealed goal or getting sucked into a dangerous musical acceleration with no escape in sight. She might well meet with the same fate as the Francophile sister-in-law of South Vietnamese president Diem, dubbed by American journalists "The Dragon Lady." Diem's closest advisor from 1956 until 1963 was his brother Ngo Dinh Nhu, a dandy who had spent several years studying at the Ecole des Chartes in Paris. Nhu's wife, dolled up in tight silk dresses and long red fingernails, lived at the presidential palace as its "First Lady," claiming, much like Nancy Reagan would do decades later, to be the force behind the presidential agenda.[48] The United States was unwillingly allied with this last gasp of French Orientalism in South Vietnam, yet the decadent and controlling behavior of "The Dragon Lady" was "rewarded" with her American-sanctioned execution. ("Off with her head!")

Over the course of the sixties, the United States became more and more entrenched, not only in the messy, personalized politics of the South Vietnamese government, but in the quagmire of Cold War geopolitics. "White Rabbit" *feels* like escalation (with no foreseeable end in sight), a feeling that exactly paralleled America's mode of operation in the war in Vietnam. Although the counterculture wanted nothing to do with the dialectical politics of us versus them, democracy versus Communism, and appeared to adopt a "no rules at all" agenda as its alternative, the language to express this agenda had already become a tool in the dialectical game. Manfred Mann's 1965 song "With God on Our Side" builds ominously, with sparse piano accompaniment that depicts an intensifying chronological and sociological narrative about the horrors of war. And in 1967, folk singer and activist Pete Seeger wrote "Waist Deep in the Big Muddy." His lyrics quite explicitly drew on the trope of escalation. Describing a World War II platoon that sinks deeper and deeper into Louisiana's Big Muddy River, the song—because of its timing—was intended and read as an allegorical indictment of the Vietnam War. Seeger was originally scheduled to sing it on the *Smothers Brothers Comedy Hour* in 1967, but CBS canceled his appearance because of the song's implications.[49]

In the song's first stanza, "where it all began," the platoon is "knee deep in the Big Muddy." The platoon "keeps slogging" according to the captain's orders, and by the end of the second stanza it is "waist deep in the Big Muddy." The captain says to the men that they simply "need a little determination," but that gets them "neck deep in the Big Muddy" and the captain tells them to continue pressing forward. This gradual buildup, from knee deep to waist deep to neck deep, was a metaphor for the insidious method of war in America's longest overseas hostile operation. Vietnam was built up slowly with thousands more troops sent each year, never able to turn back.

While Jefferson Airplane's music and the counterculture's sound in general would not have been allied with any single, overt political position (instead refusing to take sides), "White Rabbit" can be heard as embodying the *feeling* of an escalating war. The textural buildup of instrumental and rhythmic layers entices the listener into the music's plot; flamenco's harmonic signature of a descending half-step is inverted to literally climb up the scale or escalate; the bolero pattern provides a hypnotic "ideology"; and Slick yells to "push on" (i.e., "feed your head"). Repeated again and again, we march in deeper and deeper. Certainly the song offers no explicit political agenda, in contrast to "Waist Deep in the Big Muddy," but its feeling of escalation implicitly addresses America's mode of operation in Vietnam. As Seeger predicted, "We'll be drowning before too long."

By 1967, protests against the Vietnam War were on the rise, and a heterogeneous mix of people was considered part of a large antiwar movement. There were pacifists who opposed war in any historical situation. There were far-left and far-right radicals who opposed all government-sponsored actions, including the war. There were white middle-class youth, mostly students in the New Left and the SDS, and poor African Americans who opposed the war because it exemplified how America used and discarded the less fortunate to drive an exploitative capitalist system. Protests and antiwar actions were publicized on television. The TV viewer witnessed footage of scores of marchers, saw hearings of individuals who refused to pay the portion of their income tax that went to support the Defense Department, heard boxer Muhammad Ali refusing his induction orders and accepting the consequence of a prison sentence for his civil disobedience, and learned of three army enlisted men (the Fort Hood Three) who challenged the constitutionality of the war by refusing to fight. Thousands evaded the draft by going to jail or Canada, thousands more participated in antiwar rallies, and many engaged in small-scale protest actions like holding up troop trains. Protest, in all these forms, brought the gravity of the Vietnam War to the public consciousness and countered the government's rosy we-are-on-a-winning-track story. Polls in 1965 showed widespread popular support for the war, but by the summer of 1967 a majority of polled Americans, as well as mainstream publications like *Time,* said that it had been a mistake to go to Vietnam.[50]

Sixties' musicians produced a plethora of songs that evoked musics of countries explicitly *not* engaged in the Communism-versus-democracy politics of the Vietnam War, songs that might be considered representative of the second type of countercultural exoticism. The spacey, distorted, quasi–Middle Eastern section in Steppenwolf's "Magic Carpet Ride" seemed to reinforce the lyrical message that "fantasy will set you free." The notion of escaping mainstream alienation in Donovan's "Hurdy Gurdy Man" was reinforced through echoing and distorted Eastern effects on the zither and East Indian sitar. And the Yardbirds' "Heart Full of Soul," considered the first song in a category that was later labeled "raga rock," boasted Jeff Beck imitating a sitar on the electric guitar, redefining the boundaries of the electric guitar's role in rock and roll. Added to the rolls of raga-psychedelic-Eastern-exotic rock explorers was an unexpected newcomer.

After spending his youth in Los Angeles and then joining the navy for three years, guitarist-singer-songwriter Joe MacDonald moved to Berkeley, California, in 1962, ostensibly to attend college. MacDonald had grown up in a radical left-wing family and been immersed in American politics. Soon after his arrival in Berkeley, he became part of a folk music culture, played on the burgeoning people's radio station KPFA, formed two rock bands, and started up an underground magazine called *Rag Baby,* which he edited. He quickly found a way to fuse his interests and piloted a "talking" issue of *Rag Baby* that was distributed on cassette rather than newsprint. The edition, timed for release to coincide with a major Berkeley teach-in in May 1965, combined spoken and musical commentary about political issues, including two songs MacDonald wrote and sang.[51]

Two things inspired MacDonald and his close musical

companion Barry Melton (who had a similar political up-
bringing in New York and then Los Angeles with a union father who was baited by the FBI) to develop a "more serious"
rock band in late 1965. The first was the success of *Rag Baby*'s
talking issue. The second was a moment of revelation. In early
1966, MacDonald and Melton toured with Students for a
Democratic Society (SDS) as the newly created folk band
Country Joe and the Fish. After the tour, Melton recalls, "We'd
gone to the Pauley Ballroom, on the Berkeley campus, and
seen Paul Butterfield Blues Band play. We were loaded on acid
and decided that we had to make Country Joe & the Fish into
a rock 'n' roll band."[52] The very name of the band—Country
Joe and the Fish—had left-leaning political undertones. "The
Fish" derived from Mao Tse-tung's reference to "the fish who
swim in the sea of the people," and "Country Joe" had numerous variants, most notably as an allusion to the nickname
of Joseph Stalin during World War II. True to name, Country
Joe and the Fish's collection, *Songs of Opposition,* was out just
in time for the first large-scale anti–Vietnam War protest in the
East Bay in October 1965. MacDonald and Melton took part in
the protest, marching on the first day from Berkeley toward
Oakland, only to be turned away by Oakland police at the border between the two cities. The next day, marchers hoped to
avoid a repeat of the previous day's dispersal by the police.
MacDonald and Melton dropped acid and performed on the
back of a flatbed truck in the protest parade, but as they and
thousands of protestors reached the border, the presence this
time, not only of the police, but of the Oakland chapter of the
Hell's Angels made sure that the peaceful event would fail.[53]

If ever there was an instance of historical karma for Country Joe and the Fish, the simultaneous occurrence of the "Tribute to Dr. Strange" concert in San Francisco and the anti–Vietnam War protest march in Berkeley was it. Melton and
MacDonald didn't remain for long in the East Bay social and
political scene. Despite the band's name, political affiliations,

participation in protests, and allegiance to leftist political organizations, Country Joe and the Fish were not so consumed by politics, protest, and social causes as their image implied. Doing a musical about-face, the next *Rag Baby* issue, also recorded, included the distinctly apolitical rock song "A Thing Called Love" and a druggy tribute to marijuana based on classical composer Grieg's "Hall of the Mountain King" called "Bass Strings." The issue became something of an ID card for the band, allowing them passage into the San Francisco scene. They secured their first gig at the Fillmore Auditorium as a substitute band in August 1966, and soon were sharing bills with local San Francisco bands. By late 1966, Country Joe and the Fish signed with Vanguard Records for their first album, *Electric Music for the Mind and Body.* Vigorous self-promoters, the band advertised their performance schedule each week in the alternative newspaper *Berkeley Barb* and made sure that radical deejays had their music to play on FM radio stations. While on the surface everything about Country Joe and the Fish seemed to resonate with a Berkeley-style, politically active ethos, their music told a different story. It was picked up alongside Jefferson Airplane's on FM airwaves directed at the counterculture and cheered on as quintessential psychedelic San Francisco rock music at the Human Be-In in January 1967.

Given the timing, it appears that Country Joe and the Fish at least partly suppressed their political image in order to profit in the music industry. After signing with Vanguard, the band moved to San Francisco and into the counterculture by transforming their array of politically charged signifiers into emblems of the exotic. In the band's defense, Melton remarked that "success never diminished our opposition to the Vietnam War and our support of progressive causes. In some sense the success of Country Joe and the Fish, and that of our musical contemporaries, directly reflected the success of the antiwar movement. As opposition to the war in Vietnam became the cultural mainstream, so did our music."[54] Obviously, Melton wanted to believe that profit never clouded the band's support for political causes. But by juxtaposing the band's economic success with the expansion of the antiwar movement into the mainstream, Melton sidestepped an explanation of why explicit political jargon disappeared from the band's musical repertoire. In addition to the curious defensiveness with which Melton dealt with the group's economic achievements, it is interesting that he saw the need to explain himself in the first place. If their opposition to the Vietnam War was "never diminished" by success, then it must have been expressed musically.

Country Joe and the Fish adopted an exotic musical tinge at the time they moved to San Francisco. Their second album, *I Feel Like I'm Fixin' to Die,* was released in May 1967, and although the album title (taken from their anti–Vietnam War song from the *Rag Baby* talking issue) aimed to capitalize on the band's political notoriety, the album itself did not include the song, nor any other overtly political music. More representative of the album's flavor is a track entitled "Eastern Jam." Like the songs "Masked Marauder" and "Section 43" from *Electric Music for the Mind and Body,* "Eastern Jam" was a popular instrumental track that was heard frequently, both in performance and on FM radio. From the obvious allusion in the title to the evocation of musical gestures that came to characterize the "East," "Eastern Jam" draws on a chaotic mixture of elements to signify the exotic.

The song begins with a held note in the bass guitar followed by delicate, unmeasured flurries on the high hat. The opening is in metrical limbo until a muted pattern in the tom-toms provides a rhythmic upbeat, intimating that a more regular meter is to come. Percussive, yet not intrusive, the tom-toms sound more like hand-hit drums in a communal drum circle. On first hearing, this aloof fifteen-second improvisation is by no means "Eastern." To the countercultural listener acquainted with the mix of musical styles played on FM radio at the time, it probably sounded like jazz. The casual exchanges between the voices in addition to the elusive meter and mellow timbres together encoded what the second half of the song's title had already suggested. This connection to (and adoration of) modal and free jazz, in particular, was flaunted openly by musicians, critical voices, deejays, and promoters in the counterculture. Instrumental tracks by other major counterculture bands, like the Grateful Dead's "Feedback" on *Live/Dead* and Jefferson Airplane's "Embryonic Journey" on *Surrealistic Pillow,* for example, owed their free forms to contemporaneous "avant-garde" jazz styles. KMPX often played long improvisatory sections of albums by musicians such as Albert Ayler, John Coltrane, Elvin Jones, Miles Davis, and Ornette Coleman. Promoters Helms and Graham frequently invited these same musicians to participate in the Fillmore and Avalon shows alongside countercultural bands (including Country Joe and the Fish). As jazz and pop music critic Frank Kofsky noted at the time, "The structure of jazz meshes with the whole bias of the San Francisco scene toward 'freedom.'"[55]

In 1971, historian Ben Sidran observed that "the most basic common denominator of the black musical tradition [is] the striving for personal freedom through complete collective catharsis."[56] Countercultural music wanted to aurally capture a piece of this "freedom" and appropriated modal and free jazz as part of its Otherworldly palette to represent a new, unexplored, and idyllic world of social connections. To the extent that the experimental musical practices and personal ideologies of jazz artists contributed, in Sidran's terms, "to the basis of a lifestyle that was a negation of Western analytic process," such aesthetics also resonated with the counterculture's interest in non-Western spiritual philosophies.[57] Saxophonist John Coltrane, for example, who died at age forty-one in 1967 having already become the dominant jazz figure of the time, in his late works—including *A Love Supreme, Meditations,* and *Stellar Regions*—linked his personal interests in Eastern religious philosophies with musical experimentation in non-Western song forms and Indian modes. Some songs, like "Chim Chim Chimee" and "The Promise," explored hypnotic patterns in such depth that a listener would have been certain to hear, and perhaps even experience, the subtext of religious trance and exaltation. "Avant-garde" jazz employed non-Western sounds, forms, harmonic practices, and instruments as sonic alternatives to the seemingly rigid structures of feeling signaled by Western religious traditions. Countercultural music, by appropriation, could indirectly assume similar qualities. By 1968, Country Joe MacDonald had completely immersed himself in this improvisatory exoticism: "We don't want to play songs anymore. We want to improvise. There is a different relation between people and a band that improvises."[58]

About fifteen seconds into "Eastern Jam," an electric bass enters with a solo supported by a characteristic backbeat, the kind of rhythm-and-blues pattern that one would more likely expect from Chuck Berry. While the bass solo relaxes into a comfortable R & B groove that remains a riff throughout the rest of the song, its melodic language, rather than sounding bluesy, employs jazz harmonies to signal a vaguely Eastern musical identity.[59] A guitar solo enters at forty-three seconds into the song with a slightly distorted sound subjected to heavy reverb. Improvising phrases, motives, and streams of arpeggiated chords on the harmonic material established by the bass, the guitar line roams around as if slightly intoxicated while showing off a musical adeptness with skilled ornamentation and skewed notes. Like the bass riff, the rhythm and articulation of the guitar solo is rooted in the same jazz idiom that began the song, yet it disguises itself in harmonic language that had come to signify the "East." As musicologist Ralph Locke has observed, the "residual" aspects of non-Western musics that appear most different from Western musical practices are the ones that signal the exotic.[60]

The guitar solo exemplifies Locke's formulation with a

"modal" pitch orientation and slippery ornamented notes that together signal a South Asian, possibly Indian, Other. This particular musical identity is reinforced at about two minutes into the song by a new instrumental layer. As the guitar proceeds on its extended solo, soaring into higher and higher registers, a pitched percussive pattern emerges that seems to mimic an Indian sitar. Country Joe and the Fish had experimented specifically with the sitar, and then with Western instruments imitating Indian instruments, on their first album. Not surprisingly, this pitched percussive pattern also includes a familiar home pitch, like a typically Eastern drone. Three minutes into "Eastern Jam," the guitar solo reaches its conclusion and a new guitar melody enters immediately to take its place. The song remains in the same key and the drone persists (preserving an Indian backdrop), but this solo takes on a different and more aggressive timbral, harmonic, and ornamentive identity that, through movies, television, and stage productions, had come to be the aural stereotype of the menacing Eastern Other.[61]

Songs like "Eastern Jam" not only relied on clichéd aural stereotypes but maintained them as viable sounded tropes for the emerging spiritualized jazz-rock that would enjoy huge popularity in the early seventies.[62] The counterculture's ability to musically juxtapose non-Western and Western gave listeners an escape from Western rationality and rigidity of the status quo by affirming an Eastern irrationality through exoticism. This technique of juxtaposition also allowed the counterculture to detach from a brand of nationalism built on a history of slavery and ethnic cleansing. But there was always a safety net for the counterculture because taking the Other as an alternative did not require relinquishing access to mainstream power. This is often what is most deceiving about exoticism. The Other is defined and absorbed under the guise of finding a new pleasure and freedom that is lacking in the familiar world. But that exploration is buffered by a sense of hubris—our counterculture is better than the normative culture because we possess not only the familiar world but the experience of Other cultures that are different and enlightening.

Certainly, it seems likely that songs such as "Eastern Jam" are alluding to the transcendental experience that the counterculture perceived to be embodied in the East. India, in particular, had come to be seen as mystical, and its signifiers were used to denote spiritual escape from the perceived rigid values of the dominant Judeo-Christian culture. The British Invasion bands had helped to make this possible.[63] Not only were the Beatles, as one critic remarks, "the main publicists for Indian culture (however imperfectly understood)," they also showed how profitable exoticizing India could be.[64] In this regard, countercultural bands that played exoticized music had an economic motivation—copy what the Beatles do and make money.

Adopting India wholesale from British cultural figures such as the Beatles also had political implications. Britain had had a long relationship to India as its primary colonizer, while the United States had displayed little political interest in India. In 1946 Congress passed a law allowing South Asians entry into the United States. The allotment was for an annual quota of one hundred people, indicating that South Asia was not a high priority on the American diplomatic agenda. Although a meager percentage of the American population was of South Asian descent by the fifties, India had started to become a feature of American domesticity—Indian décor and textiles added color to many living rooms and quickly became a symbol of "Eastern" mysticism.[65] This association was fortified by the publication of works such as *Autobiography of a Yogi* by Paramhansa Yogananda. Yogi Paramhansa had emigrated to the United States in 1920 and eventually settled in Southern California, where he established a spiritual center in Encinitas. By the midfifties, classical violinist Yehudi Menuhin began to curate an Indian classical music collection. Around the same time, both sarod player Ali Akbar Khan and sitar player Ravi Shankar toured the United States. Shankar opened a branch of his Kinnara School of Music in Los Angeles in 1963, in addition to the one already established in Bombay, and soon gained popularity within the counterculture. Participation in the school required a comprehensive course of study—three main disciplines of voice, sitar, and tabla, the history and development of Indian music, and an intense study of the legends, mythology, and religion of India. Shankar's influence spread further by 1967 due to his publicized connections with Menuhin, including their collaborative record *East Meets West*. The counterculture's interest in India was not as transformational as Shankar had hoped, though. Richard Goldstein ironically reported to the *Village Voice* that "hip has become mass-cult, and Ravi Shankar finds himself not the prophet of an elite, but the universal guru. His following wants Buddhahood on a long-play record. Tao on tap, a bath in the Ganges without getting wet. And they want Ravi Shankar to sock it to them."[66]

Music journals and magazines, in a less ironic tone than politically inflected newspapers, also played an important role in defining India as a commodity promising instant enlightenment. From 1967 through 1971, *Jazz and Pop* magazine featured dozens of articles and advertisements linking India to countercultural music. Feature-length articles such as "Transcendental Meditation Benefits Musicians" were mixed in with advertisements by guitar-maker Coral for the new "electric sitar." One page after another praised popular musicians, such as George Harrison and members of Jefferson Airplane, for being influenced by Ravi Shankar.[67] After George Harrison studied for a month with Ravi Shankar in Bombay, the reviews of Harrison's appropriation of Indian sounds into a Western idiom were glowing.[68] And by 1968 *Down Beat* boasted several articles about Ravi Shankar and two articles on "raga-rock."

While these journals celebrated the Indian influence on

popular music, Shankar voiced his skepticism. His 1968 auto-biography noted that "many people these days think that Indian music is influencing pop music to a high degree. But my personal opinion is that it is just the sound of the sitar and not true Indian music that one finds in pop songs . . . they [are] using our music as part of the drug experiences and understanding of India's ways [is] shallow. Wearing beads and bells and flowers and carrying joss sticks [comes] across as a mimicry and a mockery of the real thing."[69] Just as Indian décor was an exotic accoutrement to many American homes in the fifties, so were Indian sounds in popular music of the late sixties. Buddhist studies scholar Robert Thurman explains that the Western impression of Indian and Tibetan Buddhism as mystical inevitably included prejudices that equated this mysticism with social apathy and ethical laziness.[70] One problem was that these prejudices were not always coded as negative. Indeed, appropriating the identity of a "mystical" Other could be used as an excuse to retreat from practical social concerns. India was, in part, a romanticized spiritual construct of non-Western gods, fertility, sex, and lavishness, where the rigidity of the Protestant work ethic was absent. If anything, it represented an American spiritual vacation.

Certainly the American counterculture made incongruous connections between East and West. On the one hand, it evoked India without representing, or even acknowledging, its reality of poverty, overpopulation, and racial-religious wars between Hindus and Muslims. But, on the other hand, India was not America's paradigmatic exotic Other, as it was for Britain. For centuries England was closely tied to the political and social realities of its colony, so exotic appropriations of India in British music, such as the Beatles' "Within You without You" or "Norwegian Wood," were more allied to a traditional Orientalist practice of "possessing" a colony. American culture, and the counterculture in particular, had relatively little historical connection to India, so unlike "White Rabbit"—

whose string of exotic connections stems back to an established French and then American Orientalist narrative—the appropriation of India in countercultural music was not an afterecho or reshaping of nineteenth-century Orientalist tropes.

Certainly songs such as "Eastern Jam" were profitable imitations of the British "accent" in music and sounded analogs of spiritual transcendence. But they also revealed the counterculture's own role in America's neocolonial political situation. Because America was not engaged in a colonial relationship with India, India could become a reservoir of guilt-free Orientalism. In a political sense, though, there were dozens of countries that were out of reach of America's hegemonic fingertips. What was special about India then, as opposed to Mongolia or Gabon, for instance? In 1955 Prime Minister Jawaharlal Nehru helped establish India as the largest and most powerful nonaligned nation.[71] At the weeklong Bandung Conference in April 1955, delegates from twenty-nine countries of Asia and Africa expressed their dissatisfaction with the treatment of Asia and Africa by the rival superpowers—namely the United States and the Soviet Union. The conference hosts—Indonesia, Myanmar, Sri Lanka, India, and Pakistan—took the lead in a consensual conclusion that "colonialism in all of its manifestations," including Soviet policies and Western colonial pressures, should be condemned. Nehru, in particular, claimed the spotlight, definitively stating India's position in global politics:

We do not agree with the Communist teachings, we do not agree with the anti-Communist teachings. . . . I never challenged the right of my country to defend itself if it has to. . . . If we rely on others, whatever great powers they might be, if we look to them for sustenance, then we are weakened. . . . So far as I am concerned, it does not matter what war takes place; we will not take part in it unless we have to defend ourselves. . . . Every step that takes place in reducing the area in the world which may be called the *unaligned* area is a dangerous step and leads to war. . . . Are we, the countries of Asia and Africa, devoid of any position except being pro-Communist or anti-Communist?[72]

As neither a client state nor an enemy of America (or the Soviet Union at the time), Nehru described an India that stood for nonalignment. His forceful argument outlined nothing short of India's political agenda for the upcoming decades. India would not be reduced to pro or con and would not engage in the dualism of Western hegemonic political games. So in perhaps one of the most significant misreadings of global politics, the counterculture evoked India as if the absence of superpower alignment meant the absence of politics. India seemed the most direct contrast to places like Vietnam (or Korea)—two-sided, pro or con, Communist or democratic, down to their very geographical boundaries. For the counterculture, India appeared to have dropped out of the global power struggle, exemplifying on the world stage what Timothy Leary had advised the counterculture to do at the Human Be-In.

For Country Joe and the Fish, in particular, India was the ticket out of the dialectical left-right politics of Berkeley and into a nonpolitical countercultural wonderland in San Francisco. Before entering the countercultural scene in San Francisco, Country Joe and the Fish were deep in the dialectical movement tradition—engaging with explicitly political agendas, and making music that was movement-oriented. Given this reputation, the band would seem the least likely to step outside of the political complex. But, as historian Robert Cantwell caustically points out, by the sixties "a new millennialism, an apolitical and anti-intellectual mix of Zen mysticism, peyote-cult animism, and pueblo-inspired tribalism, became the wellspring from which a new youth culture flowed."[73] Whether Cantwell paints an accurate portrait of the counterculture, or merely describes how it appeared on the surface, clearly Country Joe and the Fish assumed some degree of "apoliticalness" and "anti-intellectualism" to gain favor.

In Gabriel García Márquez's popular 1967 novel *One Hundred Years of Solitude*, the distinction between the factual history and invented mythology about the novel's town, Macondo, is blurred. Franco Moretti proposes that such blurring or "rewriting [of] an event in mythical form is tantamount to making it meaningful: freeing it from the profane world of cause and effects, and projecting into it the symbolic richness of the archetype."[74] Likewise, consuming the exotic afforded the counterculture a method of engaging with politics indirectly, without seeming to deal in the real world of "cause and effects." Members of the San Francisco counterculture were largely inactive with regard to American politics. Unlike the Berkeley activists across the Bay, for example, they were not, for the most part, fully engaged in anti–Vietnam War activities until the end of the decade. But they were certainly aware of the gravity of Cold War politics and the impact of the Vietnam War at home. Underground newspapers that spoke for the New Left assumed a forceful anti–Vietnam position and were circulated in San Francisco.[75] So while the counterculture's promoters employed the exotic to construct a veneer of Otherworldliness, they also used it as protection. On the surface, exotic signifiers marked the counterculture as nonpolitical, nonmainstream, nonmaterialist, and non-Christian. Songs such as "White Rabbit" and "Eastern Jam" suggested that participation in the Otherworldly or mystical spaces that they offered could provide the fantastical qualities that modern dialectical civilization lacked. The exotic allowed the counterculture to appear to exist in an idealistic anti-Occidental frame—a frame that remained intact when political reality was not overtly challenged but kept at arm's length.

"White Rabbit" and "Eastern Jam," like Márquez's *One*

Hundred Years of Solitude and J. R. R. Tolkien's *Lord of the Rings* (a huge success when published in paperback in 1965) advertised exoticism's promise of escape, but there was a catch. The traditional Orientalist narrative manipulated in "White Rabbit" reveals the horror of America's mode of operation in Vietnam, and the nonaligned exoticism in "Eastern Jam" strives to be aligned with the nonaligned to avoid the perils of dialectical Cold War nation-building. But both are neocolonial strategies subversively engaged in politics because ultimately there is no way to detach completely from the realities of a consumer capitalist system and simultaneously consume exotic products and sounds to appear outside the system. When Yossarian, the main character of Joseph Heller's *Catch-22*, attempts or imagines multiple scenarios to get out of catch-22 reasoning, he ultimately can only escape the absurd political bureaucracy and mindless violence of World War II by running away to a place that is outside of the dialectical war complex. In the final chapter, Yossarian decides to join his bombardier friend, Orr, who has deserted the army and made it to Sweden. Marked as a neutral haven, Sweden is nonetheless caught in the political paradox of *Catch-22*. It is marked as an exotic escape, a solution to catch-22, but only in relation to the political powers engaged in war games. Yossarian is trapped by paradoxical, circular reasoning yet again, "jeopardizing his traditional rights of freedom and independence by daring to exercise them."[76] In a way, this was also the counterculture's Catch-22. To craft a nonpolitical space, it had to engage with an Otherworldly exoticism that itself is inevitably marked by dialectical, sociopolitical realities.

Chapter Four

The Natural Persona

Freedom, the Grateful Dead, and an Anticommercial Counterculture

In July 1969, Columbia Pictures released the movie *Easy Rider,* cowritten by the film's two starring actors, Peter Fonda and Dennis Hopper, directed by Dennis Hopper in his directorial debut, and aurally illustrated by a rock-and-roll soundtrack featuring the folk-turned-psychedelic rock band, the Byrds. Fonda's and Hopper's characters, Wyatt and Billy, are long-haired, drugged-out bikers from Los Angeles who take a cross-country trip through the South in order to reach New Orleans for Mardi Gras. Their travels bring them into contact with a range of people—a rancher and his family, a hitchhiker, prostitutes, "rednecks," a lawyer for the ACLU, and "hippies" on a commune. Before reaching the promised land of New Orleans, the freedom-loving, self gratifying Harley riders explore a host of environments from the natural landscapes of Monument Valley to the open highways of the Southwest, from small-town streets to local graveyards. Like their namesakes, Wyatt Earp and Billy the Kid, the film's heroes are rebels, not because of crimes they have perpetrated and consequences they have avoided, but rather for crimes they have not committed and punishments about which they are naive. Theirs is a tale of freedom, not action, a world of anything goes, not of rules and penalties. There is no need to wage a war against mainstream conformity when the goal is to do whatever we want, whenever we want, wherever we want.

Easy Rider's popularity at the Cannes Film Festival and with young audiences that year spoke to a quality of yearning that permeated popular culture at the end of the sixties. The film nostalgically lauded a countercultural sensibility that had seemed viable only a few years before its release. Even as the final credits roll down the screen, potentially shattering the movie's two hours of fantastical freedom with the names and achievements of those who had constructed it, the longing for a countercultural autonomy still holds on with the sound of the Byrds' "Ballad of Easy Rider." The ballad rides the movie out to its end—"All I wanted was to be free / And that's the way it turned out to be." In one sense, the film's popularity can be attributed to people's general desire to enjoy freedom and pluralism vicariously through fictional characters. But with *Easy Rider,* there was something more tangible and more palpable going on. Moviegoers were emboldened with a nostalgic idea not only that the film's characters were victorious in their quest for unlimited freedom, but that, with the right music and attitude, they too could ride out the credits of the constructed world around them and be self-made, unfettered, and free.

The irony that lingers around *Easy Rider* and other stereotypical depictions of the countercultural sensibility is that the illusion of freedom that drives it is the same one that propels the very nationalistic, goal-directed concept of the American Dream. The dream, countercultural or national, is about having the freedom to be whatever you want to be. The problem for the counterculture before it became a media spectacle during the 1967 Summer of Love was that, if anything, it defined itself by what it was not—not allied to the mainstream, not allied to any one thing. So while the freedom of the American Dream is goal-directed, defining a course of action to get from what you are to what you want to be, the freedom of the counterculture was the availability of all courses of action to get to no place in particular. Inevitably, the counterculture included scores of items also found in the mainstream—women, men, sex, food, drink, drugs, clothing, shelter, laughter, humor, and so on. The difference between the counterculture and the mainstream, then, was in how those items were used, treated, and valued. The fact of sharing the motivating ideal of freedom with the mainstream was not a blight on or blow to the counterculture because it didn't conceive of itself in dialectical opposition to the mainstream. What was important for the counterculture was to distinguish itself and its brand of freedom from that of the mainstream. Nature was the key to making that distinction.

In 1932, Aldous Huxley published *Brave New World,* a book that, thirty-five years later, was as widely popular with the San Francisco counterculture as its author was. A futuristic fantasy, the novel depicts a horrifying totalitarian world of twenty-four-hour surveillance, complete mechanization, test-tube babies, and enforced cultural conformity. Within this narrative, Huxley offers advice on how to stop civilization's progress toward such a potential apocalypse: "[Do] anything not to consume, [go] Back to Nature."[1] Huxley's narrative draws a direct relationship between consumerism and symbolic freedom in order to guarantee the success of *Brave New World*'s thesis. The tangible prospect of a technology-driven, inhuman future could only be stopped by a retreat to the utopia offered by nature, and this retreat to nature could only be achieved by not consuming.

Huxley's instruction to reject consumer culture by returning to nature is not necessarily reflexive. In other words, a rejection of consumer culture does not *require* a return to nature. Composers in the fifties like Karlheinz Stockhausen, for example, had relied on technology to define themselves at the forefront of an anticommercial avant-garde. Yet technology was malleable. It played a more complicated role for cultures linked to popular music because the musical technology required to produce many forms of popular music had become associated with commercialism on account of the music's consumer appeal. Rock and roll, in particular, saw technology as a consumable product of culture rather than of nature.

Cultural theorist Raymond Williams explains that "one of the most powerful uses of nature has been in [the] selective sense of goodness and innocence . . . nature is what man has not made, though if he made it long enough ago—a hedgerow or a desert—it will usually be included as *natural*."[2] When the things that "man has not made" (or made "long enough ago") signify "goodness" and "innocence," then a technological culture, such as the counterculture, which defined itself by what it was not, played a precarious game of construction. The counterculture would somehow have to distinguish itself from the mainstream's predominant and most obvious mode of freedom—namely, consumer capitalism.

To refuse allegiance to materialist values and refuse participation in mass society did not automatically imply a rejection of consumer capitalism. Could the counterculture be unassailable by popular consumer culture (as a sign of its freedom) and still be a friend to technology? Nature became a mediator of sorts, as the counterculture systematically obscured its very real reliance on technological advancements and capitalist structures of mainstream America via a complex, and often contradictory, engagement with them. In the same way that technology was ambiguously coded depending on whether it was deemed a consumable commodity or "naturalized" by its context (as in the Be-In poster), nature, too, came in a variety of discursive forms, allowing the counterculture to interact with commercial culture and disguise its own consumerism.

For the developing counterculture in the safe haven of San

Francisco's Haight-Ashbury district, Huxley's advice—do anything not to consume, go back to nature—might have seemed an insoluble contradiction. On the surface, the countercultural way of life appeared completely different from the mainstream's, and both groups were content, in a sense, with that distinction. In terms of ideological orientation, however, the two groups existed in the same industrialized capitalist country and invested in value systems that were not so far apart. Freedom to buy a new dishwasher with money earned from a nine-to-five office job was the same as freedom to buy a concert ticket to a Jefferson Airplane show with money earned from work in a local boutique or money given as a graduation present. The counterculture needed to distinguish itself, and, perhaps even convince itself, that it was based on a unique brand of freedom that was everything mainstream conformity was not. So the insular counterculture constructed, identified with, and consumed a congeries of natural signifiers in its attempts to appear free of that which seemed commercial.

Robbie Robertson, best known as lead guitarist and lyricist of the Band, was born in Toronto. At the age of fifteen he joined up with an American from Arkansas, Ronnie Hawkins, and played rockabilly for five years until their band, the Hawks, was noticed by Bob Dylan in 1963. Hawkins left, but the five players comprising the group that would become the Band four years later took an offer from Dylan to accompany him on his tumultuous 1965–66 tour. Except for Robertson, the Band's members played multiple instruments, together able to incorporate an encyclopedic array of musical styles, textures, and effects into their songs. This ability was certainly appealing to Dylan, as it was to the burgeoning countercultural bands, but it carried little weight, even negative weight, for audiences during the tour. Pluralism, agility, and most of all, amplification, were not hallmarks of folk purity to audiences wanting Dylan's signature raspy acoustic folk stylings.

That Dylan and the Band were heckled from one concert to the next was not surprising given his reception at the 1965 Newport Folk Festival in July, prior to his going on tour. With the Paul Butterfield Blues Band backing him up, Bob Dylan infamously broke away from his acoustic past to "go electric" on the festival's stage. His use of amplification and an electric guitar shocked listeners in part because folk-based protest music had previously been associated with the "naturalness" of acoustic sounds.[3] Whether betraying nature's purity or forging new potential for nature's meaning, Dylan's break ushered in amplification and electronics as a mainstay of folk-rock groups and psychedelic rock bands across the country.

As the United States escalated its involvement in the Vietnam War, using technological weaponry on a massive scale against a largely agrarian and less elaborately armed guerrilla force, the aggressive amplified sound of the counterculture had a particular resonance with these increasingly destructive historical circumstances. Performances at the Fillmore Auditorium featured bands like the Grateful Dead and Jefferson Airplane, well stocked with electric musical instruments and elaborate state-of-the-art amplification systems, playing against a backdrop of strobe lights, colored light shows, and enlarged photographic images displayed by multiple slide projectors. But promoters, advertisers, and critics often downplayed the music's connection to technology, keeping the counterculture detached from what might be considered mainstream political and commercial signifiers. In spite of the electronic mediation of most Fillmore Auditorium performances, many critics perceived, or at least depicted, a different, more bucolic scene. During his extended stay in the Haight-Ashbury district in 1967, *Village Voice* reporter Richard Goldstein offered the following description of the "San Francisco sound":

> The big surprise in this music has nothing to do with electronics or some zany new camp. Performers in this

city have knocked all that civility away. They are down in the dark, grainy roots. . . . The sound of the Grateful Dead, or Moby Grape, or Country Joe and the Fish, is jug band scraping against jazz. . . . Their music, they insist, is a virgin forest, uncharted and filled with wildlife. This unwillingness to add technological effect is close to the spirit of folk music before Dylan electrified it.[4]

In part, Goldstein's assessment is based on a comparison between the pop-experimental electronic music scenes in Los Angeles and on the East Coast and the stylistic eclecticism of the San Francisco sound. Goldstein accurately observes that "added technological effects," such as tape loops and electronically synthesized sounds, were rare in the counterculture's music. Yet to insist that the music's "surprise" attributes had "nothing to do with electronics" and then to paraphrase approvingly the notion that the music was "uncharted virgin forest," seems critically suspect and ideologically naive at best. Even more incongruous is Goldstein's likening of the countercultural sound to "the spirit of folk music before Dylan electrified it" because few things stand more obviously as precursors to the countercultural sound than Dylan's electric performance at the 1965 Newport Folk Festival. Goldstein's inconsistent mix of metaphors is, in a sense, a reflection of technology's inconsistent role in cultural definition. If technology represents commercial artifice, then the technologically mediated music of the counterculture was in danger of being dismissed as fake, "unnatural" showmanship. In such a situation, critics like Goldstein were in a position to rescue countercultural music from the appearance of a commercial commodity, disguising its connection to technology with naturalizing descriptive language.

Ironically, the counterculture's allegiance to an anticommercial image—however manufactured—would prove to be one of its most marketable commodities, profitable for the record companies, advertisers, the underground press, and countercultural musicians. Major record label distribution helped to spread this image and, consequently, reinforce its ideological implications across the country. But this took maneuvering, especially on the part of some of the musicians. As Clive Davis, president of Arista Records, recalled at the time of the first Monterey Pop Festival in 1967, "The artists felt that it would look phony and be unrepresentative to their followers if there was any hint of interest in money or acquisition or competition."[5] In turn, artists put on their own "phony" show of disregard for profit. Davis goes on to remark that there were exceptions: "some groups, the Dead being one, were noneconomically motivated."[6]

The band that Davis deemed as "noneconomically motivated" was the same one that enjoyed social and economic success for thirty years while simultaneously being blessed with labels such as "true community musicians" and "the quintessential countercultural rock band." The Grateful Dead advertised an image of itself as a collection of anticommercial unprofessionals, and obviously people such as Davis were convinced by this image. At Ken Kesey's Acid Tests beginning in 1965, the Trips Festival of 1966, San Francisco Mime Troupe shows, the Human Be-In in January 1967, their open-door ranch in Novato, and their shared home at 710 Ashbury Street in the heart of the Haight-Ashbury district, the Grateful Dead's band members became the core of San Francisco's countercultural community in the midsixties. The high-tech band, however, went far beyond their San Franciscan musical contemporaries in crafting a "green," communal image. And perhaps they had to take extreme measures with their image in order to balance the extent to which they indulged in cutting-edge musical technology. They traded upon the ambiguous relationship between commercialism and technology, with elaborate natural referents as their bargaining chips.

The band, for example, often gave free performances in

the Panhandle of Golden Gate Park on the edge of the Haight-Ashbury district. Centered in the middle of San Francisco's urban landscape, the park is a huge garden, a green space that can be accessed without leaving the city. For these performances, the Dead often collaborated with a group named the Diggers, who handed out free food and supplies. From late 1966 until mid-1968, the Diggers functioned as the Haight-Ashbury's social workers, city planners, street entertainers, and welfare providers. Associating themselves in name with the original seventeenth-century English farming radicals, the Diggers orchestrated elaborate street happenings, produced and distributed hundreds of leaflets, and transformed the Haight-Ashbury district into a "free city" with several "free" stores that gave away clothing, household items, and food.

The contrast between the original Diggers and the Haight-Ashbury Diggers is notable. Neither planners nor builders, the seventeenth-century group was made up of farmers, radical in ideology but practical in their till-the-soil, back-to-nature realization of ideas. While using the same name allowed the Haight-Ashbury group to be associated with a "back to the earth" philosophy, there wasn't anything particularly natural, such as farmers or farmland, about the group. On a practical level, the San Francisco Diggers attempted to make living in the Haight-Ashbury district free of charge for its residents: yet there were also ideological implications to their "free city" agenda. Historian Dominick Cavallo observes that "the Digger belief that everything should be free was inseparable from a naïve and rather traditional faith in the power of American abundance and technological ingenuity . . . [They] assumed American enterprise and technology could create unlimited abundance and leisure for everyone."[7] In reality, it wasn't nature that enabled the counterculture to "liberate" itself from capitalism's work-buy-sell agenda. "American abundance" was distributed to Haight-Ashbury residents for free by a nonfarming group in the middle of a highly commercial city that had been founded on violent and scarring resource extraction.

The "noncommercialism" of the counterculture's "natural" associations had deep contradictions. Countercultural participants wore Native American attire, ruffled Edwardian clothing, and old Levi's jeans (all obtained for free at the Diggers' stores) as a way to reject the cookie-cutter fashions of the modern American middle class. But wearing such items, along with homemade clothes and knitted accessories, made them no less invested in the consumerism of a free, democratic, and capitalist America. At best, the fact that they didn't buy new mass-produced items of clothing was a show of nonmaterialism, which has only since been equated with countercultural noncommercialism. Though it may be clear that rejecting materialist values by living in a free city is not equivalent to rejecting consumer capitalism, the counterculture had to draw distinctions somewhere. Its brand of freedom had to be uniquely countercultural.

The Diggers were highly invested in the project of defining countercultural freedom. They worked within the countercultural community as if it were a tabula rasa of American freedom, and the Grateful Dead, in many ways, provided the aesthetic backdrop to the Diggers' stage of commercially liberated abundance. "In 1967, the Grateful Dead's equipment weighed thirteen hundred pounds and fit into [a] van." By May 18, 1968, at "the Santa Clara Fairgrounds show, it weighed around six thousand pounds and still fit in a van, a much larger one."[8] Clearly, the Grateful Dead had a fervent appetite for technology—an appetite constructively linked to their Digger-like notion of freedom and illustrated by the story of the Grateful Dead at the first Monterey Pop Festival in June 1967. The band lobbied for the festival to be a nonprofit affair and agreed to play only if the proceeds went to a worthy cause.[9] On this score, festival coordinators were reassuring, but during the festival itself, the band faced another profiteering twist. When it came to signing film and record releases, the Dead refused.

Though they had stepped outside of the media loop, the Dead still made their position of noncommercialism known. They took CBS and the Fender Corporation—ostensibly the festival's corporate sponsors—to task. CBS and Fender had lent a million dollars of equipment to the festival in return for free advertising. The Dead sent a telegram to the corporations and a copy to critic Ralph Gleason at the *San Francisco Chronicle*. With Gleason's help, they advertised their intentions: on the last day in Monterey, the band would "liberate" some of the "corporate" equipment in order to provide a week of free concerts to the people of San Francisco, and then return it when they were done. The Dead's *fantasy* scenario became a reality. On the last night of the festival, the equipment had been left unguarded because members of the Dead's crew had given LSD to the security people, and were able to load the equipment.

The week of free performances that followed in San Francisco's Golden Gate Park was a huge success. The band built a makeshift stage, patched extension cords to a nearby house for electricity, borrowed a generator, coordinated with both the Diggers, who were dispensing food, and the Hell's Angels, who were guarding the equipment. When they were done, they telegraphed CBS and the Fender Corporation (which had become one in a corporate merger) and returned the equipment. Carol Brightman describes the whole incident as "a guerrilla action": it "served to polish the Dead's image as rock 'n' roll Robin Hoods, dedicated to the principle of *free* music—of liberating the surplus of the rich to blow the minds of the young."[10]

In one sense, Brightman's analogy is right on the mark. For all intents and purposes, Golden Gate Park in 1966–67 "belonged" to the counterculture and its bands as a space rarely violated by the mainstream. In this liminal place, alternatively seen as a makeover of Robin Hood's forest, the Dead could share nature freely with their listeners. Such incidents substantially reinforced the Dead's image as the people's band. The natural setting helped to downplay the band's consumption of the very corporate symbols they purportedly despised. And while the successful, fun, communal performances in a beautiful outdoor milieu represented freedom and liberation, the corporations that produced, sold, and bought the technology became negatively branded as perpetrating consumer culture.

The fact that the Dead were using corporate-made, sophisticated, musical technology to create their music received minimal critical attention. In part, it was because the cultural signifiers of naturalness drew the electric guitar-centered music into the fold. Appropriating natural signifiers made the counterculture seem at a distance from consumer capitalism (and closer to a more original America), while giving it access to capitalism's products. A similar dance with mainstream commercial and technological culture characterized the Dead's own business dealings. The Grateful Dead decided to give each member of the band an equal voice in decision making. As major record companies began to court various San Francisco bands in late 1966, the Dead held off from signing while demanding total control over their content and production, titles, and graphic designs. Warner Brothers finally agreed to meet the Dead's demands for unlimited studio time, complete publishing rights, and an unusual approach to royalties. Traditionally, albums were filled with short songs that could easily fit the AM radio station format because record companies, commercial radio, and the music industry increased their profits when royalties were based on the number of tracks per album.[11] The Grateful Dead, however, insisted that their royalties be based on the total amount of musical time per album side.

The Grateful Dead's negotiations to put artistic control in the hands of the musicians helped maintain their anticorporate, community-based image—an image that stuck with them for another thirty years. Yet given that many of the Dead's songs included extended improvised sections, thus making them unsuitable for radio play, their negotiations were equally concerned with forming a new industry standard within which their music could make money. This double agenda also held true for live concerts. When the band performed in venues requiring ticket purchase, they assumed control of the concert arrangements. By offering a reduced single price for all tickets and first-come, first-serve seating, they welcomed the community and profited at the same time, often packing auditoriums to three times their designated capacity.

Even with the success of their agenda, luck also helped associate the Dead's technophilia with freedom and liberation rather than with consumer culture. Technology, on its own, is anything but natural, and to the Luddite, or even to the countercultural participant deeply identified with a self-image of naturalness, it can be seen to fragment the self, undermine freedom, and bind humans to notions of rational progress. So the Grateful Dead rejected industry standards of record companies, took economic control of their performances, staged incidents such as the "equipment liberation," and became revolutionaries who aggressively enacted their noncommercialism by attempting to fight corporate control. Fortuitously for the Dead, what made the music business seem so riddled with commercialism had far more to do with the corporate profiteering motive than with the actual technologies used to produce records and make sounds. So the band never had to fight the commercialism of the music industry by forfeiting their stock of musical technology in protest. Instead they showed their noncommercialism by doing what they wanted, giving away and indulging in "nature" for free, and not conforming to the industry's capitalist demands. Musical technology was, paradoxically, a hidden secret that was right in front of everybody's eyes.

The ideological and moral implications of the Dead's "natural" image continue to offer up a host of ironies. Even the identity suggested by the band's name and by the imagery of skeletons and death that adorned most of their albums seems deliberately crafted to fit a particular image. A popular association at the time was the ancient folk legend of the "grateful dead man":

> We learn of a hero who finds the creditors are refusing to permit the burial of a corpse until the dead man's debts have been paid. The hero spends his last penny to ransom the dead man's body and to secure his burial. Later, in the course of his adventures, he is joined by a mysterious stranger who agrees to help him in all his endeavors. This stranger is the grateful dead man. The only condition which the grateful dead man makes when he agrees to help the hero is that all winnings which the latter makes shall be equally divided.[12]

With such mythical associations, the Grateful Dead's image seemed culled from imaginings of a distant egalitarian folk world from the past. And with visual associations of playful skeletons on their album covers and poster art, what in medieval times had been a serious religious fascination with death was transformed into a celebratory and fanciful take on death more akin to Mexican Day of the Dead festivities. Both the visual and mythical associations exude what Umberto Eco has called a "medieval consciousness." Like other modern American communal spaces, such as Disneyland and Disney-World, there is "a total lack of distinction between aesthetic objects and mechanical objects. All [is] ruled by a taste for gaudy color and a notion of light as a physical element of pleasure."[13] Indeed, the Grateful Dead's concerts in the late sixties, and after, appeared to exhibit such a consciousness, with jugglers in velvety peaked caps, circles of drummers and guitarists, Coleman stoves for communal food, and bright tie-dyed costumes. Their concerts were already imbibed with nostalgia—for a populist aura of a time and space long ago. In Raymond Williams's terms, their neomedievalism became a stand-in for nature, in the same way that Renaissance fairs, medieval sword-fight reenactments, and Dungeons and Dragons game groups provide an ideological, if temporary, haven from modern technological capitalism. The constructedness of their natural countercultural space of freedom was within arm's reach, though, ready to be uncovered. Regardless of how much neomedievalism functioned as the antithesis to mechanical civilization, the Dead's concerts still resembled a capitalist marketplace—offering music, handmade jewelry, and attire to buy and consume.

The counterculture's retreat to "nature" implicitly negotiated the relationships among American abundance, technological progress, and the environment. But that, in itself, was nothing new. In the nineteenth century, America was fervently colonizing uncharted territory—manifest destiny linked moral and economic progress with western expansion. In part, this progress was enabled by human control over nature (and native people)—namely, the transformation of wilderness and desert into cultivated farms, and then larger cities. At the continent's western edge lay San Francisco. The city's population increased from one thousand in 1848 to thirty thousand five years later, exemplifying the "success" of manifest destiny's agenda.[14] While individualism and western expansion had, to a certain extent, been enabled by taming nature, the human development of this conquered western wilderness seemed to mark the end of the line. The West was now being stifled by cities and other ever-increasing advancements of human civilization. While the ideal of American democratic and capitalistic progress has often been symbolized by a conquest narrative that has transformed nature from wilderness, to rural farm life, to urban landscape, the counterculture, and the Grateful

Dead in particular, cleverly negotiated this narrative in their music and still appeared to celebrate nature's freedom.[15]

The song "Sugar Magnolia" was a mainstay in the Grateful Dead's concert repertoire. It was considered in mainstream popular culture to be a characteristic example of the Dead's "countercultural" music, though it didn't appear on vinyl until the 1970 *American Beauty* album. "Sugar Magnolia" and the other nine songs on *American Beauty* are described in the album's liner notes as "blues, country, and folk-styled originals," intended to reflect the album's theme of American roots.[16] The song tells the story of a man wooing his lover in an idyllic pastoral landscape. As advertised, "Sugar Magnolia" possesses many of the musical trappings of an early-twentieth-century folk ballad—a strophic form, a comfortable 4/4 meter, clearly articulated lyrics, consistent dynamics, simple melodic vocabulary, a memorable refrain, and a conversational exchange between solo voice and group. In addition, the song's instrumental riffs and tone colors allude to country music, the references to which are about as American as the use of an underlying harmonic structure derived from the blues.

The narrative of "Sugar Magnolia" is relayed in the first person by a man expounding on his lover's many positive traits, describing the activities and feelings he likes to share with her. When the song begins, however, the listener is not yet aware that "Magnolia" signifies anything but a flower. Two guitars and percussion play a five-bar instrumental introduction with a slightly laid-back tempo and subtle country twang that emphasizes the song's harmonic and melodic grounding in a bluesy tonic/dominant alteration. Into this comfortable musical setting, the story begins with "Sugar Magnolia, blossoms blooming / Head's all empty and I don't care." Like the "American roots" that are tidily encapsulated in the instrumental introduction, the lyrics speak to something rural, something distant from modern civilization. Nature is unencumbered, as the blossoms freely bloom and the mind is left unrestricted by rational thought. The musical reinforcement of the lyrical imagery almost goes unnoticed because it consists of musical characteristics—harmonization in thirds with flute chirps in the background—that have become so iconic of nature that a listener would have been hard pressed to imagine anything different.

While the instrumental introduction, first stanza of narrative, and musical setting all elaborate on the idea of idyllic nature, the next stanza does the same, but with a subtle, even underhanded twist. The narrator tries to coax his lover to join him under a willow tree so that together they "can discover the wonders of nature / rolling in the rushes down by the riverside." Certainly a pure, unspoiled nature is still present here, signaled by various characteristic features of folk music—the repetition of the same musical material as the first stanza, an ongoing gentle vocal quality, and a comfortable alteration between harmonized and solo voice that makes the setting serene and familiar. Even the euphemism for sex ("we can discover the wonders of nature" by "rolling in the rushes") sounds like frolicking fun in this pastoral, folklike milieu. At the same time, though, the easy flow of folk music sounds makes nature and woman become one and the same. The magnolia blossom of the first line is transformed into the narrator's lover: like the river, the willow, and the rushes, the woman is simply another untainted object of the natural landscape.

Folk music—be it rural white country, urban folk music, or African American blues—plays an important role not only in the shaping of nature and woman in "Sugar Magnolia," but in its representation of America. One of the most enduring representations of "the folk" emerged in relation to the radical Left of 1930s America. Liberal political factions searched for a new set of values that had roots in precapitalist and anticapitalist sources. While some found these values in an affirmation of individualistic ideals, others turned to a socialist model that celebrated the seemingly cohesive life of an idealized small folk community. This communal context offered something comforting in relation to the increasing atomization of American society and often incorporated music into its collective "progressive" causes.[17] While the music of the 1930s radical Left was an integral part of union meetings, political rallies, and workers' strikes, its proletarian function has since been romanticized, and has come to represent something untainted by commerce. This untainted purity contributed to the folk revival of the late fifties and early sixties, adding a sonic aura of seemingly honest expression as an alternative to a polished superficial culture of commodities.

Not surprisingly, allusions to folk musics and folk myths proved to be a crucial resource for the counterculture's self-image. As in the music of Bob Dylan, Joan Baez, and other early sixties folk revivalists, folk-like "simplicity" in countercultural music offered listeners an aural antithesis to the gimmickry of show business. Those who listened to folk music could feel they were supporting an anticonsumerist agenda without the organized effort connected to folk's earlier ideals. Yet in contrast to their folk predecessors and contemporaries, countercultural bands, steeped in pluralism, *included* folk musics among many other musical styles. In so doing, they were freed from the social and cultural constraints of a single musical label while appearing to have the freedom to tap the wells of an unmediated American spirit. Historian Robert Cantwell suggests that bands such as the Grateful Dead operated "in a cultural field that could still objectify the American identity."[18] In other words, the countercultural image, adorned with folk allusions, appeared untainted by the commercial and corporate elements of modern daily American life while simultaneously being tied to America's founding principles of freedom and liberty. Needless to say, the folksy appearance of the preindustrial and rural in "Sugar Magnolia" is, to a certain extent, a fabrication. The values of freedom and individualism that are nostalgically used to characterize a long-lost pastoral age were, in large part, the same values that fueled America's market-driven "democracy" at the time.

A similar set of ironies attend the lyrical parallel of nature and woman in "Sugar Magnolia." Historically, a utilitarian approach to the environment (in the form of cities, houses, technology, and industrialized agriculture) has been marked as masculine, while the earth itself, and its preservation, has been coded as feminine. Unfortunately for the counterculture, its spokespeople, its outward face to the rest of the country through music, and its location in an urban and industrial city, were all directly or indirectly masculine. To extract its image from the traditional category of utilitarian, then, the counterculture had, in a sense, to feminize itself. To do this, remarks cultural theorist Aniko Bodroghkozy, "involved focusing on the 'hippie chick.'"[19] Musicians, artists, and writers were on the job. One of the front covers of the underground countercultural newspaper, the *San Francisco Oracle*, in the late sixties, for example, was adorned with a photograph of a beautiful naked woman.[20] At first glance, the woman appears to be at ease with her natural setting, lying naked on the grass, surrounded by trees and mountains, looking up into the sky, and visually encircled by a symbolic earth. Yet, like Gustav Courbet's late nineteenth-century work *L'origin du Monde* ("Origin of the World"), which depicts a woman's crotch without the rest of her body, the focus of the *Oracle* cover from slightly above ground level, is on the woman's spread legs and vagina. Overtly pornographic, the newspaper objectifies woman as Mother Earth. Although this is, in part, a celebration of nature's life-giving qualities, it is at the expense of reducing woman to her procreative potential.[21]

If technology and environmental destruction symbolized urban man, his antithesis was the natural woman who preserves nature, refrains from violence, and produces life. So, to evoke nature as woman was to appear, at least on the surface, to be nonmasculine, nonmodern, and, even antitechnology.

Environmentalist John Miller argues that the representation of nature as a life-giving woman often reveals a culture's desire to identify with a "pre-industrial agrarian epoch" or Paradise Lost.[22] While songs like "Sugar Magnolia" gave voice to such a feminized, "agrarian" concept of community (however idealized, sexist, or inaccurate), many in the Haight-Ashbury district, including the Grateful Dead, Jefferson Airplane, and Big Brother and the Holding Company, attempted to transform these aesthetic constructions into reality. By the midsixties, groups of people in the Haight began to share housing, creating minicommunes, and become part of extended families whose individual members they had never known. Certainly the Grateful Dead (followed by the Diggers) were a formative influence in this trend—not only in the example they set by living communally, but in their rhetoric during performances. The Dead's bassist Phil Lesh often encouraged audiences to share the band's philosophy of community: "It is the dream and hope of The Grateful Dead that small moral communities continue to grow. These families represent the true nature of all future people who are presently subjugated by the paid-off and unaware community."[23] The Dead-inspired lifestyle, of course, was as far from a "rural" setting as possible since communal living took place in apartments and houses in a major American city.

Communal living situations were coded as more natural and less consumerist, appearing to be a symbolic alternative to the commercial, urban lifestyle of mainstream America. But the reality of "social retreat" offered cruel ironies, especially given that the practical running of such enclaves was seldom prioritized. The large California communes that began in the sixties, such as Seacrest, disintegrated because the ideology of living freely conflicted with the responsibilities necessary for day-to-day existence.[24] Lacking an internal economy, these groups became dependent on food stamps, welfare, and governmental services—programs administered by the very mainstream social system they claimed to be detached from. Many of the smaller communal living situations in the Haight-Ashbury district fell prey to the same decline, pointing to a larger ideological paradox that governed many communal living situations.[25] In nineteenth-century antebellum days, hundreds of communities—like the Shakers and Brook Farm—emerged, advocating for socialism, abolitionism, and, in some cases, feminism. A key difference with the sixties groups was an emphasis on individual freedom and pleasure (rather than a societal cause) that ultimately was realized at the expense of group unity and coherence. Without shared communal ideals enforced by rules, sixties groups were more fleeting and economically vulnerable.

A handful of songs touched on this downside to the counterculture's alternative lifestyle. The Grateful Dead's "Truckin'" describes the self-destructiveness of living the low life, and Bob Dylan's "Maggie's Farm" hints darkly at the lack of ethical and practical responsibility that a communal lifestyle could engender. Even in *Easy Rider* there is a brief respite from its nostalgic yearning when it depicts the commune-dwellers as starving, looking for dead animals on the side of the road, and sowing seeds in barren, sandy soil. Perhaps Grateful Dead biographer Carol Brightman is accurate in her assessment that the Dead's "deep-seated suspicions of the corporate world" were ultimately rooted in the band's "horror of 'selling out.'" If so, then shaping a natural, feminized, preindustrial community around them could quell their fears.[26] But no matter how much the music depicted idealized fantasies of oneness with nature and aesthetic qualities apparently missing in an increasingly masculinist utilitarian environment, nature was still accessed by things "man-made." Even in "Sugar Magnolia," where the listener has a ringside seat to a man's courting ritual by the river with a woman who, by name, is part of nature, everything is through the eyes of and at the service of the male narrator. Magnolia "takes the wheel" when he has been drinking too much. She pays for his speeding tickets. She, as representative of nature, is "everything" that he "needs."

As in the Band's "Up on Cripple Creek," the ideal woman is a "drunkard's dream" because she takes care of him. ("She mends me." "She defends me.") "Sugar Magnolia" thus reinscribes a masculine, utilitarian approach to nature. While the song uses folk, blues, and country to represent the naturalness of "America's roots," these sounds also constitute an unwavering musical disguise. Within this constant medium, the story is relayed through the man's perspective. The musical setting allows the song to be situated in the natural, "unchanging same" worlds of blues and folk, but we never hear Magnolia's own voice.[27] She is constructed solely as man wants her to be using a nature-serves-man, utilitarian approach. This is even more apparent in the following stanza when the narrator compares Magnolia's dancing to jumping "like a Willys in four-wheel drive." Because she can do such things, she consequently "can make happy any man alive." Magnolia, as a stand-in for nature, is not only being explored by technology, she becomes the technology that serves man—transformed into a truck, giving the man a "good ride." The song as a whole feminizes the American pastoral and then betrays it. The eroticizing of technology (like the masculine, hormonal thrill of destruction using weapons of war) is an exaggeratedly masculinist way to use the feminine.

Two and a half minutes into "Sugar Magnolia," the vocal line leads into what the listener expects to be the concluding verse to the song, sung by a solo voice over a dominant harmony. Instead of a conclusive consequent phrase sung by the group, though, the song suddenly modulates up a whole step, and the antecedent phrase that seemed headed toward resolution becomes a tool for modulation into another antecedent phrase. Again sung by a solo voice, the "natural" course of musical events (antecedent to consequent, solo to group) is subverted. Man, not nature, is in control.

"Sugar Magnolia" represents a preindustrial, folklike fantasy of nature that occurred early in the Grateful Dead's musical repertoire. The band "progressed" from there and conquered new ground, using its modern technological tools, venturing into a postapocalyptic, chaotic wilderness that could be tamed. This change in musical output, in many ways, paralleled the change in makeup and orientation of the counterculture itself. The idyllic days of a private Haight-Ashbury district were gone, and the Dead sought out new territory to explore, without tourists. They spent more time in Marin County away from the city and encouraged a kind of gypsy following that would continue to grow and ultimately be with them for decades. The Dead's 1968 album *Anthem of the Sun* breaks new musical ground by featuring an entire side that is essentially electronic music.[28] Similarly, a track entitled "The Eleven," from the band's 1969 *Live/Dead* album, ventures into uncharted territory with a heterogeneous mixture of features, including a circuitous form that eludes the listener as to the song's beginning and end, episodes of intricate metrical counterpoint, unpredictable harmonic motion, wildly juxtaposed melodic layers, and a narrative ripe with hallucinogenic imagery and allusions to the Bible.

The title's "Eleven" derives from the song's use of the unusual eleven-beat meter. Each measure is broken into a fast grouping of 3–3–3–2. At the beginning of the song, however, the eleven-beat structure is hidden. For the first three minutes, metrical chaos unfolds, slipping in and out of 4/4 time. While this improvisatory whirlwind of cycling polyrhythms offers no well-defined melodic characters, it is not cacophonous or atonal. As with "Sugar Magnolia," this opening entertains blues-based conventions that had become characteristic of the

Grateful Dead's sound. Like some traditional blues musicians who drop beats and shorten measures, the patterns in this opening similarly stretch metric boundaries. Here the patterns are shaped by additive processes: each of the three instruments adds notes to its particular motive to create an unpredictable new meter.

Unlike a blues band, however, the three instruments develop their motives and patterns independently, withholding any possible collective goal toward which they might be building. In this sense, the opening musical depiction of vastness and chaotic space leaves no firm ground on which to stand. As if to test the listener's ability to discover order, we hear the lead guitar teasingly emerge and recede with clear melodic passages. These blues-based riffs provide momentary focus, but their forceful attempts to push out into the open are repeatedly subsumed by the surrounding instability.

While this opening sounds nothing like signature Dead songs such as "Truckin'" or "Friend of the Devil," Brightman notes that "the sudden eruption of harmony in the midst of chaos [was] a leitmotif of the Grateful Dead's music." This "leitmotif" was so important to the band's relationship with their audience, she argues, that "when it was missing from a set or failed to incite wonder, the performance fell flat. [In these cases] there were no sudden flashes of insight into . . . the cosmos—which might be memorialized in the line of a favorite song but originated in these moments."[29] If the opening of "The Eleven" is engaged with a "leitmotif" that enables "insight into the cosmos," it stands in stark contrast to the comfortable, rural setting of "Sugar Magnolia." For the countercultural participant, it more likely resembled aspects of "free jazz" that were conspicuously broadcast on the same FM radio stations as San Francisco rock music.

In the sixties, improvisational rock and experimental jazz were genres linked by critics, promoters, musicians, and the media as symbiotic in their chaotic nature. In 1966, *Newsweek* described the music of the San Francisco bands as having "the spark and spontaneity of a free-for-all jam session: unlike most rock 'n' rollers . . . [these bands] improvise freely."[30] Ralph Gleason, the jazz and rock critic who helped the Dead orchestrate their post–Monterey Pop "equipment liberation," remarked that "the Dead was really a jazz band."[31] In 1967, Richard Goldstein wrote in the *New York Times* that fans heard jazz as rock and rock as jazz particularly when the music was full of sound meshes and improvisation.[32] The Dead's bassist Phil Lesh and lead guitarist Jerry Garcia backed up such assessments, claiming that the music of jazz artists such as John Coltrane and Sun Ra fundamentally influenced their approach to musical experimentation.

While folk music sounds and lyrical descriptions of the outdoors served as explicit natural references in the early days of the musical counterculture, the experimental jazz signifiers of the post-1967 culture revealed a more covert engagement with nature. Albums such as Sun Ra's *Janus* and Coltrane's *Stellar Regions* and *Ascension* contributed to a conception of outer space as a territory waiting to be experienced by human beings, resonating with the counterculture's spirit of individualistic freedom. Sun Ra, for example, positioned himself as an Afro-alien, coming from space to reclaim the earth that had been taken from the African peoples. The counterculture, by appropriation, could similarly assume "space" (and then the earth) as a stand-in for nature. Of course, space could only be accessed with the latest technology. The space race initiated by the Soviet launch of *Sputnik* in 1957 quickly turned into a competition of nationhood, technology, and men, with Alan Shepard becoming the first American in space in 1961. More followed throughout the decade, culminating in 1969, with Neil Armstrong and Buzz Aldrin, in Apollo XI, becoming the first men to walk on the moon. Apollo XI was a genuine rocket ship that had transformed science fiction into reality for millions of people around the world. Sun Ra's technology was also a rocket ship, but its purpose was to reclaim a cultural and racial space that had been denied to his community. The counterculture's technology was strangely similar to the space race technology in what it seemed to represent—a tool for a masculinist thrust into uncharted natural territory.

The question, musically speaking, was whether this sublime, uncharted chaos could be tamed. "The Eleven" seemed to answer yes. Intimations of a solid melodic character emerge from the chaotic opening, only to fall back in. At last a melody emerges out of the fray, pieced together from its previous attempts. Soon the other instruments find a similar sense of order in their own patterns—an order that will ultimately unite all the instruments to produce a coherent narrative. The lead guitar wavers in and out of a 4/4 ostinato pattern until, at three minutes and twenty seconds, Jerry Garcia effortlessly transforms the same 4/4 ostinato into the song's eleven-beat riff.

Emerging from the chaos and grounded in this unusual eleven-beat meter, the main melodic protagonist appears representative of a do-it-yourself modern individualism. Phil Lesh, who studied with Luciano Berio at Mills College in 1965, touted the band's experimental sound as "Dragon music—esoteric, asymmetrical music that could only be intellectualized by a few and then most inaccurately. It was truly cliché-free, uncontrived music, even beyond the free-form structures of Miles and Coltrane."[33] "The Eleven" certainly possesses some of the qualities that Lesh ascribes to it. Without a recognizable form, standard meter, or the distinct tonal narrative common to most rock and roll songs—and indeed, to most of their own songs—it defies a fixed categorization as blues, jazz, or rock. But Lesh makes an extra leap by putting the Dead in outer (musical) space, distancing them from any cultural influences and dismissing the possibility of anyone understanding their sound. Perhaps he was trying to craft an image of unmediated inspiration—the band as a medium through which "cosmic" insights flowed.

At three minutes and fifty-five seconds, a key change in the song signals a rhythmic and harmonic unification in the instruments and a sustained recognizable tonic in the guitar. The eleven-beat is reinforced by a repeated harmonic progression (I-IV-V-IV) that brings out the 3-3-3-2 grouping. Within a few seconds, the eleven-beat feels comfortable as a groove: it has become naturalized and now allows room for the lead guitar to improvise a melody over the repeating chord pattern and drum rhythm. After the improvisatory baton is passed to the most contemporary piece of technological musical equipment in the band—the electronic synthesizer—the overall density begins to decrease in preparation for the upcoming, yet unexpected, song lyrics at five minutes and forty-seven seconds.

The lyrics seem to flow naturally in the eleven-beat meter, defying a melodic sense of anticipation and resolution. The sung section of "The Eleven" miraculously appears and then disappears. The narrative is condensed into less than one minute of a nearly ten-minute song, appearing like an inspired instant of mythical revelation—the transformation of biblical prophecy into a psychedelic experience. The narrative begins as a conversation between a main harmonized vocal line and a solo background voice. The line is sung syllabically, as the background voice politely waits to reply to the main voice. As this call-and-response scenario continues, it becomes less polite, as the main harmonized vocal line jumps back in and overlaps the last two beats of the previous response given by the background voice. This eager anticipation emphasizes the import of its line—"*now* is the *time* of *returning* / with our thought jewels polished and gleaming" (emphasis added). While the background vocal line is playful with its jumbled mix of objects ("eight-sided hat rack") and mischievous emotions ("whispering," "hallelujah"), the main vocal line presents the advice to grasp the moment ("now") in order to discover lost wisdom ("thought jewels").

This lesson, however, is hard won. The background vocal waits until the main vocal has finished and sings playfully once again. But the main vocal insists on being heard, this time overlapping with the last three beats of the background vocal line and usurping the playfulness of the background vocal. The two lines begin to meld together, losing their call-and-response quality. The main vocal sings "now is the test of the boomerang," holding "now" for six beats to emphasize the moment. If the "boomerang" signifies throwing caution to the wind and faith in the object's return, the background vocal appears eager to pass the test during this "night of redeeming," and overlaps with the main vocal, until finally, the lyrical narrative concludes with the main voice and background vocal singing two different lines of text concurrently.

As the vocals finish at six minutes and twenty-seven seconds, the binary, back-and-forth experience of conversation has been transformed into a collective experience of other realms: "foreign dominion," "whalebelly," "coral sands," "the waters"—these nature-coded signifiers are so fantastical that their "redeeming" capacity seems only accessible in some kind of altered state. While redemption is typically associated with Christian deliverance from sin, "to redeem," in a secular sense, means to "make amends" or "restore oneself." Whether through a religious or LSD-inspired revelation, "redemption" in this context implies some kind of bid for personal transformation.

By conflating natural, psychedelic, and religious imagery, this bid for redemption becomes a tangible possibility. While Huxley was writing *Brave New World,* he experimented under a psychiatrist's supervision with the hallucinogenic drug mescalin.[34] Realizing the potential for alternative and enhanced realities, he continued his hallucinogenic experimentations and eventually relayed his experiences in the famous book *The Doors of Perception.*[35] Comparing it to mystical revelation, Huxley argued that the experience of hallucinogenic drugs pushes back the screen that the mind erects when in an everyday state and allows new perceptions to flood in.

Huxley's experience of "going back to nature" by consuming drugs was not uncommon. Psychiatrists funded by governmental agencies had been experimenting with these drugs, in labs, on people, and on themselves, since the first half of the twentieth century. In scientific circles, mescalin and LSD were used to further research into the popular field of psychoanalysis.[36] Psychoanalysts hypothesized that LSD created a sense of oneness with nature, allowing the user to let go of the trappings of the ego. By the late sixties, Timothy Leary, Richard Alpert (Ram Dass), and Allen Ginsberg became crusaders for the positive effects of LSD, touting it as a way to get back to nature and escape the materialism of modern society.[37]

Songs such as "The Eleven" rely on this mythologized yet tangible connection among nature, LSD, and spiritual/revelatory insight. LSD seemed to offer personal meetings with the transformative experiences that nature promised. Yet this chaotic model of nature was made attainable by things manmade: LSD was one of the most manufactured drugs available to the counterculture. Unlike marijuana, or even cocaine, LSD was solely a product of the laboratory. In this sense, the counterculture's ability to tap into the revelations of nature and the cosmos was made possible by the "generous support" of Dow Chemical, Bell Laboratories, Monsanto, and the Central Intelligence Agency.

The end of "The Eleven" leads immediately into a strong unified eleven-beat phrase in all the instruments. Over the same I–IV–V–IV harmonic progression played previously, the lead guitar repeats a measure-long melodic motive above the collective texture, emphasizing the rhythmic ostinato of 3–3–3–2. The meter and key are now decipherable. The instruments dig into the 3–3–3–2 rhythm as if in a trance. Together they repeat the same progression and melodic motive for over a minute and a half. This hypnotic, almost minimalistic episode diffuses any expectation of closure, as if stuck repeating a closed groove on an LP. Finally the trance is broken and obscured as the lead guitar slips into a flurry of improvisation. The song descends into a chaotic mixture of melodic and rhythmic motives and there is no conclusive gesture to indicate where "The Eleven" ends and the next track begins.

The song's narrative—from a chaotic opening to a brief vocal section to the emphatic and extended episode of repetition to the final recapitulation of the chaotic nature of the opening—is uncommon. Conventionally, a recapitulation marks the end of a piece's journey by returning to the secure home that was established in the beginning. In this case, however, a return to the chaotic vastness of the beginning poses a logistical problem in that a return to the opening instability dissolves the eleven-beat melodic subject that was formed over the course of the song. But rather than evoking a failure of identity, the return to chaos marks the primordial void as a safe haven of origins, a world unmediated by modern civilization. The lyrics evoked the revelatory hallucinogenic experience. The repetitious eleven-beat episode drove the point home. And once that point was made, the original, chaotic space was ready to be "redeemed" in a final return to the void.

> I saw a Deadhead sticker on a Cadillac.
> —Don Henley, "The Boys of Summer"

In a scene from *Easy Rider,* the character George describes for Billy how the Venutian society (comprised of aliens on Venus) is more evolved that the one on earth. "They don't have no wars, they got no monetary system, they don't have any leaders, because, I mean, each man is a leader. I mean, each man—because of their technology, they are able to feed, clothe, house, and transport themselves equally—and with no effort." The portrait of the counterculture (aka the Venutian society) recounted above is discerning in that it associates competition, profiteering, and consumerism with mainstream America while allying technology with an egalitarian and effortless lifestyle where individualism and freedom are prized. What's important about this portrait is that, because individualism ("each man") was so often linked with the natural, technology just gets folded in, naturalized, as a tool to achieve freedom. This is exactly what countercultural bands, including the Grateful Dead achieved. Songs like "Sugar Magnolia" and "The Eleven" make nature's pastoral and revelatory qualities available through a sleight of hand that minimized the import of the very mechanisms of their production.

Of all the countercultural bands, the Dead had the most technologically advanced equipment to produce their sound and the most powerful manufactured LSD to drive their imaginations. The band encouraged concertgoers to tape-record their performances, making the vision of dozens of tape-recorders held high in the air by the audience, recording their concerts, an integral feature of any Dead show. Because this "free" activity was not commercially motivated, the tape recorders (bought by relatively affluent countercultural participants), became in a sense naturalized. The Dead's concerts might very well have been communal folk festivals, but they were experienced within the cocoon of technology and consumerism.

The counterculture constructed and consumed "the natural" as uncontaminated, unmanufactured, and unmediated even as it acquiesced in, rather than actively rebelled against, its indulgence in the modern commercial world. Certainly the Dead, and the counterculture as a whole, were detached from mainstream commodity consumer culture. Yet this detachment was not particularly grounded in political critique. Ultimately it was about the semblance of being spiritually elevated, about not wanting to *appear* to be caught in such mundane things as consumerism, about not selling out. What is problematic though is that appearance is so often based in commercialism. To refuse the conformity of the mainstream requires buying into a new look that, at least for a certain length of time, represents being outside the system. So Huxley's suggestion to "do anything not to consume, go back to nature," was misunderstood by the leading edge of the counterculture. "Go back and consume nature" was what they did.

Ultimately, we might understand the culture represented by the Grateful Dead and its music as an attempt to rediscover an American frontier. In late 1967, as the Haight-Ashbury district became a media spectacle and people came to experience the very frontier that had been advertised across the country in the counterculture's music, the Diggers and many countercultural bands fled the scene. Faced with the possibility of confronting what they, in part, had wrought, the Grateful Dead also retreated, spending more time at their rural Novato ranch in Marin County. They were followed by people who have since been named Deadheads. The band encouraged this following, creating what might be seen, at least at concerts, as a movable counterculture, always on the run, never in one spot for too long, escaping a fixed locale and definition. And perhaps it was easier that way—to revive the counterculture for one or two nights each week and then return to their ranch, rather than making a prolonged investment in the culture they spawned.

Brightman describes "the Novato countryside that once seemed so wild" as it appears thirty years later: "The house that harbored Hell's Angels, visiting Beats and Pranksters, along with London rockers and fresh-faced kids from the Northwest, has been swallowed up in the suburban sprawl of northern Marin. The VW vans, Beetles, and occasional Ferrari have turned into Hondas, BMWs, and armored Humvees. The faith healers have become naturopaths, aromatherapists, and lawyers. Many of the musicians, however—the Dead, above all—remain musicians."[38] Brightman poignantly articulates what twenty-first-century Marin has come to symbolize. But her absolution of the Dead raises the question of how the ethics of people's actions relate to their historical consequences. While she does not hold the Grateful Dead (and countercultural musicians) accountable for the way their environment has been transformed over the past three decades, perhaps we should not be so forgiving. The Grateful Dead taught their listeners that it is acceptable to indulge in technology and abundance to access nature, and the community that has developed on the Dead's stomping grounds seems to have taken that lesson to heart. Marin may be a beautiful, natural haven of spiritually minded people. But as a county with one of the highest per capita incomes in the United States, their lifestyle and ability to advocate for environmental preservation is made possible by American capitalism and consumerism. Perhaps it is incumbent upon those of us who benefit from technology to reexamine how history has taught us to use it.

Chapter Five

The New Age Persona

Sex, Spirituality, and Escaping to the Now

Out of their kaleidoscopic creations, it was to be hoped,
might emerge "a shared symbolic order of the kind that a
religion provides"—the ultimate agenda of postmodernism.
—PERRY ANDERSON, *The Origins of Postmodernity*

In February 1967, soon after the Human Be-In—where acid guru Timothy Leary uttered his "Tune in, turn on, drop out" phrase—Leary and poets Gary Snyder and Allen Ginsberg, along with comparative religion philosopher Alan Watts, met for an event called the "Houseboat Summit." Advertised as a dialogue between four men widely considered to be spokespersons for the countercultural lifestyle, the summit took place on Watts's own ferryboat, which was moored in Sausalito, a town north of San Francisco on the San Francisco Bay. As a recognized mouthpiece for the counterculture, the underground newspaper *San Francisco Oracle* sponsored the summit and published a transcript of it in the March–April issue.[1] The general focus of the event was on the philosophy of and possibilities for the emerging subculture. The men generally agreed that this subculture was forming in isolated urban pockets around the country, from the Haight-Ashbury district to the Lower East Side in Manhattan to coffeehouse enclaves in Seattle, but that it would soon leave the cities to make its existence closer to nature.

Discussion quickly turned to the notion of "dropping out"—could everyone do it, how could they do it, what were they dropping out of, were they dropping into somewhere else, what did dropping out mean, and what were the implications of it for the future of humankind. The four men at the Houseboat Summit were not the only ones asking such questions. On the contrary. Even in the competitive halls of America's top advertising agencies, designers and marketers were crafting what Thomas Frank calls a "hip consumerism" that reflected a growing distaste for conformity and growing desire for individualism. Frank's explanation of the path that advertisers would take in their "creative revolution" is remarkably similar to the assessments formulated at the summit.[2] Watts argued that as creative and freethinking individuals isolated themselves, experienced their loneliness, and developed their vision, they would come to see that the rules of mainstream society were illusory and that they could transform their own visions into their own reality. Though Watts's formulation left plenty of room for interpretation and agreement, Leary was not satisfied. Unwilling to let go of the fundamental principles of individualism and unlimited variety while also refusing to relinquish his all-or-nothing "drop out" philosophy of complete escape from society and its organized structures of laws and leaders, Leary dug himself into a hole. He insisted that "drop outs" had already liberated themselves but that, at the same time, the issue for now, and for the future of this subculture of individuals with their own visions, was that they didn't "know where to go." Leary was compelled to answer a range of implied questions raised by his own response: Where *should* they go, then? Will they have leaders? Will they go toward something? Leary responded:

> They don't need leadership, but they need, I think, a variety of suggestions from people who have thought about this, giving them the options to move in any direction.[3]

In Leary's construction, a world where veteran thinkers advised new initiates in a subculture (on what to do upon "dropping out") apparently was different from a world where leaders laid out guidelines for activity and rules for cultural inclusion. Advice and suggestions, rather than laws, meant that all options and all directions were still on the table. Leary's hole kept on getting bigger. He suggested that meeting places, or "meditation rooms," in each isolated urban space should be set up so that dropouts could explore their infinite options and decide where to go from there.

> The different meditation rooms can have different styles. One can be Zen, one can be macrobiotic, one can be bhahte chanting, one can be rock and roll psychedelic, one can be lights. If we learn anything from our cells, we learn that God delights in variety . . . people would meet in these places, and AUTOMATICALLY tribal groups would develop and new matings would occur, and the city would be seen for many as transitional . . . and they get started. They may save up a little money, and then they head out and find the Indian totem wherever they go.[4]

On the surface, Leary's description fits in with everything he claimed was part and parcel of "dropping out." There were no leaders. There were many options for honing one's vision. Individuals carved out their own paths and found their own "totems." But looking more closely, we see that not only were there limited options, but certain elements *had* to be included in the package for a person to drop out. Philosophers Joseph Heath and Andrew Potter assert that this specialized inclusiveness is a hallmark of what they deem "countercultural thinking." Certain things must be integrated in one's cultural repertoire (and certain things excluded) in order for the counterculturalist to feel unencumbered by societal norms.[5] In the case of Leary and the other older gurus of the emerging subculture, items such as Zen, the macrobiotic, chanting, God, the tribal, matings, and the "Indian totem" are erected as a scaffolding of intertwined items to support the ideology of dropping out. Clearly, escape would have to be achieved through some combination of spiritual, non-Western, and sexual elements.

> In a camper, parked on Haight Street,
> with a hippie cool and keen,
> lived a minor, named Regina,
> who was only seventeen.
> There he brought her, food and water,
> and her hair he had to comb.
> She was someone's, naughty daughter,
> who had run away from home.
> They were lovers, 'neath the covers,
> but he had a greater goal.
> It was odd, he loved her body,
> but he sought to save her soul.
> —Ashleigh Brilliant, "How Delinquent
> Can You Be?" (1967)

In 1967, street singer and songwriter Ashleigh Brilliant began appearing each day at 3:00 p.m. in Golden Gate Park at the end of Haight Street. Brilliant purported that his free concerts, performed on his portable microphone, became "somewhat of an institution in the Haight, often gathering hundreds." For twenty-five cents, he handed out a pamphlet with his photo, a brief biography, and new song lyrics to familiar tunes.[6] Brilliant's concept was successful—with tunes that everyone knew and lyrics in hand, he fostered a communal atmosphere each afternoon, his audience always joining in. Above all, Brilliant's lyrics focused on Haight-Ashbury-style sex, revealing, to an extent, how the San Francisco counterculture perceived sexual politics.

The song cited above ("How Delinquent Can You Be?"),

sung to the tune of "Clementine," was part of his collection, *The Haight-Ashbury Songbook: Songs of Love and Haight*. As the lyrics illustrate, images of rape, dominant male sexuality, and women as sexual objects were commonplace in the Haight-Ashbury district. Other Brilliant songs, such as "The Intercourse Song," sung to the tune of "God Rest Ye Merry Gentlemen," only reinforce this impression: "God rest you girls and gentlemen, let nothing you dismay; science has the answers now, there's no more need to pray; for liking sexual intercourse, no consequence you'll pay, oh, tidings of comfort and joy." The lyrics praise science in favor of a traditional Christian God ("no more need to pray") for enabling free sex, with no strings attached ("no consequence you'll pay"). The three following verses, on venereal disease, abortion, and the pill, drive the point home—in the Haight, sex is a free commodity, whose immediate consequences could easily be dealt with.

Brilliant's decision to use familiar tunes allowed his new lyrical material to flow smoothly. The melodics of songs such as "Clementine" and "God Rest Ye Merry Gentlemen" were already embedded in the cultural consciousness, so they required less active attention, if any, to be learned. This quality then transferred to Brilliant's new lyrics, naturalizing the sentiments expressed, while, at the same time, inviting indifference to those same sentiments. Similar, in part, to "singing commercials," Brilliant's songs tapped into what had proven in advertising to be a successful marketing technique. By borrowing the tune of a common Christmas carol, "The Intercourse Song" easily formed a thematic alliance—one that underscored much countercultural music. As in the dropping-out ideology expressed during the Houseboat Summit, spirituality, philosophy, and sexuality (along with drug-induced euphoria) were collapsed together in a heap. Sometimes spiritual ecstasy was cast in terms of sexual climax, or vice versa. At other times, spiritual and philosophical concepts were used to substantiate an agenda of sexual hedonism. In the case of "The Intercourse Song," Brilliant appropriated a tune that originally alluded to the comfort of faith in Christ—"remember Christ our Savior"—to signal the same comfort of faith, but this time in sex. An appealing commodity, casual sex became a spiritual Christmas present.

This spiritual-philosophical-sexual alliance had been a part of many local traditions that the counterculture had access to. A columnist named Gavin Arthur, who wrote for the *San Francisco Oracle,* was one of the most immediate links to such traditions, giving shape to what would later be called the "free love" ideology.[7] By mid-1967, the newspaper edited by Allen Cohen claimed one hundred thousand copies in circulation, with articles addressing topics ranging from healthy diets to Eastern mysticism, art displays mixing multiple spiritual and sexual images, and locally designed advertisements championing San Francisco rock bands. The theme of the February 1967 issue of the *Oracle* was "The Aquarian Age." Three astrology experts—Gayla, Ambrose Hollingsworth, and Gavin Arthur—contributed to the two-part feature, and its success allowed Gavin Arthur to become a regular contributor in several issues to follow.[8] Arthur's writings consisted of extensive astrological predictions—of the type that, today, we get in the reduced form of "the horoscope section." Born in 1901, Arthur had decades more life experience than the majority of his readers, so his dazzling descriptions of astrological history, coupled with Eastern-flavored sexual psychology, often suggested new possibilities that his young followers appeared eager to experience. Within a few months, during the 1967 Summer of Love, Arthur's reputation through the newspaper allowed him to open the doors of his mansion for hundreds of young people to act out the group sexual dynamics of the psychological schools of thought he so diligently described in the *Oracle.*

Certainly, the writings of many philosophers and spiritual thinkers had begun to gain currency as serious academic reading material on West Coast college campuses. But the range of topics, and the array of contributors to the *Oracle*—including Gavin Arthur, Alan Watts, Timothy Leary, Richard Alpert, Buckminster Fuller, Ken Kesey, and a host of Beat poets—exemplified how the counterculture mixed and matched various schools of thought to craft its unique path out of mainstream society. At the time, Theodore Roszak argued that the counterculture was able to meld these strands into a coherent and crafted ideology. He described "a continuum of thought and experience among the young which links together the New Left sociology of Mills, the Freudian Marxism of Herbert Marcuse, the Gestalt-therapy anarchism of Paul Goodman, the apocalyptic body mysticism of Norman Brown, the Zen-based psychotherapy of Alan Watts, and finally Timothy Leary's impenetrably occult narcissism, wherein the world and its many woes shrink at last to the size of a mote in one's private psychedelic void."[9] This continuum "defected" from the "secular intellectuality" of the technocracy for "something sacred which stands above all men."[10] Although Roszak depicted the counterculture as everything that a rationalistic, profiteering, repressive technocracy was not, he failed to mention that the various schools of thought that the counterculture drew upon as a means to drop out could only have been available in the middle of a technocracy—a "democratic" nation, thriving on the intersection and economic trade of diverse ideas. Most countercultural participants came into contact with spiritual, sexual, and philosophical materials in the *Oracle,* but they also perused them in Ron and Jay Thelin's Psychedelic Shop. All brands of erotic and esoteric reading could be bought there, merchandised and advertised, one after another, in exemplary capitalist fashion. If anything, the Psychedelic Shop was the counterculture's discount adult bookstore without the age restrictions.

The writings of Marxist theorist Herbert Marcuse sold well at the Psychedelic Shop. His *One-Dimensional Man,* published in paperback in 1964, offered a unique combination of dense Marxist theory and musings on modern sexuality.[11] "Live intensely, have orgasms without restraint"—Marcuse suggested that sexual repression perpetuated Western capitalism and the way to break the shackles of this oppressive sociopolitical system was to establish a free sexual society. The counterculture welcomed this sentiment, and, not surprisingly, Marcuse's next paperback quickly became a cult classic. *Eros and Civilization* argued that "private disorder reflects more directly than before the disorder of the whole."[12] Marcuse's argument was that modern civilization increasingly relies on the internalization, in people, of the repressive apparatus of society. This results in the renunciation of instinctual aspects of human nature. In particular, as facets of capitalism, such as mass production and mechanization, take a greater hold on people and their bodies, sexuality is more and more repressed and substituted with an appetite for consumer goods. The remedy, of course, is not to internalize what is repressive about modern capitalist society and not to renounce human instinct. Needless to say, Marcuse became an adopted hero for the counterculture. His writings, and particularly *Eros and Civilization,* were interpreted as an invitation to celebrate subjective sexual experience as part of the counterculture's remedy for social disorder and repressed knowledge.[13]

Erotic license (enabled, in part, by hallucinogenic drugs and justified by spiritual philosophy) seemed to underscore the wisdom of the counterculture's older cultural gurus. While Marcuse addressed sex from an intellectual standpoint, philosopher and humanities professor Norman O Brown celebrated the body as a means for mystical freedom. Sociologist Paul Goodman claimed the technocracy could be dismantled through sexual liberation. The books of Wilhelm Reich suggested people tap into what he called a free-floating erotic energy. And philosopher Frederick Fritz Perls drew upon psychoanalysis and existentialism to ultimately dismiss intellectualism and endorse living "entirely in the moment." In a comprehensive study of twentieth-century sexual revolutions, historian David Allyn notes that Perls spent a lot of time in the late sixties at the Esalen Institute in Big Sur, California—a communal retreat offering classes in everything from yoga to group marriage. It was only in this setting, not in daily life, that Perls encouraged nudity as a means to be in the moment and shed the rules of conventional society.[14]

In general, the message that the counterculture took away from these thinkers, whether accurately assessed or not, was to refuse the technocracy and embrace individual, instinctual consciousness. This notion seemed best summed up by psychiatrist R. D. Laing, who argued, like Marcuse, that individuals were alienated from their authentic selves. With Laing, though, liberating the repressed self took up the entire agenda, allowing no room for social concerns or consideration of oppressive systems. In prose not unlike that which dominates the new age/self-help book industry that has sprung up in recent decades,[15] Laing indulged in a generalized theory of liberation wherein a person could counter the repressiveness of her experience by getting in touch with her childhood, unconscious, and bodily/sexual selves. The counterculture jumped on board.[16]

In addition to the philosophers mentioned above, a number of writers and poets who, as Roszak described, *"thought they had found something in Zen [Buddhism] they needed,"* gained exotic and erotic currency in the counterculture.[17] Henry Miller's early novels were an enticing commodity. Full of mystical musings, references to Zen Buddhism, astrology (*Tropic of Cancer* and *Tropic of Capricorn*), marijuana, and loads of sex, works from his sixteen years in Big Sur (1945–61) were the ones the counterculture lauded. However dismal this period of Miller's life was, and however much he considered himself to have moved on to deeper spiritual concerns in his novels of the sixties, the counterculture clung to his earlier work. In those novels could be found a brand of Zen that sanctioned hedonism, or "a new permissiveness," as musician-turned-historian Gary Valentine Lachman describes—the notion that sexism and womanizing could be tools for spiritual development.[18] Likewise, Jack Kerouac's works of "Bop prose"—including *The Dharma Bums* and *On the Road*—seemed to applaud excess with Zen phrases filling out the sexually exploitative narratives.

Even more than Miller or Kerouac, Allen Ginsberg became a kind of sexualized father figure to the San Francisco counterculture, with a visible presence on the countercultural scene. After reading his erotic poetry and chanting on stage at the Be-In, and after helping the Swami Prabhupada establish Krishna Consciousness in the Haight in 1967, Ginsberg became a frequent point of reference in the underground press. In March 1967, for example, Liza Williams wrote as if she were directly communicating with Ginsberg. "I think you have a tongue like some great bronze bell from the municipality of insight (and personally I don't care who you fuck, being delighted that you fuck with pleasure and can convey the delight of fucking, the news about loving, breathing, sweating, tasting, the humanness of contact."[19] Poet Gary Snyder, too, was familiar to the counterculture. Of the Beats, he was the most experienced in Zen. After studying Asian languages and pan-Asian culture and poetry as a graduate student, he took formal Zen instruction in Japan. Along with meditation, he described communion with nature and sexual indulgence as means to shake the foundations of the rational mind.

Miller, Kerouac, Ginsberg, and even Snyder, to an extent, did not practice "real Zen" in the sense of a pared-down existence of simplicity and internal struggle with paradox. The Buddhism they crafted was a popularized "Beat Zen" offering an "anything goes" sensibility of instant enlightenment. This Beat Zen found its mouthpiece to the masses in Alan Watts. Though Watts was, at times, critical of Beat Zen's permissiveness, he had no qualms about advertising it through lectures, books, tutorials, and therapy sessions. His version of Zen Buddhism (first outlined when he was an intellectual prodigy in the 1935 *The Spirit of Zen,* and then trumped by the 1961 *Psychotherapy East and West,* inspired by his third wife) suggested that beings were already enlightened and all they had to do to find their enlightenment was let go of the social restrictions on mind and body. In this brand of Zen, letting go of restrictions on mind and body implied letting go of distinctions between right and wrong. Without such distinctions, Zen seemed to champion a "do your own thing" mentality where moral determinations mattered far less than the appearance of being outside a rule-bound, dominant, repressive culture.

For the counterculture, popularized Beat Zen was easily mixed and matched with elements from Mahayana Buddhism and Tantric Hinduism. While the goal of Mahayana Buddhism was thought to be about unifying material and spiritual by eliminating ego and suffering, the goal of Tantric Hinduism appeared to be the same, but through ecstatic sexual union. The *Oracle* put all these Eastern methodologies and religions on par with each other, without distinction, as tools for the countercultural experience of revelation. Certainly, this reflected a degree of arrogance—all traditions should be and could be available to the counterculture—that was further reinforced by the rhetoric and actions of countercultural figures like Timothy Leary.

Countercultural leaders associated marijuana, naturally occurring hallucinogenic drugs such as peyote, and LSD in particular with their new revelatory agenda. These drugs were talked about by Leary, Watts, Ginsberg, Ralph Metzner (Leary's colleague at Harvard), and others, in terms of their medicinal qualities, touted as cures for the ailing Western psyche and its repressed consciousness. Whereas such talk served to justify people's indulgence on a day-to-day basis, it also became self-fulfilling prophecy. Leary and Metzner saw the need for experienced guidance in the psychedelic world, so, in addition to the *Psychedelic Review,* they published psychedelic interpretations of the Tibetan Book of the Dead and the Tao Te Ching and encouraged developing courses where students could learn simultaneously how to meditate, take hallucinogens, and practice yoga. In a way, this became a reality in the spring of 1967 when a woman named Amelia Newell donated the use of over thirty acres near the small town of Gorda on the Big Sur coastline to the *Oracle* for staff and friends to take retreats. People came to the land every weekend for getaways, but it quickly became a makeshift detox center. As the Haight-Ashbury district attracted more outsiders and hustlers, harder drugs, like methedrine and heroin, also infiltrated the scene. By the autumn of 1967, many longtime countercultural participants got hooked on these harder drugs and were sent to Newell's land along with truckloads of brown rice, beans, vegetables, LSD, and peyote for their recovery.[20] Whether it was the hiking in forests of Big Sur, meditation under the trees, drumming by a communal fire, taking hallucinogenic drugs, or the combination that "cured" people, is beside the point. The counterculture had convinced itself that its drugs were the way out of the mainstream world and the way into a unique spiritualized world of personal consciousness.

Timothy Leary used all available means to further this notion, becoming the country's "most notorious LSD-advertising agent."[21] The fact that he so often engaged with the mainstream world did not seem to put a dent in the idea of LSD as the counterculture's key to escape. As *Village Voice* reporter Richard Goldstein remarked sarcastically in 1967, "The government is Leary's most generous patron; it showers him with publicity. Now that he swings with the beautiful people, the feds are helping Leary reach the folks who guzzle beer."[22] Leary seemed to move from television, to interviews in countercultural newspapers, to the stage of the Human Be-In, to the mainstream press with ease. Leary, however, was not always lofty in his rhetoric. In his interview with *Playboy* magazine in September 1966, Leary was asked the following question: "We've heard that some women who ordinarily have difficulty achieving orgasm find themselves capable of multiple orgasms under LSD. Is that true?" After having earlier in the interview claimed that any LSD session "that does not involve an ultimate merging with a person of the opposite sex isn't really complete," one might have imagined that Leary's statements could get no more outrageous. He disproved that theory with a calculated response: "In a carefully prepared, loving LSD session, a woman will inevitably have several hundred orgasms." And if that wasn't enticement enough, the notion that LSD was a "cure for homosexuality" cemented a strange mixture of hypermasculinity, heterosexuality, elevated consciousness, and druggy eroticism as core to the counterculture's spiritual agenda.[23]

On the whole, outrageous and sexist sentiments such as Leary's were commonplace in the Haight-Ashbury district by late 1967. Only two years before, in August 1965 "Two young men and two young women tentatively stripped off their clothes and staged a nude 'wade-in' off a San Francisco city beach."[24] Jefferson Poland, the leader of the wade-in, had already started the Sexual Freedom League on the East Coast, and was one of the hosts for the League's first meeting in the Haight-Ashbury district in early 1966. Historian David Allyn remarks that the Sexual Freedom League opened its doors to everyone, including straight people, gay people, prostitutes, monogamous couples, S & M advocates, and swingers. The League hoped that a society where all sexual preferences and orientations were treated equally "would be less exploitative, less tempted by mass-market pornography, suggestive advertising, and other forms of commercialized titillation."[25] Ultimately such an organization, with a genuinely open-armed approach and a vigorously thought-through social agenda, failed to compete with popularizers like Timothy Leary.

By 1967 the Haight hosted dozens of live heterosexual sex shows. The Psychedelic Shop stocked the satanically inflected predictions of orgy-connoisseur Aleister Crowley and the pornographic poetry of Lenore Kandel (mentioned on the Be-In poster). Kandel's poetry collection, purportedly an idyllic celebration of liberatory "free love," included a dark sexual fantasy entitled "Invocation of My Demon Brother." Perhaps it wasn't so surprising that, by the end of the decade, the countercultural sensibility had been transformed by cultural heroes into explicitly antimainstream mantras such as "We want our fuckolution and we want it now."[26]

Hank Harrison, one of the earliest biographers of the Grateful Dead and a Haight resident in the late sixties, described the scene as "[being] alive and getting laid. Girls and boys were actually indulging their bodies."[27] While Harrison's statement appears simply blind to the sexual politics behind "free love," Barry Melton of Country Joe and the Fish displays how this revisionist "naïveté" has filtered into nostalgic reflections on the counterculture. "Free love" in 1966–67, according to Melton, was "a genuine attempt by a handful of young people to redefine much of what was taken for granted about the way human beings relate to one another."[28] Allen Cohen went one step further, drawing an equation between sexual/sensual exploration and perceived spiritual experiences, with drugs as the catalysts to set the reactions in motion: "Although there were many spiritual paths being explored and invented in the Haight, the preponderant view favored an intense sensuousness. Experiences with both LSD and marijuana seemed to unveil a world of sensory splendor and spiritual depth that had been absent from most people's Judeo-Christian expectations. Our religions, philosophies, and social conditioning had not prepared us to experience such things, as the whole planet being one living and breathing organism with our own beings melting into it, or every atom of our bodies merging with our sexual partners' body and experiencing their thoughts as ours, as if there weren't two different beings, or seeing God or gods and talking to them, or realizing that you and every one else was God."[29]

In these and other reminiscent accounts of the counter-culture's "free love" agenda, there is an underlying implication that somehow loosening the sexual rules of society was an expression of the counterculture's alternative approach to spirituality rooted in the body. With such attention focused on the counterculture's spiritualized sexual practices, it's worth asking the degree to which sexual mores (and spiritual disciplines) were actually revised by the counterculture. Un-like Harrison, Melton, and Cohen, cartoonist Robert Crumb (who designed the *Cheap Thrills* album cover) assessed the sex-ual dynamics of the Haight-Ashbury scene in 1967 with his typical wry realism: "It was much more open than any other place. But the air was so thick with bullshit you could cut it with a knife. Guys were running around saying, 'I'm you and you are me and everything is beautiful, so get down and suck my dick.'"[30] Chester Anderson, like Crumb, was another mainstay of the counterculture who bore witness to the po-tential for exploitation that the "free love" philosophy carried with it. Anderson was, in journalist-activist Abe Peck's words, the Haight's "resident critic." After writing for the *San Fran-cisco Oracle,* he founded the Communications Company, which distributed leaflets on all sorts of topics around the Haight on a daily basis. In April 1967 he delivered a scathing report entitled "Uncle Tim's Children," directed at Timothy Leary and his it's-all-easy-with-LSD philosophy. "Pretty little 16-year-old middle-class chick comes to the Haight to see what it's all about & gets picked up by a 17-year-old street dealer who spends all day shooting her full of speed again & again, then feeds her 3000 mikes [micrograms of acid] & raffles off her temporarily unemployed body for the biggest Haight Street gang bang since the night before last. . . . Rape is as common as bullshit on Haight Street."[31] (The similarities between Anderson's report and Ashleigh Brilliant's everybody-join-in song "How Delinquent Can You Be?" are unnerving.)

Debunking the rosy picture of young people "indulging their bodies," Anderson reveals that the ethical politics of "free love" were far from egalitarian. Only a month before the publication of Anderson's leaflet, journalist Jerry Farber, in a column for the *LA Free Press* in March 1967, showed that a nonegalitarian and crass approach to sex was more common to a male-dominated, countercultural sexuality than many of its participants perhaps wanted to admit. "Sex shows up in the classroom as academic subject matter—sanitized and abstracted, thoroughly divorced from feeling. . . . What's missing from kindergarten to graduate school, is honest recognition of what's actually happening—turned on awareness of hairy goodies underneath the petti-pants."[32] Undeniably, Farber articulates a position that is anything but "sanitized" and "abstracted"—so he could never be accused of sympathizing with the establishment. But, at the same time, he implies that sexual "feeling" is "recognition," in particular, of women's genitalia as means for male pleasure. Farber would likely have been pleased to hear that Marco Vassi, a psychology instructor at the Experimental College at San Francisco State University in the late sixties and early seventies, was teaching what Vassi called "Kundalini Buddhist inspired relaxation seminars" that, more often than not, ended in group gropings and orgies.[33] Yes, everyone was having sex, but for women (and girls), their contribution to the "free love" ideology *had* to be their bodies.

As historian Aniko Bodroghkozy notes in her study of the media's portrayal of "rebellion" during the sixties, the underground press consisted mainly of middle-class, white men who marginalized women, often deliberately. "Male perspectives prevailed in a movement that frequently made sense of its rebelliousness as a means to assert manhood."[34] Magazines and newspapers increasingly became littered with personal sex ads, caricatures of naked women, and jibes at women's liberation. Photographs of women showed their breasts, often without the rest of their bodies, portraying them as disembodied objects. And, as historian Beth Bailey explains, if women didn't want to "contribute their bodies to the Cultural Revolution" they had hang-ups, and if they did, they became the flesh-and-blood property of the men with whom they had sex.[35] "Free love" offered women a familiar double-bind. Sexual hedonism had become an important countercultural marker of freedom, of "dropping out" of the mainstream, and women had to embrace it or their cultural allegiance would be questioned.

Not surprisingly, Theodore Roszak observed this trend in the underground media and on the streets, citing the following example: "The San Francisco *Oracle* gives us photos of stark-naked madonnas with flowers in their hair, suckling their babies." Here was the old formula for acceptable sexual behavior. Men could crave sex and women could be sex objects or nurturing parents, but not the other way around. Unfortunately Roszak's mild assessment failed to comment on the counterculture's embrace of this classic double standard. He remarked that "the effect is not at all pornographic, nor intended to be so."[36]

But, of course, it was pornographic, just in a new countercultural guise. When mainstream cultural and social institutions openly or implicitly made rules that put men in positions of dominance and women in submissive and nurturing roles, then the counterculture wanted nothing to do with that mainstream system. Such rules were seen by the counterculture as devices used for the oppression of women and men who otherwise might be interested in getting in touch with their repressed selves. So to escape from that system meant dropping the rules. As rules were dropped, "free love" filled in the gaps— a nonsystem that purportedly had no rules, no artificial restrictions, and no social conventions. "Free love" wasn't particularly concerned then with equal treatment or egalitarian practices as it was in Jefferson Poland's Sexual Freedom League. It was, in typical countercultural fashion, about what it was not. And that meant not being bound by sexual rules, sexual conventions, or sexual restrictions associated with the mainstream. It's fair to say that, even a genuine attempt at a culture without rules, constraints, or conventions with regard to sexuality, which is borne out within a larger patriarchal network that has relied on the systematic exploitation of women for its survival, is destined to fail. In mainstream society, women were abused and exploited, and the biased legal system gave them minimal recourse to fight back and scant protection from their aggressors. In the counterculture, women were abused and exploited, and the lack of rules gave them little voice and little protection within their culture. "Love" might have been present in the "free love" world, but "freedom," for women at least, was little more than a charade.

Countercultural music often captured the complexity of "free love"—both its rule-less verve and underlying charade—in its pluralistic and sensualistic juxtaposition of elements. Jimi Hendrix, among others, exemplified this erotic pluralism, and fans and critics alike recognized how powerfully he used it. "Although he had been adopted by the British faction of the flower-power syndrome as a kind of high priest, guitarist Hendrix, through the screaming power of his music, belongs to the other side of the love-generation coin. Violence."[37] Remember Hendrix's "Purple Haze." The opening of the song is aurally gritty and dirty. The throbbing quarter notes are unrelenting, assertively leaping up an octave on the offbeats. This phallic riff takes shape in the first two measures of the song with a bass pedal on E and an A-sharp in the lead guitar—together forming a grinding dissonant tritone (the devil's interval) that creates isometric tension from the outset. The top note of the tritone soon disappears as Hendrix moves into the opening blues strain—at times indecipherable with bent notes, pentatonic harmonies, and distortion—and the bass and percussion continue to pound away at the underlying riff.

In her work on Jimi Hendrix, musicologist Sheila Whiteley reads this combination of musical elements as the "feeling of muscle and crunch common to most Hendrix numbers."[38] This "muscle and crunch," together with Hendrix's use of distortion, fuzz, extreme dynamics, and feedback, served as an aural analog to both the sexual experience and the hallucinogenic experience. The powerful opening bars of "Purple Haze" seem musically to represent the raised perception of one's heartbeat during an acid trip or the literal intensification of the heart pounding during sex. Likewise, Hendrix's characteristically wild and virtuosic improvisations simultaneously pointed to the quality of timelessness associated with drug-induced hallucinations, the phallic freedom of orgasmic release, and the ungrounded and surrealistic nature of "spiritual" insight.

The matrix of drug, sexual, and spiritual elements available in a song like "Purple Haze" reflected the counterculture's ideology back to itself, but it also displayed that chaotic mix to the rest of the country, making the counterculture vulnerable to media co-optation. The counterculture *was* concerned with stimulation and inspiration in the moment—opting for the pleasures of now over the prospect of delayed gratification—and free love, LSD, "psychedelic" music, and non-Western spiritual philosophies were seen (and heard) as available means for immediate transformative experiences. If mainstream society kept order by repressing individuals, then pleasure was the key to liberation—liberation for themselves, that is. The counterculture never claimed to want to change the system or advocate for the rights of women, workers, or underprivileged persons. Yet no matter the extent to which the counterculture was *not* about greater societal concerns, its route to "dropping out" was still attached to the workings of mainstream culture. It seems that the hubris of the counter-culture's decadence—in drugs, sex, and spiritual traditions—masked an array of lived contradictions. Nemesis would not be far behind.

Musicologist Robert Fink has suggested that "changes in the cultural sphere often precede and presage transformations in the material sphere."[39] Countercultural music seemed soaked in hubris, oozing potentially catastrophic outcomes. Jefferson Airplane's first album, *Surrealistic Pillow,* included the first songs from the Haight-Ashbury to top the charts, and the band became musical poster-children for San Francisco in the late sixties. The Beatles helped to further advertise a counter-cultural aesthetic around the world on June 25, 1967, when twenty-four countries were linked by global satellite to broadcast a live television performance of their song "All You Need Is Love." By then, the word was out. Jefferson Airplane's second album, *After Bathing at Baxter's,* released in December 1967, had instant countercultural appeal. Lead singer Grace Slick recalls that the album's six months of recording sessions lacked "the fun of frivolous mutual excess" that had been present at the start of the Airplane's success. The San Francisco counterculture was no longer an isolated ethos. As she laments, "We just couldn't get a good bacchanal going for lack of interest in what we'd become."[40]

The second album was an eclectic mix, including a four-minute track entitled "ReJoyce." Jefferson Airplane, like Hendrix and Ashleigh Brilliant, employed a variety of musical means to encode the complex sexual politics of the counter-culture, and songs such as "ReJoyce" served as musical primers on "free love" and "dropping out" and were harbingers of their consequences. Like philosopher Marshall McLuhan's groundbreaking work from 1968, *War and Peace in the Global Village,* "ReJoyce" makes extensive reference to the work of writer James Joyce.[41] Drugs, however, not literary modernism, characterize the opening of the song. "Chemical change like a laser beam" leaves the light of ordinary reality "shattered." And lest any listener miss the connection between psychedelics and sex, LSD's hallucinogenic effects are narrated by Grace Slick with an alluring foreplay of throaty tones. She anticipates the drugs (or the sex) to make her "warm," waiting, on the verge, for them to be "inside" her. After the drugs begin to take effect, the lyrical narrative of "ReJoyce" delights in a world of plurality where everything is available—including references to most of the major characters in Joyce's *Ulysses* (Mulligan, Saxon, Steven, Bloom, Molly, and Boylan), jibes at the Vietnam War as "good business," mockeries of commercialism ("Sell your mother for a Hershey bar"), spouted quasi-Eastern philosophy, and more sex.

Certainly Joyce's *Ulysses* contains most of the elements that surface in "ReJoyce." In particular, one of the novel's main plot-lines is sexual, concerning the antihero and cuckold Bloom, who is wandering the streets of Dublin as his wife Molly prepares for a four o'clock rendezvous with her lover Boylan. More than a mere retelling of *Ulysses* though, "ReJoyce" exemplifies the heterogeneous strands that coalesced to form the counterculture's hallucinogenic ethos of "free love": on first hearing, the listener could conceivably identify with any one of the sexualized characters—from Boylan the "counterculture stud" to Molly the "sexually liberated woman."

Joyce's literary technique has been termed stream-of-consciousness, which allows for, among other things, the narrative of the story to move freely in and out of a character's inner consciousness. The musical textures of "ReJoyce" similarly meld and transform subjectivity unpredictably over the course of the song. A nonlinear narrative combined with sudden moments of repetition magically blends into an eclectic mix of musical features. The song begins with a slow, meterless opening, marked by wafts of electronically distorted sounds. Later, an anxious march of *Ulysses*' characters enters in a quick 4/4 tempo. The middle of the song offers an exotic instrumental interlude of sorts, with a sinewy melody, ripe with augmented seconds, played by a wind instrument: the episode is meant to mimic what in American vaudeville shows and cinema had become characteristic sounds of a Middle Eastern snake charmer. An obsessive section of repeated lyrics and disconcerting parallel-fourth harmonies leads to a conclusion of suddenly drawn-out notes that seem to want to glue the preceding episodes together.

On the one hand, this somewhat chaotic interplay of lyrical references and musical styles can symbolize freedom. As Timothy Leary said at the Houseboat Summit, the countercultural participant has dropped out but, in so doing, has tuned into an array of options in every direction. The intertextuality of "ReJoyce" makes it difficult to categorize, so it escapes being confined into one musical box. Instead it celebrates an eclecticism often interpreted as depth of insight into elusive aspects of the self. In a study of Led Zeppelin, musicologist Susan Fast argues that because musical techniques such as reverberation, echo, and distortion are expansions of the "sonic palette," they serve as "metaphor[s] for the expansion of consciousness into uncharted territory."[42] In "ReJoyce" this "uncharted territory" is at once drug-induced, spiritual, and sexual. Grace Slick, like both Robert Plant and Jimi Hendrix, vocally tows a fine line between control and abandonment, as if enacting that indescribable moment before orgasm, the letting go of rationality for the experience of an intangible LSD hallucination, or the struggle of perceiving the body while having an out-of-body experience. Her ornamented singing style and unpredictable points of climax, the blurred timbres and mesh of dissonant instrumental sounds, and the juxtaposition of wildly different musical textures simulate the sexual experience as if inseparable from drug-induced hallucinations and spiritual ecstasy. In this respect, then, songs like "ReJoyce" and

"Purple Haze" allude to the collapse of physical boundaries, gratification in the moment, development through immediate experience, and abandonment of opposing forces.

What's strange about "ReJoyce's" pleasure-filled narrative is its pessimistic ending. What should be made of the long drawn-out notes—grasping to hold the disparate parts of the song together—which lead to the final line, "It all falls apart"? Neither does it seem to reflect the "peace, love, and flowers" story that so many sixties histories tell nor resonate with Molly's affirmative "yes" when she eventually sexually reunites, in her fantasy, with her husband at the end of *Ulysses*. Inasmuch as the intertextuality of "ReJoyce" can be heard as exploration of uncharted territory and the spiritual dimensions of sexual abandonment, it can equally be heard as a disjointed tale of desire and consumption that ends in broken pieces.

Conscious or not, it's possible that this kind of narrative was part of the appeal of songs like "ReJoyce." Sandy Pearlman, a writer for the underground music magazine *Crawdaddy*, noted in 1967 that "the most basic live sound of Jefferson Airplane is dense and complex, often highly turbulent . . . [The songs] are complex and sound complex."[43] Certainly aspects of "ReJoyce" fit this definition. The strange mixture of gender politics and authorial voices that play out in the song is compelling in its complexity. In *Ulysses*, Bloom is the lead character whose inner thoughts we hear directly, but in "ReJoyce" he is constituted only through Slick's description of him. It is Slick who explains that Molly has gone to meet her lover, Boylan. It is Slick who describes the "amazing" things that Boylan can do with his manly endowment. And it is Slick who shapes the apparently quirky and pathetic character of Bloom, who does nothing except avoid sex by sleeping turned around in their marital bed with his head buried near Molly's feet. Bloom's function in the song's narrative, as well as Boylan's (as a disembodied sexual object—"crotch"—that provides what Bloom can't), both seem to heighten the drama of female sexual desire. Couple this character construction with the Middle Eastern interlude at the center of the song. While such exoticism can be heard as a sign of taboo sexuality, it is usually coded as feminine, sensuous, dangerous, and alluring.[44] Here its musical qualities of asymmetrical pitch and rhythm, augmented seconds and fourths, and metrical instability describe a feminine Other who inspires both sexual obsession and fear.

So Grace Slick gives voice to all the male characters in the narrative, effectively describing for her listeners the perception of male sexuality by a woman. And although she, the character of Molly, and the female Other signaled by the instrumental episode, collectively give the impression that women are in control, their power still derives from their sexuality. This scenario represents the often precarious position that women in the counterculture held. Their type of sexuality could figuratively and literally threaten both the normative patriarchal culture and the hyper-heterosexual, hyper-masculine counterculture. Women with sensual allure or sexual power had the potential not only to upset the balance of normative gender and sexual relations in society, but to imperil men directly, at least from men's perspectives, who wanted to be in control of crafting their unique countercultural escape from society.

With the likes of Jimi Hendrix, Mick Jagger, and Eric Clapton, for example, rock music had no shortage of macho posturing. But theirs was also an androgynous sexuality (if only for show) that arrogantly possessed both femininity and masculinity. The aura they gave off was that they were so masculine and so macho that they had the power to possess everything else, including femininity. Ironically, but not surprisingly, the mainstream hurled insults at the counterculture, not for its all-consuming masculinity, but for its so-called androgyny and feminization. Men in the counterculture did not fit a traditional image of muscular, unemotional masculinity, but had long hair, loose shirts, flowing bell bottoms, and lithe physiques. They appeared to be in touch with their emotions, receptive to non-Western spiritual traditions, and ready to be ungrounded in fantastical druggy worlds. But like their male rock music heroes, men in the counterculture possessed this flexible masculinity at the expense of women.

More often than not, countercultural men who felt threatened used female sexuality against women to reinforce their own masculinity. And violence was part of that threat. In Hunter S. Thompson's quasi-autobiographical, half-fictional novel *Fear and Loathing in Las Vegas: A Savage Journey to the Heart of the American Dream,* for example, the machismo at the center of the dropped-out, countercultural American Dream is captured through the fear and loathing of women. There is sheer contempt for female characters such as the hotel cleaning lady and the runaway teenager, and that contempt is acted out, among other ways, through direct violence.[45] This violent machismo, particular to the subcultural atmosphere of the end of the sixties, was shared by Hell's Angels and leftist political types alike. The novel sees women, like drugs and alcohol, as things to be used to excess and then discarded, as tools for refusing to face reality. In one of the novel's most menacing instances of despising women, the character of Gonzo takes a bath with the intention of committing suicide. Jefferson Airplane's "White Rabbit" blasts at high volume again and again in the background. Grace Slick's piercing voice provides the backdrop, the narration, and ultimately the reason for his pathetic failure as a man.

Reflecting back, Allen Cohen argues that he and the *Oracle* staff attempted to reshape a normative gendered hierarchy by giving the counterculture an alternative vision of women as revered goddesses. Though he acknowledges that "there was still much to be desired in the position of women in Hippie culture," the fact that women's roles were shaped predominantly through sex seemed to be no cause for alarm. Instead he flows into a reverie about how women were respected "as a result of men and women experiencing each other in their symbolical divine aspects during psychedelic visions." His idealizing of countercultural women in sexual union with men doesn't stop there. He argues that because there was a "pervasive atmosphere of sexual and psychological freedom," women were able to find a new kind of personal power. This sexual power, along with "the politicization of women in the movement against the war, would lead to the women's liberation movement that began to shake the status quo in the early 70s."[46]

At best, Cohen's take on countercultural female sexuality as a driving force behind the history of women's liberation is yet another instance of revisionist naïveté. For women in the late sixties counterculture, sexually derived power was just a revised version of the double standard that prevailed throughout the fifties. Historian David Allyn describes it in the following way: "American males were told that if they were healthy they should hunger for sex, while young women were advised to resist forcefully and demand a ring. . . . Under the double standard, a woman who publicly expressed the slightest interest in sex effectively forfeited her right to say no."[47] But of course roles for women in the counterculture were shaped by more than just a rejection of (or refusal of) normative fifties sexual standards. The most prominent women in the sixties sociopolitical arena—not associated with fifties stereotypes or conservative politics—came out of the New Left and civil rights movements. In 1960, only 30.5 percent of married women worked for wages. But with the FDA's approval of an over-the-counter birth control pill in 1960, over one million women taking the pill by 1962, and an increasing percentage of women graduating from college, the numbers of working women began to change.[48] Needless to say, numbers can't eliminate entrenched sentiment, and an ideology of domesticity was pervasive. Both the New Left and the civil rights movements were male dominated, run by men who fostered sexist sentiment that was notably hostile toward feminism. But women were participants in both movements, and from their experiences they learned the language and techniques of protest that they would use to question normative gender roles and fight against their own oppression.[49]

Women's rights advocates were associated with many different camps, including existential feminists (based in the work of Simone de Beauvoir), Marxist feminists, radical feminists, liberal feminists, and socialist feminists. Two groups—liberal feminists, spearheaded by the National Organization for Women (NOW) formed by Betty Freidan in 1966, and women's liberationists, who shared a closer ideological alliance with black radicalism—were closely associated with the larger ideological changes of the sixties. NOW and liberal feminists called for the end of sex discrimination and equal treatment under the 1964 Civil Rights Act, while women's liberationists called for a complete exit from the patriarchal system. Liberal feminists viewed the liberationists as reducing the paramount struggle for women's rights into a wrangling over bedroom choices, while the liberationists saw the liberal feminists's agenda as a brand of mainstream liberalism that was bending its values to play within a totally corrupted, discriminatory system. For the liberationists everything was seen in terms of its position in the patriarchal system—men, women, masculine, feminine, capitalism, and integrationism—and they wanted out. Like the counterculture and unlike the liberal feminists, the women's liberationists were not particularly interested in reforming the system or in fighting against it. Their goal was to be outside of the system, outside of all sexual and gender boundaries.

At first glance, Grace Slick, like Janis Joplin, appeared to be outside of the system by deliberately constructing her own sexual image. As a former beauty queen who dropped out of college to come to the Haight, Slick was beautiful but naughty. Tired of her husband and just one sexual partner, she was happy to advertise the number and variety of men that she slept with.[50] And in one sense, by wanting a brand of sexual excitement that was so obviously restricted by traditional social contracts such as marriage, Slick, like Molly's character in *Ulysses*, became for the counterculture the antithesis of middle-class repressed female sexuality. And as one of few female rock musicians, she could encourage female sexual assertion, both through her music and via her position as a role model.

But in a male-dominated and heterosexist counterculture, it was not surprising that sexuality became the main avenue for women to define themselves. The counterculture's self-perception, as well as its construction in history books, is that it shattered sexual taboos under the guise of "free love." But as Alice Echols has explained, "Instead of undoing the deeply rooted sexual double standard, free love only masked it in countercultural pieties."[51] Multiple partners and sex orgies—key features of so-called alternative lifestyles—were enticing, no-strings-attached covers for traditional gender roles beneath the surface. "Free love" was constructed out of the same sexist strands of behavior familiar to the mainstream, and mirrored what Thomas Frank and Aniko Bodroghkozy both identify as the marketable sexy edge of consumer culture in the sixties.[52]

This marketable love was poignantly encapsulated by the Beatles' hit "All You Need Is Love." The small collage of quotes and musical snippets reinforce the point of the refrain—"It's Easy." From the "Love, Love, Love" part of the refrain to the quotes of the *Marseillaise* and the Beatles' own early song "She Loves You," all forms of love appear equally available and legitimate. Although the song is not particularly sexual, it offers, as scholar Ian MacDonald describes, a "non-evaluative attitude." If the Beatles claimed that all you need is a personalized ideal of love, then the counterculture, at least on the surface, appeared to be advocating for the same idea with its "free love" ideology.[53] But the Beatles' sentiment resonates beneath the countercultural surface too. Because the musical quotations are fleeting, the song describes a world where love doesn't, and ultimately, can't last—especially for a culture that wanted the new, in the now. How ironic that, in 1968, the *San Francisco Oracle* proclaimed, "Much of the shape of the future can be seen in rock aspirations today (these being, in part, total freedom and experience, total involvement, total love, peace and mutual affection)."[54] Because, as "ReJoyce" prophesized, out of its chaotic mixture of musical elements and lyrical references, "It all falls apart"—predicting the impending collapse of the counterculture under the weight of its ideological contradictions.

In a recent issue of *National Geographic,* journalist Alan Mairson recounts his visit to the East Wind commune in the Ozarks of Missouri. With about seventy-five members living on one thousand acres of land, the commune refers to itself as an "intentional community" with values of nonviolence, noncompetitiveness, and communion with nature. The members go by their first names, eat produce from their communal organic garden, share all their clothes, drink a lot of beer, frequently work in the nude, and often have unrestricted sexual relationships with each other. The founders formed the commune in 1973 based on their impression of Mao's socialist policies in China. To them, socialism meant shedding material goods, contributing work as needed, taking items as needed, and doing one's own thing.[55] In the middle of what is arguably one of the most nonsocialist countries in the world, the commune sought (and continues to seek) to be detached entirely from the governing American system. But in various ways and to the acknowledgment of at least one of its founders, this hope for detachment has not been realized.

The commune runs a nut butter business that generates

five hundred thousand dollars a year. To sustain the business and the commune itself, conventional petroleum-based energy products, raw nuts, and most of the food and drink for the residents are bought from outside the commune. And although the money from the business is used for shared necessities such as medical needs, transportation, food and drink, it is more than obvious that this socialist haven is made possible by capitalist enterprise. Its existence, along with dozens of others that are members of the Federation of Egalitarian Communities, seems to represent people's desire to drop out of the work-buy-sell-consume-commute lifestyle of mainstream America. There aren't enforced rules and, for the most part, people live out their days playing music, drinking, hiking, having sex, and talking about their ideals. In part, this seems exactly what Timothy Leary envisioned on the stage of the Human Be-In and at the Houseboat Summit in 1967. Drop out of the system and tune into your own system. But at the same time, it illustrates exactly what Leary would not admit to— that subcultures that have stemmed from or are akin to the counterculture have so many strings attached to mainstream culture that dropping out of society is not only impossible, but is used as an excuse to be lazy and self-indulgent.

The older gurus of the counterculture argued that freedom is limited by the mainstream and its institutions and principles. To access freedom then required emancipating the self from the system—escaping—by reviving repressed instinct and inner consciousness. "Free your mind," as the Beatles said. "Feed your head," as Jefferson Airplane advised. Find "somebody to love," as Grace Slick suggested. The music illustrated exactly what countercultural leaders encouraged—to elevate the personal over the social, to indulge one's own desires rather than change society for the better. And that which was non-Western and nontraditional became the backdrop for these countercultural journeys into the self. But ultimately, as the story of the East West commune perhaps illustrates, escape was illusory. One didn't throw off the shackles of modern capitalist society and suddenly access a more authentic existence by doing yoga, taking LSD, following astrology, and having more than one sexual partner. The spiritual-sexual-hallucinogenic-philosophical Otherworld of the counterculture was inevitably tied to the mainstream world, and those ties couldn't be broken. Dropping out was bound to be more of a romanticization of the different rather than actual difference.

Chapter Six

Helter Skelter

Lessons from the End of the Counterculture

In 1968, a relatively new band named Steppenwolf released their first album and earned huge popularity with the album's hit track, "Born to Be Wild." Taking advantage of the spotlight, the band quickly released their second album that same year, *Steppenwolf the Second,* featuring the song "Magic Carpet Ride." Both songs exuded a kind of hybridity, evidenced not just by their crossover appeal with both underground music audiences and Top 40 radio listeners, but in the multiplicity built into the songs themselves. What was happening in Steppenwolf's music was also happening in the music of several other more established bands.[1] It wasn't that songs had never been crossover hits before or that there hadn't been songs where the influences of more than one musical style could be heard. Rather, it was that well-established popular music categories, clear-cut musical styles, and specific target audiences were getting out of focus.

Earlier in 1967, Jefferson Airplane's music had exemplified the psychedelic counterculture sound. Throughout the early sixties, Bob Dylan's music had been inseparable from the folk music genre. Diana Ross had been a key shaper of the Motown sound. Otis Redding had pushed soul music into the spotlight. The Beatles and the Rolling Stones had carved out two distinct musical poles of the British Invasion sound. But then, at the beginning of 1968, Otis Redding listened repeatedly to the Beatles' *Sgt. Pepper* album and released the blues, soul, and popular ballad "Dock of the Bay." The Rolling Stones, too, responded to the popularity of the Beatles' album by breaking from their mainstream "bad boys of the British Invasion" role with their 1967 album *Their Satanic Majesties Request* and their mid-1968 hard-drugs-influenced, blues rock song "Jumpin' Jack Flash." And then there was Steppenwolf's "Magic Carpet Ride." It was exaggerated psychedelic counterculture on tap with a pop-ish dance rhythm, childlike appeal, and a recurring message of "fantasy will set you free." Even the Top 40 listener could jump on board, take the imaginary ride, and indulge in the undemanding message. Something about the pluralistic, refusal-to-be-aligned sensibility of the counterculture had seeped out into the greater popular music world and was taking on a life of its own.

As we have seen, from late 1965 through the beginning of 1967, the San Francisco counterculture didn't identify itself in opposition to the system, didn't claim to be an alternative to the mainstream, and didn't view itself as a movement that would change the dominant capitalistic structure. It hoped to live out its new tribalism distinct from the system. Pluralism, nonalignment, and negation were its tools for shaping a distinct existence and a self-image that appeared natural, politically disengaged, sexually liberated, color blind, spiritually minded, and free of consumerism. In actuality, though, the countercultural lifestyle and image needed both the semblance of autonomy as well as access to the system for its driving sensibility to be realized. The counterculture relied on pluralism to refuse association with any one category while also drawing on, sometimes surreptitiously, sometimes unknowingly, various aspects of the mainstream system to sustain itself. With pluralism, the counterculture believed that it could drop out of system. However, because it continued to use threads of mainstream consumer culture to craft its image, the counterculture tempted fate in ways that contributed to its own demise. The counterculture that existed in the Haight-Ashbury district from late 1965 through mid-1967 dissolved and spread out. What had seemed to be a self-contained entity of refusal became more of an infectious, multifaceted ethos of rebellious pluralism. As one Grateful Dead biographer noted, "By 1970, Haight-Ashbury's bacchanal was history."[2]

In addition to the Woodstock Festival, there are two familiar stories—about the Altamont Festival and about Charles Manson—that are often cited in historical accounts as markers of the end of the sixties. Certainly, historians of all types tend to focus on specific dates and events as symbolic points of change. And typically these points serve as historical constituents of a teleological history. Joel Selvin, for example, refers to the Monterey Pop Festival as a marker of a culture "on the cusp of innocence." Similarly, Carol Brightman implies a teleological order of events when she writes: "Looking back, Monterey may be seen as the last way station—after the Acid Tests, the Love Pageant Rally, the Be-In, and countless smaller gatherings—in a two-year ceremony of innocence that marked the flowering of the counterculture."[3] In such historical accounts, Altamont and Charles Manson are often cited as evidence verifying the standard radicalizing narrative of sixties history, where civil rights causes naturally turn into racially militant power-grabs, free speech advocates inevitably become defenders of obscenity, and peace-loving countercultural activity manifestly becomes violent and chaotic.

It is certainly undeniable that the Altamont Festival and Manson's activities boiled over with violence and chaos, but there is something more to be drawn from these stories than a teleological inevitability implied by good/bad, black/white, this-led-to-that dialectical histories. In these two stories is a reflection of the countercultural sensibility and the paths it took as it dispersed through and took root in society as a whole. In part, these stories are examples of the collapse that songs such as "ReJoyce" foresaw. Their pluralistic and incoherent strands—like those that often made up the counterculture's exotic, outlaw, natural, and new age personas—show how the countercultural sensibility made itself vulnerable to media co-option, to unraveling into an ethos that could incubate and tolerate such violence.

On August 9, 1969, Charles Manson and his "Family" members—now often referred to as "Charlie's Angels"—began the apocalypse on Cielo Drive in Los Angeles, leaving five people dead. Manson, orchestrating a maniacal and racist killing spree that lasted two nights, was driven, both psychologically and logistically, by his frequent acid binges and sexual orgies. He believed he was receiving secret messages through the Beatles' *White Album*. "Helter Skelter"—the title of a Beatles song—was scrawled in blood on the wall of one of his victim's homes. Manson had developed his unique taste for sex, drugs, and rock and roll, in, among other places, the Haight-Ashbury district. In 1967 he was released from prison, headed to San Francisco, slept on the streets until finding an apartment to crash in, and there began developing his "Family" plans. By late 1967, Manson had gotten hold of an old school bus in which to house his growing family of adolescent girls and young women. In stark contrast to the brightly painted school bus named "Furthur" of Ken Kesey and the Merry Pranksters, the Manson Family bus was painted black. And while Furthur's summer expedition across the country in 1964—taking off with Kesey riding shotgun and Beat poet Neal Cassady at the wheel—could be understood as idyllically celebrating the freedom afforded by acid and "free love," Manson became obsessed with sex, drugs, and rock and roll as means for controlling and using others.

After Manson took up residence in the Haight-Ashbury district, he frequently played his guitar on the streets. During the several years of imprisonment preceding his stay in the Haight, Manson had been developing his musical skills. In one of dozens of accounts of Manson-related history, biographer Karlene Faith remarks sympathetically that, during this period, "Manson constructively translated alienation into song." Such constructive use of music, Faith goes on to explain, was resonant with the sensibility that Manson soon encountered in the Haight: he "discovered a counterculture that appeared to use musical sounds to express agonies and longings but which also, like Eastern religions, encouraged kindness, compassion, and positive attitudes."[4] Faith's assessment of music's role during this period of Manson's life is confirmed by Manson's own recollection of that time. He describes: "I started playing my music and those on the street, they liked it, and they had smiles that were real. . . . Their minds were there, buzzing, everybody was making music, and we grooved on it . . . all the people around me had beards and were giving out love. It buzzed, it made you tune in with it and once you were in with it you saw it was everything."[5]

Not "everything" for Manson, however, was "smiles," "love," and "constructively translated alienation" during this period in the Haight-Ashbury district. His experiences and relationships provided many of the seeds out of which later actions would grow—as if he took the counterculture with him and transformed it over time to his own ends.[6] The notion of being a major rock star, for example, appears to have taken shape during Manson's time in San Francisco, despite the extent to which countercultural figures outwardly advocated for an insular counterculture detached from the mainstream. At the Houseboat Summit, Timothy Leary warned people that "above all, avoid mass movements, mass leadership, [and] mass followers."[7] Perhaps the hypocrisy underlying such statements by a man who did nothing if not sell the idea of counterculture in every radio, television, and magazine interview he could, resonated with Manson. Leary's rhetoric seemed to imply that all things to do with the masses were bad, but his actions showed that if engagement with the masses was about promoting the counterculture, then that activity and that person were exempt from the rule. Obviously being a major rock star involved the masses, and because Manson had developed, by this point, a near pathological desire for mainstream rock stardom, he went to the only place that had it to offer—Los Angeles. Yes, he would likely have a mass following and be immersed in mass culture as a rock star, but presumably he would be exempt because he would be toting his convoluted version of a countercultural sensibility with him.

On April 12, 1968, Manson, together with a group of young women and two men, left the Haight and traveled through Washington, Arizona, Nevada, Texas, New Mexico, and finally down the coast of California. After a trip of guitar playing and singing, unconditional sex with all the women, and one on-board birth, they neared Santa Barbara and Manson announced, "I'm going to cut a record in Los Angeles."[8] Upon reaching Los Angeles, Manson's prospects for becoming a rock star were real. Intent on shaping sex, drugs, and rock and roll into his own divine trinity, Manson tried to win the support of musicians and reconnect with his ex-cellmate Phil Kaufmann (friend of the Flying Burrito Brothers and the Rolling Stones). In the summer of 1968, Manson and his Angels took over the home of Dennis Wilson, drummer for the Beach Boys. Manson wanted, and imagined he deserved, the kind of fame that groups such as the Beach Boys and the Beatles enjoyed, and Wilson, in these contorted plans, was a stepping-stone to Manson's fame.

After skipping out on the Monterey Pop Festival and a

failed album *(Smile),* the Beach Boys turned to the teachings of the Maharishi. It is not surprising that the prospect of spiritual enlightenment failed to quell Wilson's keen interest in sex and drugs. With record and television producer Terry Melcher (and his assistant Gregg Jakobson), Wilson formed what Gary Valentine Lachman calls "an LA-style Hell Fire Club" called the Golden Penetrators.[9] At his home, Wilson introduced Manson to Melcher and various musicians (including Neil Young and members of the Mamas and the Papas) in exchange for sex with Manson's "girls." According to several accounts, Manson was getting the good end of the deal because women were a dispensable commodity to him, existing, to paraphrase onetime Manson-follower Leslie Van Houten, "to fulfill their one and only role as slaves to men."[10] As one anonymous male follower of Manson explained, "Charlie would have maybe half a dozen of the girls, all running around naked up there, and he would give them to guys to ball or whatever . . . pass them out to people he figured could get him into the music business."[11]

The Beach Boys did release a song by Manson in December 1968 on their *20/20* album. Originally entitled "Cease to Exist," the Beach Boys changed it to "Never Learn Not to Love" and gave Wilson the writing credits instead. And although Jakobson recorded some of Manson's demos in August 1968 and Manson himself took a trip up to the Esalen Institute on August 3, 1969, to play for "influential" people there, he was repeatedly rejected. His plans for musical stardom failed to materialize, and "Never Learn Not to Love" was the closest he came, in the late sixties, to achieving his goal of musical stardom.[12]

In part, desire for stardom on the part of a relatively unknown musician exemplified the counterculture's utopian sensibility—everything and anything was available and possible. Yet it also illustrated how the counterculture, when not tied to a particular geographical location, was transformed into a countercultural ethos that could easily become a profiteering mechanism. Beginning with the Monterey Pop Festival, countercultural happenings intimated the possibility of larger-than-life privilege for musicians. In the Haight, Janis Joplin, Jerry Garcia, Grace Slick, and other countercultural musicians had been part of the community, but the possibilities of stardom would soon set them apart from their audiences. As Carol Brightman notes, "The festivals, especially Woodstock, two years later, sold records, millions and millions of them, which in turn helped franchise magazines and rock pundits. All together, they fueled an industry whose properties, the stars, would become nearly interchangeable so long as returns outstripped investment."[13] As it turned out, it wasn't just the stars that were interchangeable, but the musical venues, the audiences, and their values.

On December 6, 1969, The Rolling Stones put on a free concert, referred to as the Altamont Festival, at the Altamont Speedway in Livermore, California, the eastern limits of the San Francisco Bay Area. In an arena distinctly different from the cultural hotbed of San Francisco with its signature dance halls, the festival in Livermore showed, in one sense, how the vibe of the San Francisco counterculture would play out in the rest of America. The concert was not originally intended to feature just the Rolling Stones, nor was its setting supposed to be outside of San Francisco. In November 1969, the Grateful Dead had suggested to the Rolling Stones that they join in a free concert in San Francisco's Golden Gate Park. During recent years, the park had housed thousands of free concerts, most notably the Grateful Dead's weekly jam sessions. Jerry Garcia had the idea that a free concert, which included another big-name band, would help ease the tensions between rival biker gangs in the area. The Rolling Stones agreed, offering to finance the free beer, T-shirts, and food, and proposing that the San Francisco chapter of the Hell's Angels cover security.

This suggestion, in and of itself, was not unusual. The Angels had provided security for many events, from Ken Kesey's

Acid Tests in 1965 to the 1967 Human Be-In to various other free concerts in the park. The Angels had become enshrouded in the romantic aura of the outlaw. Appearing to celebrate the freedom of those on the margins, they became the counterculture's unofficial guardians. The problem with the Altamont Festival was that because the Grateful Dead couldn't secure Golden Gate Park for the concert date, the music, along with the Angels, would be moved out of the protected home turf of the Haight-Ashbury district. And as if this change wasn't enough, in nationwide news a few days before the concert, Charles Manson and his own "Angels" were arrested and charged for the murders in Los Angeles. It is true that the Altamont Festival and the Manson Family murders had no connection in any practical sense. But for many, they seemed to share in the same decaying culture.

According to Carol Brightman's account, a sign was posted anonymously in the Grateful Dead's office a few days before the Altamont Festival reading, "First Annual Charlie Manson Death Festival," referring to the upcoming free event.[14] Violent cult behavior was clearly becoming a marketable commodity. Like Manson, the Hell's Angels at Altamont were high on an assortment of drugs. Like Manson, the Angels were becoming known for their sexual free-for-alls with underage girls. And like Manson, the Angels weren't known for their appreciation of racial diversity. Armed with pool cues and knives at the concert, the Angels beat several people (including Marty Balin of Jefferson Airplane) and killed a black man named Meredith Hunter. Although, from the stage, Mick Jagger did not see the knife used to kill Hunter, he did stop singing "Under My Thumb," and watch the mob develop, helpless in the face of their violence. The Grateful Dead had shown up separately to the Altamont Speedway and stayed apart from the scene to watch the Rolling Stones begin their set. They didn't play. Instead, they left, as if horrified at what a peaceful, loving counterculture had become outside of the Haight-Ashbury district.

Like the Grateful Dead, historian Todd Gitlin, who attended the concert, remembers that he was "oppressed by the general ambiance" of the scene at Altamont. In a chapter of his widely read account of sixties history entitled "The Implosion," he laments: "It wasn't just the Angels . . . Who could any longer harbor the illusion that these hundreds of thousands of spoiled star-hungry children of the Lonely Crowd were the harbingers of a good society? . . . The star-struck crowd was turned on, not to each other, not to the communal possibilities, but to the big prize, the easy-ticket."[15] To Gitlin, Altamont was more than an event gone wrong—it was the countercultural "illusion" of peace and love unveiled. Perhaps Gitlin's disdain for this "illusion" is, in part, influenced by his bias toward political activism. Not only was Gitlin a part of the New Left, but his historical accounts of the sixties repeatedly applaud those movements that explicitly attempted to affect sociopolitical change. On the one hand, the counterculture cannot really be criticized for its lack of political activism because it didn't claim to be interested in the norms of American life, much less in changing society or engaging in political activity. But on the other hand, the counterculture's seemingly "nonevaluative," egalitarian, nonjudgmental philosophy had some horrible practical consequences. When a Hell's Angel was brought up on charges for Meredith Hunter's murder at Altamont, not one witness came forward to testify, and the suspect was acquitted. How could there be no witness from an event that hosted thousands? Gitlin's response implies how inexcusable it was for those who identified with the countercultural philosophy to acquiesce in the face of racism and violence.

The ethos surrounding Altamont can be seen as an epitaph for the counterculture in the same way that literary historian Marianne DeKoven describes former Hell's Angel Hunter S. Thompson's depiction of Las Vegas in his novel *Fear and Loathing in Las Vegas* as an epitaph for the sixties as a whole.[16] At first, the mainstream, neon, crooning-style materialism of

Las Vegas seemed anathema to a rebellious and activism-driven sixties culture. Instead Vegas inspired fear and loathing of its excesses. But by the end of the sixties, Thompson's quasi-countercultural main characters are dripping with excesses of their own—violently abusing women, carrying a trunk load full of drugs, speaking uncontrollably through their continuous druggy haze as if stricken with verbal diarrhea, and primed at every turn to score huge riches in Las Vegas. Thompson's narrative speaks to a significant ambiance of "alienation" that was recognizable at the end of the decade. But it doesn't, as DeKoven suggests, represent a direct betrayal of the countercultural dream. The desire for riches, drugs, sex, music, and gambling in 1969 Las Vegas was about indulging oneself, about elevating personal pleasure over practical concerns, much as a group Tantric yoga session or psychedelic Acid Test or all-night concert at the Fillmore Auditorium during 1966 was. The difference between the two types of indulgence is a matter of degree. Somewhere between the first Family Dog dance at Longshoreman's Hall at the end of 1965 and the Altamont Festival, the perception of the countercultural sensibility became absurdly exaggerated. Altamont was a dark satire of the counterculture, in the same way that a political cartoon amplifies a person's recognizable features, transforming the whole person, often uncomfortably, into a caricature beholden to his grotesque features. As the countercultural sensibility became amplified and exaggerated, excesses such as racism and violence filtered in.

What had happened to the counterculture to elicit such exaggeration? The 1967 Summer of Love spawned articles in *Time, Newsweek,* and *Life* magazines, spreading the counterculture out and bringing visitors in. Thousands of tourists and drifters (Charles Manson included) came to experience the Haight-Ashbury district, but because they came as onlookers, they had no investment in the community that had been established there. They aimlessly filled the streets, wanting to indulge in the countercultural atmosphere of "anything goes" and "do your own thing." Incidents of gang rape and teen pregnancy increased, venereal disease became rampant, and quick-fix drugs, like cocaine and heroin, ousted the counterculture's idyllic LSD. The Diggers saw that the Haight was changing and in the fall of 1967 organized a "Death of the Hippie" parade. Allen Cohen, editor of the *Oracle* at the time, remembers that thousands of people had made the "pilgrimage" to the Haight that summer, and that the local groups, shops, and organizations couldn't hold up under the strain. After the summer, the newspaper supported the "Death of the Hippie" parade and hoped that burying a "coffin filled with hippie paraphernalia and flowers signifying the death of the media generated hippie" would contribute to the rebirth of the "Free man and Free city."[17] As the parade participants chanted, "Hippie, the devoted son of mass media," they buried the store sign of the Psychedelic Shop in a gesture symbolizing the death of something once unique.

In *When We Were Good: The Folk Revival,* Robert Cantwell argues that there was something inevitable about the countercultural sensibility becoming reified as a fixed rebellious ideology. "As soon as it found expression, always self-consciously, in response to the public construction put on of 'disillusioned' and 'rebellious' youth by journalists and critics in the parent generation . . . it had lost its freshness and originality, had become a kind of ritual formula unconnected to the genuine wellsprings of the revivalist mood."[18] According to Cantwell, a middle-class white youth culture, carved out of economic and educational affluence from the beginning, was bound to become "a dazzling consumer spectacle." Cantwell crafts his assessment in retrospect, but Theodore Roszak witnessed something of this transformation at the time. Youth "have been pampered, exploited, idolized, and made almost nauseatingly much of. With the result that whatever the young have fashioned for themselves has rapidly been rendered grist for the commercial mill and cynically merchandised by assorted hucksters—*including* the new ethos of dissent."[19] Roszak saw that "genuine" countercultural impulses dissipated with increasing attention. The media presented the counterculture as an excessive, adolescent party, and many indulged in the new image, paying little attention to what the countercultural lifestyle had been about in the first place.[20]

But something else happened beyond the media's takeover of the Haight-Ashbury, and it was buried in the countercultural sensibility, in the hidden story of the Psychedelic Shop sign. By the end of 1967 the owners of the Psychedelic Shop, Ron and Jay Thelin, had closed it and moved out of town. Underground columnist for *Ramparts* magazine Warren Hinckle noted in March 1967, before the Summer of Love, that both the Thelins and the staff at the *San Francisco Oracle* had considered making their respective operations nonprofit. For the Psychedelic Shop, the Thelins thought that a nonprofit cooperative would help preserve the freedom of the Haight-Ashbury way of life, allowing participants to get high on life without the shackles of consumerism. And the *Oracle* staff considered that if their newspaper was a guide, of sorts, for the countercultural change in consciousness, then "to reconstruct our world" would be better done without the influence of capitalism.[21] But as Hinckle implies with a fair degree of cynicism, the shop and the newspaper were paying lip service to something they didn't really intend to do. Ultimately merchants and advertisers, publicity and profit, were more valuable to the Thelins and the *Oracle* staff, creating what Hinckle calls "the myth of utopia" to attract new consumers to the Haight. People came to the Haight to live and consume the very "posture of unrelenting quietism" that the counterculture had announced through its music, newspapers, musicians, and stores.[22]

Even before the Summer of Love, and well before Altamont, the Monterey Pop Festival hinted at what the counter-

culture was turning into. As the last act of the festival weekend, the Mamas and the Papas and Scott McKenzie had sung,
"If you're going to San Francisco, be sure to wear some flowers
in your hair . . . all across the nation, there's a big vibration."
In one sense, the song "San Francisco," which Papas singer
John Phillips had written with the festival in mind, revealed
how the Haight, San Francisco, the counterculture, and
"peace, love, and flowers" were becoming collapsed together
to signal a loosely defined style, quality, or "vibration." In another sense, a Los Angeles pop group singing "San Francisco"
(as if they were as countercultural as any of the San Francisco
rock groups at the festival) was a musical foreshadowing of the
events to come. Altamont and Manson exemplified what
could happen when the countercultural sensibility became an
empty signifier, disconnected from the fragile communal
ecosystem within the Haight-Ashbury district.

In Los Angeles, Manson had a mixed reception. Many in
the music scene thought that he had talent, but his proneness
to unpredictable bursts of violence, lack of interest in developing social skills (to put it mildly), and unwillingness to practice or prepare for producers and recording sessions made him,
ultimately, an unattractive commodity. Even before igniting
the fuse of his apocalyptic vision, Manson was an outcast
whom people (other than those he had drawn into his cult)
wanted nothing to do with. His behavior was certainly alien-
ating, but perhaps people's apprehension of him also had to
do with what Manson represented. Not only was he a night-
mare image of what the San Francisco counterculture had inspired, but it said something that his version of the countercultural sensibility could find its twisted realization in mass-
mediated Los Angeles.

In an interview with Ralph Gleason in 1967, Jerry Garcia
remarked on the differences between San Francisco and Los
Angeles:

Why is it that San Francisco is so much groovier of a place? Why has the scene blossomed so fantastically? For one thing, everybody's in it. . . . In the early dances, everybody was a part of the band. Everybody was stomping on the floor. And waving their arms around . . . They don't have any dance things in LA. The extent of the dancing in Los Angeles is ten feet off the floor in a glass cage. Everybody watches, like the movies. Except you go to be watched as well. Their scene is real isolated, you know. They don't have a community in LA . . . For the millions of people down there, there is no place where you can go and cool it and just like be there and not have to worry about what you're doing there. Or worry about someone asking you what you're doing there.[23]

As a mainstay of the San Francisco scene, Garcia tried, above all else, to preserve the image of a detached and unique counterculture through negation. In his assessment, Los Angeles was everything that San Francisco was not. Los Angeles lacked dancing, community, and an atmosphere that enabled people to be comfortable and themselves. Implicitly unlike San Francisco, Los Angeles's music scene then appeared decadent, where people participated *to be seen,* rather than, in Be-In fashion, just *to be.*[24]

Musicians with geographical allegiances were not the only ones to voice such criticism. Reporter Richard Goldstein explained: "Traveling up the coast from the ruins of the Sunset Strip to the Haight is a Dantesque ascent. Four hundred miles makes the difference between a neon wasteland and the most important underground in the nation."[25] And Joan Didion, resident of Los Angeles at the time, remarked on its "glamorous veneer of unreality" in the late sixties: "The public life of liberal Hollywood comprises a kind of dictatorship of good intentions, a social contract in which actual and irreconcilable disagreement is as taboo as failure or bad teeth, a climate devoid of irony."[26] Garcia, Goldstein, and Didion all focus on a quality of commercial superficiality, implying that tensions were kept hidden beneath the surface in Los Angeles. If there is any accuracy in their depictions, then perhaps Los Angeles *was* the perfect venue for Manson to fill up the countercultural vessel he toted from San Francisco. The rootless, loner persona he had crafted from years in prison and traveling on the road resonated with Hollywood—a place that lived by transforming loners and nobody's into stars. But it could just as easily be argued that Manson might have realized his vision had he stayed in the Haight. The Haight was rapidly catching up with him, and the consumerist and superficial qualities of the Los Angeles scene that Garcia and Goldstein criticized would describe San Francisco (and Altamont) soon enough.

What turned the countercultural sensibility into a marketing-friendly "vibration"? Perhaps it was, as Gitlin suggests, the appeal of the counterculture's underlying "illusion [of] consumption," where all things were indiscriminately valuable. In 1966–67, the San Francisco counterculture had perceived itself to be living a kind of carnival. This type of existence, as literary theorist Mikhail Bakhtin describes, sees "the suspension of all hierarchical precedence [to be] of particular significance. . . . Free, familiar contacts were deeply felt and formed an essential element of the carnival spirit. People were, so to speak, reborn for new, purely human relations."[27] The counterculture's music, its ballrooms, its outdoor concerts, its musicians, and the community they drew around them all illustrated how the culture's embrace of drugs, sex, nature, non-Western spirituality, and carefree philosophy sustained such a carnivalesque way of life. The mode of existence in the Haight was not tied to moral imperatives or individual responsibility. Those who identified with the countercultural scene were not oriented toward politics, ethics, civil rights, or general societal concerns in oppositional terms. In appearance, the counterculture offered an openness and variety that seemed unique and insulated from the influences of the outside world. And to whatever degree the counterculture saw itself as reliant on the larger capitalist system, it still held the belief that its style of community and its sensibility could refuse allegiance to anything mainstream.

"Tune in, turn on, and drop out," said Timothy Leary. He had hoped that this notion would inspire the creation of a host of "tribal" communities full of people who had dropped out of school, work, and society to be one with nature and each other. Detachment, individuality, freedom, escape, and disengagement were the delectable fruits earned from dropping out. But ultimately, there wasn't a way to totally and completely drop out of the system. Instead, the counterculture became a "myth of utopia," an "illusion of consumption," because it both naively and arrogantly thought that it could drop out when, in reality, it depended on, mimicked, and replicated various aspects of the system to exist. Countercultural bands—including Jefferson Airplane, Country Joe and the Fish, Sopwith Camel, the Charlatans, Big Brother and the Holding Company, and, eventually, the Grateful Dead—willingly signed contracts with the major record labels. Countercultural spokespersons openly advertised their nonjudgmentalism and political apathy to the country—tempting media attention from beyond the borders of the Haight-Ashbury district. The countercultural ideology of free love claimed sexual openness, but gave men alone full license to indulge their appetites. Consequently, oppressive gender relations were reinforced, and the role of women as sexual objects was approvingly reflected back to the mainstream media. The goallessness of Eastern spirituality was embraced by popular leaders such as Allen Ginsberg and Alan Watts, while recognition of the ways it manifested in highly structured Eastern cultures was conveniently overlooked. This willful ignorance placed non-goal-oriented philosophies on the flip side of the religious coin as convenient alternatives to a Judeo-Christian tradition and Protestant work ethic. And while such philosophies augmented the counterculture's aura of detachment from the mainstream, this same aura, further glorified by LSD, drew thousands of tourists and hustlers to the Haight. LSD seemed to offer the possibility of heightened consciousness that, in traditions like Buddhism, would take years of spiritual development to achieve. The difference, in reality, was that LSD could not offer consciousness as a permanent state of being, but only for the duration of the drug trip. Rather than extended spiritual preparation, the solution for the culture that wanted to "sit back and let the evening flow" was to trip more often. "Better Living Through Chemistry"—the counterculture ostensibly adopted the same slogan as major war supplier and chemical company DuPont.

The San Francisco counterculture considered itself to be a unique, insular, even utopian system and advertised itself as such. It tempted the rest of the country to come to its home, to indulge in its mode of existence, and to sustain what would prove to be an unsustainable philosophy. People heard the call ringing in the counterculture's music and flooded into the Haight during the Summer of Love. What Timothy Leary didn't foresee was that people came not for his vision of the future, but for easy access to the carnival life now. For them, the countercultural sensibility that Leary had helped craft was just a quick route out of normative existence, where there would be no rules and no constraints imposed by capitalism's work-buy-sell agenda. What they saw was that the expansion of consciousness was easier to attain with drugs than through extended dedication to a spiritual practice; that ecstasy was easier to attain with multiple partners than with long-term dedication to one partner; and that radical plurality was tolerable. With rebellious individuality as a driving mechanism of capitalist democracy, the appeal of the countercultural sensibility was quickly recognized and transformed into a marketable carnival where everyone had free reign to "do his own thing."

"There is no good and no bad. There is no difference between you and I. There is only one thing and that thing is everything . . . it doesn't matter what you do—it's all perfect and the way it is supposed to be."[28] That utopian statement was not made by Timothy Leary in a speech promoting the benefits of LSD, or by Jerry Garcia encouraging his audience to enjoy the show, or by John Lennon playing off the lyrics of "Lucy in the Sky with Diamonds." It derives from a 1971 interview with a psychotic cult leader and mass murderer named Charles Manson. He harnessed a countercultural sensibility and filled it with his own dark psychoses, in direct parallel with the media's move into the Haight-Ashbury district during the Summer of Love. As the counterculture became commercialized, it became nothing but pure image, ready to fit anyone's ends. As an enthusiast of drugs and sex, and a nonconformist who acted as if unbounded by mainstream norms of any kind, Manson was the most extreme incarnation of what Ashleigh Brilliant sang about—a dark marketing executive for the all-purpose countercultural family dream.

Pioneers of the counterculture like Allen Cohen still maintain that the counterculture "spread a message of peace, love and community . . . across the country and across oceans . . . and [brought] secret and ancient traditions of transcendental and esoteric knowledge and experience into the mainstream of cultural awareness."[29] Of course Cohen's is a nostalgic view of what proved to be one of the most formative times in modern American history. But it is also a plea, of sorts, which asks that the counterculture not be forgotten as having impacted the world with its message. Philosophers Joseph Heath and Andrew Potter argue that the "freedom to resist tyranny, to fight against unjust domination, is not equivalent to the freedom to do whatever you want, to have your own interests prevail. Yet the counterculture assiduously eroded this distinction"[30] Clearly Heath and Potter are trying to highlight the difference between the freedoms fought for in sociopolitical causes and those that characterize countercultural activity. Both Cohen's message and Heath and Potter's message hold some truths. True, the freedom to fight injustice is not equivalent to the countercultural freedom of anything goes. But, equally important to note is that the counterculture didn't try to make them equal. The counterculture existed within the capitalist system and often used ideas, symbols, and tools from the mainstream to construct its image. But it never represented a huge threat to society because it was never out to challenge society in the first place. It was only after the Summer of Love, after the counterculture became popularized, after its sensibility got transformed into an empty vessel for human excess, that the distinction between these freedoms was eroded.

Charles Manson justified himself with countercultural platitudes, but his apocalyptic revolutionary vision of a race war (and rape and murder as means to that end), was nothing short of a crazed teleological agenda, exemplifying dialectical thinking (black verses white) at its most extreme. Needless to say, Manson did not achieve his final goal of racial separatism, though he "won" some of his morbid battles, accomplishing rape and murder before going back to prison. The countercultural sensibility had undergone a metamorphosis, becoming a philosophy that countenanced extreme excess. In Manson's world, whatever he deemed to be not countercultural was repressive, and any acts that he perpetrated to counter that imagined repression were acts of countercultural revolt. In a true carnival, where reality is suspended, a magician saws a box in half and afterward, the person inside the box miraculously emerges whole and unscathed. The carnival that Manson envisioned, however, was maniacal, not magical, violently oppositional, not fantastically unencumbered, and when he sawed that box in half, he did it in reality because he had transformed the countercultural sensibility into license to do anything.

At Altamont, on Cielo Drive, and on the streets of the Haight-Ashbury at the end of 1967, people were treated with cruelty, knowingly exploited and discarded, and violently oppressed because the perpetrators of those horrific crimes had contorted the countercultural sensibility into a crucible to carry their excesses. The carnival sensibility that had allowed plurality and refusal, that had introduced people to magical, unseen worlds, and that had given the hope of something existing outside the mainstream agenda, was transformed into an ethos of passivity, an excuse to act without responsibility, a justification for excess, a license to acquiesce in the face of inhumanity. In its own space and on its own terms, the counterculture didn't dwell in the kind of marketable permissiveness that would tolerate such extremes. With the benefit of hindsight, neither should we.

Notes

CHAPTER ONE

1. For specific examples of this goal-oriented rhetoric, as well as particulars about the multiple campaigns of the civil rights movement, see Martin Luther King, Jr., *Where Do We Go from Here: Chaos or Community?* (Boston: Beacon Press, 1967) and *Why We Can't Wait* (New York: Mentor, 1964). In addition, for transcripts of several of King's speeches as well as a comprehensive historical analysis of the progress of the civil rights movement from the early fifties through the late sixties, see Taylor Branch, *Parting the Waters: America in the King Years, 1954–63* (New York: Simon and Schuster, 1988), *Pillar of Fire: America in the King Years, 1963–65* (New York: Simon and Schuster, 1998), and *At Canaan's Edge: America in the King Years, 1965–68* (New York: Simon and Schuster, 2006).

2. Todd Gitlin, *The Sixties: Years of Hope, Days of Rage* (New York: Bantam, 1987), xiv. See also Todd Gitlin, afterword to *Reassessing the Sixties: Debating the Political and Cultural Legacy,* ed. Stephen Macedo (New York: Norton, 1997).

3. See, for example, Howard Zinn, *The Zinn Reader: Writings on Disobedience and Democracy* (New York: Seven Stories Press, 1997); Doug Rossinow, *The Politics of Authenticity: Liberalism, Christianity, and the New Left* (New York: Columbia University Press, 1998); Alexander Bloom, ed., *Long Time Gone: Sixties America Then and Now* (Oxford: Oxford University Press, 2001); Gerald Howard, ed., *The Sixties: The Art, Attitudes, Politics, and Media of Our Most Explosive Decade* (New York: Marlowe, 1995); David Halberstam, *The Best and the Brightest* (New York: Ballantine, 1993) and *The Powers That Be* (Urbana: University of Illinois Press, 2000); Gerald Howard, "Looking Backward: The Sixties Seen from the Eighties," in Howard, *The Sixties.*

4. See, for example, Harvey C. Mansfield, "The Legacy of the Late Sixties," in Macedo, *Reassessing the Sixties*.

5. One of the most popular types of sixties histories follows a documentary-style format that tends to move chronologically through the decade by sociopolitical movement or situation. See, for example, Bloom, *Long Time Gone;* David Burner, *Making Peace with the 60s* (Princeton: Princeton University Press, 1996); Debi Unger and Irwin Unger, *The Times Were a Changin': A Sixties Reader* (New York: Three Rivers Press, 1998); and Peter B. Levy, ed., *America in the Sixties: Right, Left, and Center* (London: Praeger, 1998). These histories typically include chapters on the civil rights movement, the student movement, free speech, black power, the Vietnam War, women's liberation, environmental causes, and often conclude with examinations of cultural/ideological "movements" such as the counterculture.

6. Theodore Roszak, *The Making of a Counter Culture: Reflections on the Technocratic Society and Its Youthful Opposition* (New York: Anchor, 1969), 42.

7. See Philip Deloria, "Counterculture Indians and the New Age," in *Imagine Nation: The American Counterculture of the 1960s and '70s,* eds. Peter Braunstein and Michael William Doyle (New York: Routledge, 2002), 159–88.

8. See Franco Moretti, *Signs Taken for Wonders: Essays in the Sociology of Literary Forms,* rev. ed. (London: Verso, 1997) and *Modern Epic: The World System from Goethe to García Márquez* (London: Verso, 1996).

9. Moretti, *Modern Epic,* 142.

10. In Moretti's terms, Bloom doesn't revolt against the mainstream system so much as "run parallel to it" (*Signs Taken for Wonders,* 246).

11. Deloria makes this argument in "Counterculture Indians," 162.

12. See Allen Cohen, "Additional Notes on the S.F. Oracle: For the *Haight-Ashbury in the Sixties* CD-ROM. Part 2," located at http://www.rockument.com/WEBORA2.html, consulted August 10, 2007.

13. Transcripts of the first three parts of "The Houseboat Summit" from February 1967—Part One: Changes; Part Two: To Drop Out or Not; Part Three: A Magic Geography—are located online at http://www.vallejo.to/articles/summit_ptl.htm. All quotations from the summit come from this website. The original transcript in its entirety can be found in the *San Francisco Oracle,* March–April 1967.

14. Jerry Hopkins, "A New Lifestyle: Do Your Thing," *Communication Company,* April 6, 1967, 18.

15. Theodore Roszak's term for the counterculture's relationship to the mainstream was "refuse." See his explanation of how the counterculture "refused the technocracy" in *Making of a Counter Culture*, xii–5.

16. Richard King, *The Party of Eros: Radical Social Thought and the Realm of Freedom* (Chapel Hill: University of North Carolina Press, 1972), 8.

17. Bill Graham, *Exposure Magazine*, May 1988, quoted in Gayle Lemke, ed., *Bill Graham Presents the Art of the Fillmore: The Poster Series, 1966–1971* (New York: Thunder's Mouth Press, 1999), 61.

18. Martha Bayles, *Hole in Our Soul: The Loss of Beauty and Meaning in American Popular Music* (New York: Free Press, 1994), 217.

19. See, for example, Terry Anderson, *The Sixties* (New York: Longman, 1999); Rossinow, *The Politics of Authenticity;* Jennifer L. Roberts, "Lucubrations on a Lava Lamp: Technology, Counterculture, and Containment in the American Sixties," in *American Artifacts: Essays in Material Culture,* ed. Jules David Prown and Kenneth Haltman (East Lansing: Michigan State University Press, 2000). Roberts's definition of the counterculture resembles that issued by the International Counterculture Archive at the Gelman Library of George Washington University, online at http://home.gwu.edu/~yoffe/. Mark Yoffe, curator for the archive, offers a general definition of counterculture as "groups and movements existing within any modern society and in any country which find themselves in opposition to governing and accepted mainstream ideology, values and the approved and sanctioned forms of self expression. Counterculture is a culture of opposition and minorities. It can be highly political and/or purely artistic, but it inevitably finds itself in opposition to the mainstream political thinking, aesthetic perceptions, styles, and forms and ways of self expression."

20. Robert Christgau, *Any Ol' Way You Choose It: Rock and Other Pop Music, 1967–1973* (Baltimore: Penguin, 1975), 23.

21. As we know, modern technology was abundant and amplification and electric instruments were vital components for creating the semblance of a "unique" San Francisco sound.

22. Thomas Frank, *The Conquest of Cool: Business Culture, Counterculture, and the Rise of Hip Consumerism* (Chicago: University of Chicago Press, 1997), 29.

23. See Frank, *The Conquest of Cool;* David Brooks, *Bobos in Paradise: The New Upper Class and How They Got There* (New York: Touchstone, 2000); Joseph Heath and Andrew Potter, *Nation of Rebels: Why Counterculture Became Consumer Culture* (New York: HarperBusiness, 2004).

CHAPTER TWO

1. See Alice Echols, *Scars of Sweet Paradise* (New York: Henry Holt, 1999), 84, 116. On page 201 there is a picture of the Charlatans and their "Old-timey" look.

2. Information on the Red Dog Saloon was synthesized from a number of sources, including *Rockin' at the Red Dog: The Dawn of Psychedelic Rock,* a Mary Works Production (Monterey Video, DVD, 2005); Joel Selvin, *Summer of Love: The Inside Story of LSD, Rock & Roll, Free Love, and High Times in the Wild West* (New York: Cooper Square Press, 1999); and Echols, *Scars of Sweet Paradise,* 115–16. Echols covers similar material to do with the Charlatans, the Red Dog Saloon, and the initial events that glued together a new San Francisco counterculture in "Chapter 1: Hope and Hype in Sixties Haight-Ashbury" of her book *Shaky Ground: The '60s and Its Aftershocks* (New York: Columbia University Press, 2002), 17–50.

3. For further information and a recent extensive written and pictorial history of the Fillmore district, see Robert F. Oaks, *San Francisco's Fillmore District (Images of America)* (San Francisco: Arcadia, 2005).

4. The history of the Majestic Ballroom turned Fillmore Auditorium and the role the location had in the musical development of the burgeoning counterculture is chronicled in a number of sources. See the Virtual Museum of the City of San Francisco online at http://www.sfmuseum.org; Joel Selvin, *The Musical History Tour: A Guide to over 200 of the Bay Area's Most Memorable Music Sites* (San Francisco: Chronicle Books, 1996); Lemke, *Bill Graham Presents;* and Echols, *Scars of Sweet Paradise,* 117–23.

5. See Peter Braunstein and Michael William Doyle, "Historicizing the American Counterculture of the 1960s and '70s," in Braunstein and Doyle, *Imagine Nation,* 12. Braunstein and Doyle suggest that the Haight was "often regarded as cruel mockery by the black, Hispanic, and immigrant residents of [the Fillmore], who dreamed of attaining entry into the very material world the hippie children had casually—and provisionally—repudiated." Although Braunstein and Doyle indiscriminately describe the feelings of the residents of the Fillmore, their conceptual point here is valuable—that a degree of arrogance is involved when a middle-class white culture appropriates the veneer of oppressive circumstances that other groups have to suffer with throughout history.

6. The Panthers spawned a more generalized black power movement with spokespersons across the country. Stokely Carmichael, of the Student Non-violent Coordinating Committee (SNCC), for exam-

ple, sought to expose the racist foundations of America's institutions by means of racial separation, both economically and culturally. "We are not going to take the oppression of white society any longer. Black people in the US have no time to play nice polite parlor games. . . . Some white Americans can afford to speak softly, tread lightly, employ the soft sell and put-off because they own society. For black people to adopt their methods of relieving our oppression is certainly ludicrous. We blacks must respond in our own way, on our own terms, in a manner which fits our temperaments. . . . The plain fact is that as a people we have absolutely nothing to lose by refusing to play such games." See Stokely Carmichael in *To Free a Generation: The Dialectics of Liberation,* ed. David Cooper (New York: Collier, 1969), 169–70.

7. See Michael Eric Dyson, *I May Not Get There with You: The True Martin Luther King, Jr.* (New York: Touchstone, 2000).

8. *The Digger Papers,* a free pamphlet distributed in 1968, 6, 19, Bancroft Archive Library at the University of California, Berkeley.

9. Joseph Berke, "The Creation of an Alternative Society," in *Counter Culture: Bhudda Bhudda,* ed. Joseph Berke (London: Peter Owen / Fire Books, 1969), 1–17.

10. Gitlin, *The Sixties,* 349.

11. See Hunter S. Thompson, *The Hell's Angels: A Strange and Terrible Saga* (New York: Random House, 1967). Thompson repeatedly refers to the Angels as "outlaw motorcyclists."

12. George Lipsitz, *The Possessive Investment in Whiteness: How White People Profit from Identity Politics* (Philadelphia: Temple University Press, 1998), 118.

13. Greil Marcus, *Mystery Train: Images of America in Rock 'N' Roll Music,* 4th ed. (New York: Plume, 1997), 69.

14. Chester Anderson, cultural journalist/critic and local Haight-Ashbury resident in the late sixties, made the following sarcastic assessment of how white cultures—like the counterculture of which he was a part—rely on stereotypes of "black culture" to shape themselves: "The spades . . . are our spiritual fathers. . . . They gave us jazz & grass and rock & roll. . . . If it weren't for the spades, we would all have short hair, neat suits, glazed eyes, steady jobs & gastric ulcers, all be dying of unnamable frustration." The quotation comes from the *Communications Company* flier written by Chester Anderson and distributed around the Haight-Ashbury district (February 1967), cited in Abe Peck, *Uncovering the Sixties: The Life and Times of the Underground Press* (New York: Pantheon, 1985), 47.

15. Dave Marsh, *Fortunate Son: Criticism and Journalism by America's Best-Known Rock Writer* (New York: Random House, 1985), 57.

16. See Lemke, *Bill Graham Presents*, for more information about the specific musical schedules at the Fillmore throughout the late sixties.

17. See *Crawdaddy*, July–August 1967, 12.

18. Sam Andrew, "Recollections of Janis: Seen through the Eyes of Big Brother," at http://www.bbhc.com.

19. "Jerry Garcia, the Guru," interview by Ralph Gleason, in *The Grateful Dead Reader*, ed. David G. Dodd and Diana Spaulding (Oxford: Oxford University Press, 2000), 32.

20. Echols, *Scars of Sweet Paradise*, 235.

21. See Philip Tagg's paper "Popular Music Studies versus the 'Other,'" delivered December 14, 1996 at the symposium "Music and Life-World: Otherness and Transgression in the Culture of the 20th Century." The transcript of the paper is reproduced online at www.mediamusicstudies.net/tagg/articles/cascais.html, consulted August 10, 2007.

22. Ironically, the Haight-Ashbury might have housed the only audience, prior to the counterculture becoming a nationwide trend by the end of 1967, that was comfortable with a white woman seriously and explicitly adopting a black image. When Joplin and Big Brother played their first big out-of-town gig in Chicago, it was, as historian Joel Selvin remarked, a "total disaster." Part of the problem was that the local and acclaimed blues artists like Muddy Waters and Buddy Guy were playing just around the corner in the city that had given birth to their blues, and Joplin and her white "hippie" band seemed like freakish imitations in comparison. See Selvin, *Summer of Love*.

23. See *Crawdaddy*, October 1967, which includes an article on Motown entitled "A Whiter Shade of Black" and an article on Frank Zappa entitled "White Noise?"

24. One of the many links between Joplin and the blues queens whom she idolized was a focus on sexuality, including bisexuality. Sheila Whiteley, in *Women and Popular Music: Sexuality, Identity and Subjectivity* (New York: Routledge, 2000) explores this particular link (55–56, 66–68) as well as the dynamics of Joplin's negotiation of sexuality within the counterculture.

25. The familiar image of Joplin with bracelets, furs, feathers, rings, no makeup, loose clothing, and often a bottle of whiskey was immortalized in a photo session with photographer and "Haight street scenester" Bob Seidemann. The result was a now famous poster of "the first hippie pin-up girl," a naked Joplin draped in strings of beads. For more information about Seidemann and the photo session see Echols, *Scars of Sweet Paradise*, xix, 138. The book also includes a

reprint of the poster on the third page of photographs between pages 200 and 201.

26. For a discussion of the blues as a music of displacement, see Ronald Radano and Philip V. Bohlman, eds., *Music and the Racial Imagination* (Chicago: University of Chicago Press, 2000).

27. Hazel V. Carby, "'It Jus Be's Dat Way Sometime': The Sexual Politics of Women's Blues," in *Unequal Sisters: A Multi-Cultural Reader in U.S. Women's History,* eds. Ellen Carol DuBois and Vicki L. Ruiz (New York: Routledge, 1990), 241. The article was originally published in *Radical America* 20, no. 4 (1986): 9–24.

28. While Joplin flaunted stylistic and personal connections with African American blues musicians and singers, she generally failed to credit white singers like Joni Mitchell and Joan Baez for opening up the sixties stage for women. She made arrogant remarks such as, "I can sing like Mimi Farina if I want to or like Joan Baez, but they did it first. Why shouldn't I do my own thing first?" Quotes from Janis Joplin are collected at the site http://www.bbhc.com/firstper son.html. Accessed March 2006.

29. Brian Ward, *Just My Soul Responding: Rhythm and Blues, Black Consciousness, and Race Relations* (London: UCL Press, 1998), 248.

30. See Echols, *Scars of Sweet Paradise,* 214, 234–37. For example, Echols relays the story of Joplin's friend Linda Gravenites, who explained Joplin's heroin habit as a deliberate attempt to craft a Billie Holidayesque, "blues-singer mystique."

31. Joplin's 1967 version of "Ball and Chain" moves from a relatively calm intonation, recognizable notes, and measured delivery to moments of insistent hammering (i.e., "oh whoa whoa whoa whoa") and pining gestures lingering on the third to a final verse laden with an extreme and contrasting vocal production of something between speech, song, and whisper. Sheila Whiteley, in *Women and Popular Music,* 54–55, provides an insightful analysis of this version in terms of its narrative of the "turbulent self-awareness of the punishing nature of love." She argues that it "moves the traditional aesthetics of the blues sensibilities into the underlying dilemmas of the 1960s' woman" (55).

32. Ward, *Just My Soul Responding,* 248.

33. Released in August 1968, *Cheap Thrills* sold a million copies in a month.

34. See Echols, *Scars of Sweet Paradise,* 208–9. The so-called live track on the album entitled "Turtle Blues" included two caricatures by Crumb, one with a dialogue box reading "Turtle Blues 'Vibes' courtesy of Barney's Beanery." As Big Brother and the Holding Company assembled "Turtle Blues," they decided to infuse "live" ambient tav-

ern noise into the track. Two members went down to the actual Barney's Beanery in Hollywood with a recorder to retrieve their extra sounds. But on returning to the studio, the band concluded that the recording expedition to Barney's had not produced material up to their expectations. To remedy the situation, everyone in the studio got drunk, turned on the recorders, made lots of noise, and got captured on tape. Twenty-five years later, Big Brother's bass player Peter Albin remarked: "What we tried to do was give the impression the whole album was live and we succeeded. Consequently, even though it wasn't a total live album, we didn't want to take that feeling away from the audience." The Albin quote is from an interview with Sam Andrew and Peter Albin during the Big Brother Twenty-Fifth Reunion Tour, reprinted online at http://web.wt.net/%7Eduane/bigbro.html, consulted August 10, 2007.

35. Robert Christgau, *Grown Up All Wrong: 75 Great Rock and Pop Artists from Vaudeville to Techno* (Cambridge: Harvard University Press, 1998), 64. The quote is from an article written in 1975.

36. See Echols, *Scars of Sweet Paradise*, 207–8. "Whatever the roots of Janis's studied approach—her vanity, her insecurity, her intelligence, or a background in folk rather than in improvisational jazz—it was certainly effective, even if curiously at odds with her self-presentation as a blues singer who just 'feels things'" (208).

37. See Henry Louis Gates, Jr.'s seminal work, *The Signifying Monkey: A Theory of African-American Literary Criticism* (Oxford: Oxford University Press, 1988) for an extensive theory about troping as a form of "signifying."

38. Billie Holiday, Sarah Vaughn, and Charlie Parker, among others, began to popularize "Summertime" in the late thirties and forties, and by the fifties and early sixties it was a standard with musicians such as John Coltrane, Ella Fitzgerald, and Miles Davis. "Summertime" is included on several recordings of Joplin and Big Brother and the Holding Company, in addition to compilation discs that include Joplin's work with the Full Tilt Boogie Band. On the *Cheap Thrills* album, "Summertime" was recorded in the studio. On the *Joplin in Concert* album, "Summertime" was recorded live by the LSD guru Stanley Owsley at the San Francisco Carousel Ballroom on June 23, 1968.

39. The members of Big Brother had eclectic musical training and a fairly extensive relationship with jazz influences. While attending San Francisco State University in the midsixties, Sam Andrew had played in underground folk-rock bands and studied jazz and classical music. Big Brother's other guitarist, James Gurley, also shared an eclectic musical background. After training in Detroit in the blues and bluegrass scenes, Gurley became obsessed with John Coltrane

and worked feverishly to translate Coltrane's insights on saxophone into guitar. He fused the two worlds of bluegrass guitar and Coltranesque intensity and virtuosity with a unique finger-picking approach to the electric guitar. Once he moved to San Francisco, Gurley also took up electronic music experimentation. His interests altered the musical direction of Big Brother, and before Joplin joined the group, he encouraged the band to explore the musical possibilities available at the burgeoning Tape Music Center in San Francisco. Twisting knobs on synthesizers and playing with reverse tape loops, Big Brother prepared for their appearance at the January 1966 Trips Festival. Even after Joplin joined the group and took center stage, Gurley's experimentations with sound continued. He discovered that his Standell amplifier had a spring reverberation system that made an explosive sound when dropped. Needless to say, this became one of his trademark moves.

40. See Echols, *Scars of Sweet Paradise*, 208. Big Brother's rendition of "Hall of the Mountain King" from Grieg's *Peer Gynt* suite was also popular with the counterculture. Their version basically generates a series of bluesy variations on Grieg's theme.

41. In 1949–50, Miles Davis and musician-arrangers Gil Evans and Gerry Mulligan spawned what was called "cool," the ubiquitous sound of the fifties that marked a significant shift away from post–World War II bebop. Many historians have theorized why there was this sudden shift in jazz aesthetics. Grover Sales, in *Jazz: America's Classical Music* (New York: Prentice-Hall, 1984), concludes that "cool jazz seemed well suited to the aesthetic needs of both its players and its audience, a fitting *obbligato* to the cautious emotional climate engendered by the Korean War, bomb shelters, Sputnik, the Hiss and Rosenberg cases" (162). The parallels between cool jazz's "emotional restraint" and the reserved atmosphere of Cold War America are reasonable, but also important were the subtle racial dynamics of cool jazz's popularity with a mainstream white audience. LeRoi Jones, in *Blues People* (New York: Morrow Quill, 1963) argued that cool jazz derived much of its melodic and harmonic material from bebop, while its lyricism, middle range, classical-music allusions, and mellow vibrato-less timbres, coupled with a behind-the-beat rhythmic regularity, shifted jazz away from bebop's rhythmic innovations. Foregrounding the influences of the European classical music tradition, West Coast cool jazz marginalized, deliberately or not, the musical markers of black intellectualism, independence, and innovation associated with bebop. Note the influences of some of the key players associated with cool/West Coast jazz. Pianist Dave Brubeck, for example, studied with composers Darius Milhaud and

Arnold Schoenberg and incorporated fugue and rondos forms, Bach-like counterpoint, and quotations from Chopin and Wagner in his music. Often referred to as "contrapuntal jazz," the music of the Brubeck quartet, including trumpeter Chet Baker and alto sax player Paul Desmond, was especially popular with a predominantly white college crowd. The term *contrapuntal jazz* is often coupled with the term *chamber jazz:* The Modern Jazz Quartet, for example, led by classically trained black pianist John Lewis, announced its connections to the European art music tradition both in name ("Quartet") and in style, with long-playing albums, Debussy-like textures, and written-out compositions.

42. The cool melodic lines in the instruments appear rhythmically flexible in part because of the facile use of triplets and sextuplets in relation to the solid harmonic foundation of the song in G minor. Strangely though, the guitar and backup guitar, while often enjoying a flowing rhythmic counterpoint, have awkward harmonic moments with false relations between F/F-sharp and B/B-flat. This awkwardness gets worked out as the song progresses due to the relentless and clichéd emphasis on G minor. A descending tetrachord (G, F, E, E-flat) becomes Big Brother's harmonic hook throughout the song, and there are periodic returns during the first half of the song to half cadences on D and neighbor chords based on the minor sixth degree (D to E-flat). Only in one instance does the song break out of G minor. The band modulates to G major with four beats of unified, clearly articulated, arpeggiated, idyllic-sounding G major chords after Joplin has sung the first stanza and not yet entered with the second. This G major moment is only possible *after* a buildup of aggressive articulation and dynamics and in direct contrast to the subjectivity that Joplin offered in the first verse.

43. Gershwin's version of "Summertime" is in B minor with repeated I–II chord progressions achieved through parallel motion as the two chords oscillate back and forth. The chords are ostensibly half-diminished seventh chords—minor triads built on the first and second degrees with major sixths added for color—and very vaguely produce a V–I effect. More significantly perhaps, derived from a major sixth added to a minor triad for color, the chords advertise their harmonic nonfunctionality and alignment with recognizable stylistic features of musical French impressionism.

44. Marshall McLuhan, *War and Peace in the Global Village* (New York: Bantam, 1968), 10.

45. George Lipsitz, "Who'll Stop the Rain," in *The Sixties: From Memory to History,* ed. David Farber (Chapel Hill: University of North Carolina Press, 1994), 218.

1. See George C. Herring, *America's Longest War: The United States and Vietnam, 1950–1975*, 4th ed. (New York: McGraw-Hill, 2001).

2. See John Lewis Gaddis, *Strategies of Containment: A Critical Appraisal of Postwar American National Security*, rev. ed. (Oxford: Oxford University Press, 2005).

3. For a more detailed history about the lead-up to America's relationship with the French and subsequent involvement in Vietnam, see Frances Fitzgerald, *Fire in the Lake: The Vietnamese and the Americans in Vietnam* (Boston: Atlantic Monthly Press, 1972). The book was written soon after Richard Nixon had pulled some American troops out of Vietnam, and the American public had begun to learn of the secret U.S. bombing campaigns of Laos and Cambodia. It is a comprehensive account of the Vietnam War up until that point that addresses the complicated nation-shaping politics that were motivating France, the United States, and North and South Vietnam.

4. An interesting account of the United States' support of French colonialism and the devastating results of the patronizing and arrogant view that subsequently fueled American neocolonialism in Vietnam is Neil Sheehan's *A Bright Shining Lie: John Paul Vann and America in Vietnam* (New York: Vintage, 1989). Among other things, it reveals, from the vantage point of an army field advisor, the increasingly complex interweaving of ideologies used to fuel American involvement and strategy in the war.

5. See Edward Herman and Noam Chomsky's "A Propaganda Model," in *Manufacturing Consent: The Political Economy of the Mass Media* (New York: Pantheon, 1988), 1–35, for further discussion of the uses of anti-Communism to justify various sociopolitical agendas.

6. An example of the often stark dichotomy that ran rampant through society is explored in David Maraniss's *They Marched into Sunlight: War and Peace in Vietnam and America, October 1967* (New York: Simon and Schuster, 2003). As a kind of case study of the effects of the Vietnam War on the American psyche, Maraniss looks at the October 18, 1967, student protests against Dow Chemical recruiters at the University of Wisconsin, arguing that pro and con, establishment and radical, became increasingly apparent over the course of the day.

7. After Jefferson Airplane signed with RCA, many San Francisco bands landed contracts with other record labels. Sopwith Camel signed with the label Kama Sutra, doing so well that the label invested in the Charlatans. The Grateful Dead signed with Warner Brothers only after the company agreed to the band's unique condi-

tions. And Moby Grape signed with Columbia soon after the Monterey Pop Festival.

8. David Crosby, transcription of an audiotape later printed in the *Oracle of Southern California,* October 1967. Reprinted in Jerry Hopkins, ed., *The Hippie Papers: Notes from the Underground Press* (New York: Signet, 1968), 219–20. Located in the Bancroft Archive Library at the University of California, Berkeley.

9. See Barney Hoskyns, *Waiting for the Sun: Strange Days, Weird Scenes, and the Sound of Los Angeles* (New York: St. Martin's Press, 1996), 190–91.

10. Phil Lesh, quoted in Hank Harrison, *The Dead Book: A Social History of the Haight-Ashbury Experience* (San Francisco: Archive Press, 1973), 137.

11. See Robert S. Ellwood, *The Sixties Spiritual Awakening: American Religion Moving from Modern to Postmodern* (New Brunswick, NJ: Rutgers University Press, 1994). Ellwood is concerned with the changing meanings of spirituality in the sixties and argues that the sixties ushered in a postmodernism where the secular became sacralized as a substitute for the deteriorating effectiveness of large-scale religions.

12. See David P. Szatmary, *Rockin' in Time: A Social History of Rock-and-Roll,* 4th ed. (New Jersey: Prentice-Hall, 2000), 150–75.

13. The apparent "anticommercialism" of San Francisco's sound was not the reality for the musicians making the music. Most of the bands were eager to sign record contracts and be heard on the radio across the nation. Alice Echols observes that "San Francisco bands promoted sex, drugs, and rock 'n' roll and saw themselves as an alternative to AM teenybopper fare, but they were never averse to making money, much less at war with capitalism" (*Shaky Ground,* 41).

14. Elliot Tregel, *Billboard Magazine,* May 6, 1967, quoted in Lemke, *Bill Graham Presents,* 68.

15. John Rocco, *Dead Reckonings: The Life and Times of the Grateful Dead* (New York: Schirmer, 1999), 24.

16. Grace Slick, with Andrea Cagan, *Somebody to Love: A Rock and Roll Memoir* (New York: Warner Books, 1998), 97–98. Many scholars of the sixties have ascribed this same exoticist coherency to the counterculture, reinforcing in history the unique self-image that the counterculture maintained at the time. Doug Rossinow, for example, describes the counterculture's aims as "escape, mystic vision, or transcendence" (*The Politics of Authenticity,* 248–49). And rock music historian Edward Macan explains that "hippies placed much emphasis on uncovering new realms of perception and consciousness, especially through the use of hallucinogenic drugs and the adoption of Eastern or 'mystical' religious practices such as transcendental medi-

tation." See *Rocking the Classics: English Progressive Rock and the Counterculture* (New York: Oxford University Press), xi–xii.

17. Richard Goldstein, *Reporting the Counterculture* (Boston: Unwin Hyman, 1989), 53. This book is an edited collection of Goldstein's articles from the late sixties. The cited comment is from an article that was printed in 1967.

18. Lester Bangs, *Psychotic Reactions and Carburetor Dung* (New York: Vintage, 1987), 36–37. This book is an edited collection that includes part of Bangs's extensive oeuvre of rock criticism. The comment about Jefferson Airplane is followed up with this assessment: "It's all right to be a honky, in fact all the Marxists are due for some pies in pronto priority, but to wit on all that bread, singin' bout bein' an outlaw when yer most scurrilous illegal set is ripping off lyrics from poor old A. A. Milne and struggling sci-fi hacks, wa'al, the Creem Committee don't cotton to that, neighbor." The quote was originally printed in a November 1970 article in *Creem*.

19. Hermann Hesse, *The Journey to the East*, trans. Hilda Rosner (New York: Noonday Press, 1956), 27.

20. See Gary Valentine Lachman, *Turn Off Your Mind: The Mystic Sixties and the Dark Side of the Age of Aquarius* (London: Sidgwick and Jackson, 2001), 131. Lachman remarks that by the late sixties all of Hesse's novels were in paperback and "unduly misinterpreted" by the counterculture. One reason for Hesse's attempts to deconstruct boundaries was to show how destructive it was for people to seek a guru and a life philosophy in one person and one culture (i.e., Hitler and Nazi Germany). The misinterpretation came in the very form of hero worship that he was warning against. Hesse, still alive in the late sixties, was followed, adored, and interviewed by countercultural groups and participants. Despite his repeated efforts to disabuse his "worshippers" of their guru fantasies, he ultimately could not prevent someone like Charles Manson, for example, from proclaiming Hesse's novels to be the only "allowed" reading material for his "family."

21. See Edward Said, *Orientalism* (New York: Vintage, 1979), introduction. Said's groundbreaking work has been followed by an extensive theoretical discourse. For examples, see Michel de Certeau, *Heterologies: Discourse on the Other*, trans. Brian Massumi (Minneapolis: University of Minneapolis Press, 1986); Gayatri Chakravorty Spivak, *A Critique of Postcolonial Reason: Toward a History of the Vanishing Present* (Cambridge: Harvard University Press, 1999); Homi Bhabha, *The Location of Culture* (New York: Routledge, 1994); and Edward Said, *Culture and Imperialism* (New York: Knopf, 1994).

22. Charles Forsdick, *Victor Segalen and the Aesthetics of Diversity: Journeys between Cultures* (Oxford: Oxford University Press, 2000), 37.

23. bell hooks, "Eating the Other: Desire and Resistance," in *Black Looks: Race and Representation* (Boston: South End Press, 1992), 21–39, reprinted in *Media and Cultural Studies: KeyWorks,* ed. Meenakshi Gigi Durham and Douglas M. Kellner (Malden, MA: Blackwell, 2001) , 424–38, 427.

24. Jonathan Bellman, "Indian Resonances in the British Invasion, 1965–1968," in Jonathan Bellman, ed., *The Exotic in Western Music* (Boston: Northeastern University Press, 1998), 304.

25. Susan Fast, *In the Houses of the Holy: Led Zeppelin and the Power of Rock Music* (Oxford: Oxford University Press, 2001), 35–39.

26. Frank Kofsky, "The Scene," *Jazz and Pop,* April 1968, 20.

27. In his recent book *The End of Food: How the Food Industry Is Destroying Our Food Supply—and What We Can Do About It* (Fort Lee, NJ: Baracade Books, Inc., 2006), Thomas F. Pawlick examines, among other things, chemicals like dioxin in Agent Orange and the devastating effects such weapons had and continue to have on humanity's food supply.

28. Again, for more information concerning American interests on the Indochinese Peninsula and the connection of those interests to the political, military, and economic development of the Vietnam War see Fitzgerald's *Fire in the Lake.*

29. Ralph Gleason, quoted in Selvin, *Summer of Love,* 19.

30. Slick, *Somebody to Love,* 104. The name of Slick's group was a direct reference to President Lyndon Johnson's political agenda for America. The disbanding of Johnson's "Great Society" for the military adventure in the East is an apt metaphor for the counterculture's turn away from explicit politics.

31. Most people of the baby boomer generation who considered traveling "east" did so after 1968. Though my research on this particular phenomenon is not statistically conclusive, it appears that those who traveled to and lived in places such as India, Nepal, the Middle East, and Morocco before 1968 rarely encountered other Westerners, indicating that such journeys were embarked upon only after it had become popularized and hip in the West. Informal interviews with family members who left for places like Afghanistan and India in 1967 reveal they had little knowledge of what was in store for them because it hadn't yet been exoticized in the San Francisco Bay Area. The Himalayan import store on Telegraph Avenue in Berkeley, for example, was the only store of its kind in the East Bay in 1967.

32. The bass repeats a military-style bolero motive in 4/4 time on F-sharp for two measures and then shifts up to G for the following two measures. While the Phrygian quality of harmonic movement by

half step suggests a continued incremental ascent, the fifth measure starts again on the bottom step of F-sharp, as if it had merely been toying with the Phrygian second degree.

33. Sandy Pearlman, "Younger by Far: Jefferson Airplane," *Crawdaddy*, April 1967, 6. It should be noted that "White Rabbit" transforms Ravel's original triple meter into a duple meter.

34. Slick, *Somebody to Love*, 105–6.

35. Ethnomusicologist Peter Manuel describes flamenco as often descending harmonically through a tetrachord with a Phrygian second degree, using a bolero pattern to drive that descent. While we never hear the entire tetrachord, and the F-sharp/G fluctuation could conceivably be heard as static half-step harmonic movement, the presence of the bolero rhythm from the first measure of the song immediately marks the Phrygian harmony as flamenco. See Peter Manuel, "Andalusian, Gypsy, and Class Identity in the Contemporary Flamenco Complex," *Ethnomusicology* 33, no. 1 (1989): 47–65.

36. In 1966, Herb Alpert and the Tijuana Brass "outsold the Beatles by two to one" (Hoskyns, *Waiting for the Sun*, 117).

37. Information on Jefferson Airplane's musical activities from 1965 through 1967 collected at the site http://www.mv.com/ipusers/owsley/airplane/jabase. Accessed May 2005. Evidently, Jefferson Airplane was recording "White Rabbit" on November 3, 1966, in Hollywood, and went back up to San Francisco for concerts at the Fillmore Auditorium.

38. Hoskyns, *Waiting for the Sun*, 122.

39. Rock critic Dave Marsh has noted how Latin influences on rock music have gotten short shrift by musicians, critics, and historians: "It's worth getting perturbed over . . . how poorly the Latin forces in rock have been acknowledged, much less examined in detail. Latin music isn't just a part of the rock mixture—it's a fundamental ingredient in it" (*Fortunate Son*, 85).

40. For a detailed and insightful history of this "peaceful" time in medieval Spain, see Maria Rosa Menocal, *The Ornament of the World: How Muslims, Jews, and Christians Created a Culture of Tolerance in Medieval Spain* (Boston: Back Bay Books, 2002).

41. See Manuel, "Andalusian, Gypsy, and Class Identity," 48–55. On page 55, he explains that "the specifically Andalusian character of flamenco is clear in its Arab-influenced modal melodies and melismatic vocal style, and in its combination, or juxtaposition, of European common-practice I–IV–V harmonies with progression and chords that have evolved from modal origins (most notably, the familiar progression Am–G–F–E, in E Phrygian/major)." The progres-

sion that Manuel refers to is the same tetrachord employed in "White Rabbit," just turned upside down and transposed up a second (F-sharp–G–A–B).

42. Susan McClary, *Georges Bizet: Carmen* (Cambridge: Cambridge University Press, 1992), 30. McClary explains how Orientalist works such as Bizet's *Carmen* were not attempts at an accurate depiction of Spanish history or musical practices, but reflected European expectations of what the Other was like. "Whatever the reality of Spain's history or culture, French Orientalist's ascribed to it the same inscrutable, luxuriant, and barbarous qualities they imagined to be characteristic of the entire Middle East."

43. The melismatic contour of the guitar line defies the 4/4 time signature, while its Phrygian orientation, also a product of Andalusia, harmonizes with the flamenco character of the bass line's structure. The melodic ornamentation of the guitar line, though basically flamenco in character, is not so clear-cut: it ascends across the tetrachord (F-sharp, G, [A], B), without including the A, and descends, again through the tetrachord, touching on A to land on A-sharp.

44. Slick, *Somebody to Love,* 106–7.

45. The bass line breaks out of its F-sharp/G chord progression, making its way to the third degree of the tetrachord (A). While the bolero motive propels the song toward A on "go ask Alice" as a principal harmonic point of reference, the Phrygian quality of flamenco vanishes into a characteristically Western dominant/tonic (E/A) harmonic alteration.

46. Slick hammers on the pitch A as the accompaniment reinforces the harmonic message with a dominant/tonic (E/A) fluctuation.

47. See, for example, the memoir of Truong Nhu Tang, *A Viet Cong Memoir: An Inside Account of the Vietnam War and Its Aftermath* (New York: Vintage, 1986) and his explanation of the relevance of French cultural and political ideals (more so than Communism) to the South Vietnamese actions during the war.

48. Madame Nhu not only claimed responsibility for many of her husband and brother-in-law's political policies, but fancied herself a model for high-brow, Europeanized behavior. Among other things, "Madame Nhu had the foresight to amass a fortune in goods that might be quickly translated into European assets. It was later said that . . . she owned a large theatre on the Champs Elysees . . . [She] maintained an impenetrable façade of self-righteous hauteur" (Fitzgerald, *Fire in the Lake,* 126–27).

49. In 1968, "Waist Deep in the Big Muddy" was finally heard on the *Smothers Brothers Comedy Hour,* as the finale to a medley of anti-

war songs. The song lyrics and commentary can be found online at http://history.sandiego.edu/gen/snd/waistdeep.html, consulted August 10, 2007.

50. It is well documented that as the war in Vietnam escalated, protests to bring it to an end increased across America. Less documented are the responses of protest to the war by those who were serving in the military. Recounting his experiences as a participant-observer in the Vietnam War, David Cortright, in *Soldiers in Revolt: GI Resistance during the Vietnam War* (Chicago: Haymarket, 2005) relays a fascinating, important, and near-secret history of how resistance from GIs in the war and veterans returned from the war helped to bring the war to an end.

51. The two songs were "I Feel Like I'm Fixin' to Die Rag" and "Superbird." The first, stocked with sounds of kazoos and a merry-go-round pipe organ, was a mocking indictment of the Vietnam War and the mindless hypnotic state that people had been duped into by the government. The second, less well known, was a satirical jab at President Lyndon Johnson.

52. Barry Melton, "Everything Seemed Beautiful: A Life in the Counterculture," in Bloom, *Long Time Gone*, 153. Melton briefly discusses the band's name, as does Bill Belmont, on the official Country Joe and the Fish website, at http://www.well.com/~cjfish/bandbio.htm, consulted August 10, 2007.

53. These events in October 1965 are also recounted in Selvin, *Summer of Love*, 30–31.

54. Melton, "Everything Seemed Beautiful," 155.

55. Frank Kofsky, "The Scene," *Jazz and Pop*, April 1968, 18.

56. Ben Sidran, *Black Talk* (New York: Holt, Rinehart and Winston, 1971), 137.

57. Ibid., 129.

58. Lowell Richards, "Interview with Country Joe and the Fish: Improvisers," *Down Beat*, September 5, 1968, 21.

59. Though the avoidance of the leading tone in the solo certainly resembles most blues-derived music, the solo's outline of a D minor seventh chord in the Dorian mode makes it much more akin to jazz. This is the underlying riff that continues to the end of the song. It begins on a low D, immediately jumps up an octave, settles on the lowered seventh degree for a moment, and winds back down to the tonic through the minor third degree (F).

60. Locke explains specifically that "a minor third degree followed by a major sixth, in addition to a lowered seventh" is the "single most distinctive sign of temporal or geographical displacement in Western music in recent centuries." See Ralph P. Locke, "Construct-

ing the Oriental 'Other': Saint-Saens's *Samson et Dalila*," *Cambridge Opera Journal* 3, no. 3 (1991): 266.

61. This new solo emphasizes fourths, half steps, and augmented seconds, initially building up tension by highlighting the D/G fourth, and then playing with that fourth by angling up to the half steps E-flat and A-flat, with augmented seconds thrown in for variety. The notes grind out of the guitar, assaulting the listener with angry distortion. And while the harmonic language of the solo has an Eastern flavor, its rhythmic structure derives, again, from techniques of jazz improvisation by focusing on a riff (E-flat, G, A-flat, G) that defies the 4/4 time signature with a hemiola rhythm.

62. In 1969, for example, when guitarist John McLaughlin moved from the London blues scene to work in the burgeoning New York jazz-rock scene with Miles Davis, he also turned to Eastern religion, becoming a disciple of Indian guru Sri Chinmoy. In 1970, McLaughlin formed the Mahavishnu Orchestra, a group that combined bebop techniques, blues vocabulary, and Jimi Hendrix–inspired innovations and virtuosity.

63. In February 1965, the Yardbirds went into the studio to record a song titled "Heart Full of Soul." Though the band scrapped the first take (until nineteen years later), which included a sitar player, they released the version with electric guitarist Jeff Beck's simulation of the sound of a sitar. "Heart Full of Soul" earned the label of first rock song to include a sitar (or at least the semblance of one). Other "raga rock" hits followed. Later that year, the Kinks made the first notable popular music reference to India in the song "See My Friends." Later that same year in October, the Beatles recorded "Norwegian Wood," the first popular music song to actually use a sitar. This was followed by George Harrison's "Love You Too" on *Revolver,* which included a tonic/dominant drone over which a sitar, voice, and tabla play—and "Within You without You" on *Sgt. Pepper's Lonely Hearts Club Band.* Of course, since the Beatles were so scrutinized in the public eye, they also helped popularize the "East" in nonmusical ways by virtue of, for example, their own interest in the Indian guru the Maharishi.

64. Bellman, "Indian Resonances," 298.

65. For a further discussion of Indian-ness in 1950s America, see Timothy D. Taylor, "Korla Pandit: Music, Exoticism and Mysticism," in *Widening the Horizons: Exoticism in Post-War Popular Music,* ed. Philip Hayward (London: John Libbey, 1999). Taylor remarks that Korla Pandit's radio show, which aired in Southern California, was popular as early as 1951.

66. Goldstein, *Reporting the Counterculture,* 73.

67. See *Jazz and Pop* 6–9 (1967–70).

68. *Down Beat* magazine, for example, adored him: "George Harrison's 'Within You Without You' is perhaps the most completely successful fusion of East and West musical concepts so far effected by a Western musician." Pete Welding, "I'm Looking Through You: Beatles as Pop-as-Art?" *Down Beat,* January 11, 1968, 19.

69. Ravi Shankar, *My Music, My Life* (New York: Simon and Schuster, 1968), 93–94.

70. See Robert Thurman, *Inner Revolution: Life, Liberty, and the Pursuit of Real Happiness* (New York: Riverhead, 1998), 15.

71. Before 1955, Nehru had already been strongly inclined toward a policy of nonalignment. An interesting example of this is Nehru's acceptance of Albert Einstein's invitation to visit him in Princeton, New Jersey. On November 5, 1949, Nehru, along with his sister (who was India's ambassador to the United States) and his daughter Indira Gandhi (who would later become India's prime minister), visited Einstein and said that their conversations with him strengthened Nehru's resolve that "India must stand outside the two big blocs." See Fred Jerome, *The Einstein File: J. Edgar Hoover's Secret War against the World's Most Famous Scientist* (New York: St. Martin's Press, 2002), 116, 307.

72. Nehru's speech is reprinted in G. M. Kahin, *The Asian-African Conference* (Ithaca, NY: Cornell University Press, 1956) and online at http://www.fordham.edu/halsall/mod/1995nehru-bandung2.html.

73. Cantwell, *When We Were Good,* 309–10.

74. Moretti, *Modern Epic,* 248.

75. See, for example, David McReynolds, "What Is It to Be a Man? An Open Letter to Our Men in Service," *LA Free Press,* March 3, 1967, 46: "The 'patriots' who are so hot for the war are saying the peace movement is against you guys. That we don't support you . . . That's a line of crap. Think. If you burn a draft card you burn a piece of paper. If you burn a flag you burn a piece of cloth. But if you drop a napalm bomb you burn a human being."

76. Joseph Heller, *Catch-22* (New York: Simon and Schuster, 1961), 415.

CHAPTER FOUR

1. Aldous Huxley, *Brave New World* (New York: Perennial Library, 1932), 33.

2. Raymond Williams, *Keywords: A Vocabulary of Culture and Society* (New York: Oxford University Press, 1985), 223. The emphasis is included in Williams's text.

3. In her astute biography of the Grateful Dead, Carol Brightman notes that Dylan had "plugged in" at another public venue two years before the 1965 Newport Folk Festival, receiving similar criticism from folk diehards. Of particular significance is Jerry Garcia's reaction: "When Bob Dylan first plugged his guitar into an amplifier at the Monterey Folk Festival in the summer of 1963 . . . Jerry and Sara [Garcia's friend] walked out. They were 'stern traditionalists' who eschewed 'modernization and wanted to imitate and preserve the old forms,' Sara recalls." See Carol Brightman, *Sweet Chaos: The Grateful Dead's American Adventure* (New York: Clarkson Potter, 1998), 62.

4. Goldstein, *Reporting the Counterculture*, 56.

5. Clive Davis, quoted in Peck, *Uncovering the Sixties*, 170.

6. Ibid.

7. Dominick Cavallo, *A Fiction of the Past: The Sixties in American History* (New York: St. Martin's Press, 1999), 123.

8. Brightman, *Sweet Chaos*, 92.

9. The Grateful Dead suggested that the Diggers be the "worthy cause." When the Diggers heard of this possibility, they refused in advance, saying they would not accept money from an event that had charged admission and turned away people without tickets.

10. Brightman, *Sweet Chaos*, 124.

11. This issue was addressed in the popular music press at the time. See, for example, Harvey Pekar, "From Rock to ???," *Down Beat,* May 2, 1968. Pekar notes how experimental popular music artists felt limited by the three-minute dance song and, consequently, welcomed innovations in recording technology to accommodate their "new" musical mentality.

12. Gary Shank and Eric J. Simon, "The Grammar of the Grateful Dead," in *Deadhead Social Science: You Ain't Gonna Learn What You Don't Want to Know,* ed. Rebecca G. Adams and Robert Sardiello (Oxford: AltaMira Press, 2000), 55.

13. Umberto Eco, *Travels in Hyperreality* (New York: Harcourt Brace Jovanovich, 1990), 82.

14. Cavallo, *Fiction of the Past,* 134–35, 141–42.

15. Political and literary theorist Marshall Berman gives a fascinating and close analysis of the concept of progress as a conquest narrative as it manifests in Goethe's *Faust.* See chapter 1, "Goethe's *Faust:* The Tragedy of Development," in *All That Is Solid Melts into Air: The Experience of Modernity* (New York: Penguin, 1988), 37–86.

16. Liner notes to *American Beauty,* Warner Bros. Records 1893, 1970.

17. For an insightful and extensive discussion of the connections between 1930s radical communities and their cultural practices, see

Michael Denning, *The Cultural Front: The Laboring of American Culture in the Twentieth Century* (London: Verso, 1997).

18. Cantwell, *When We Were Good*, 149–50.

19. Aniko Bodroghkozy, *Groove Tube: Sixties Television and the Youth Rebellion* (Durham, NC: Duke University Press, 2001), 89. Bodroghkozy demonstrates that domesticating the counterculture was not a simple task. Countercultural women were expected to be both innocent and highly sexualized, rebellious yet also submissive to a patriarchal ideology, sex-starved while performing the roles of mother and homemaker in the nuclear family.

20. See the cover of the *San Francisco Oracle*, February 1968, photograph by Tom Weir. The *Oracle* was the Haight's underground newspaper and lasted for about a year. Also reprinted in Berke, *Counter Culture*.

21. Personal communication with Allen Cohen, editor of all of the *San Francisco Oracle*'s twelve issues, on September 6, 2003, revealed that the *Oracle* staff and photographer Tom Weir intended to signify "impending gloom" with the issue's cover. Cohen indicated that they knew this would be their last issue and that the Haight was starting to turn sour: hence, the woman's nakedness and "inactivity" ("she's not up and dancing") implies that she is "dead." Clearly this is an alternative reading of the *Oracle* cover that differs greatly from the one posed here. The only point of connection that might be drawn between the two readings is a bit far-fetched: if the woman is meant to be dead, then she has achieved the ultimate stage of going "back to nature" in death. Needless to say, I have not come across any other countercultural image that depicts a dead person in that pose.

22. John Miller, *Egotopia: Narcissism and the New American Landscape* (Tuscaloosa: University of Alabama Press, 1997).

23. Harrison, *The Dead Book*, 198. The Grateful Dead's position as cultural leaders grew during their time with Ken Kesey: they were the house band for Kesey's Acid Tests that were staged all around the Bay Area starting in 1965. Kesey had a brightly painted school bus named "Furthur" that he and his group of "Merry Pranksters" traveled across country in—signifying, among other things, a self-sufficient family unit searching for adventure. This too could have contributed to the later phenomenon of the Deadhead—people who followed the band around the country to attend every performance.

24. For a more extensive discussion of communes in the late sixties, see William McCord, *Voyages to Utopia: From Monastery to Commune, the Search for the Perfect Society in Modern Times* (New York: Norton, 1989).

25. An interesting historic and ideological parallel to the small

commununes of the Haight is the food co-op. Craig Cox, in *Storefront Revolution: Food Co-ops and the Counterculture* (New Brunswick, NJ: Rutgers University Press, 1994) explains that the late sixties witnessed a steep rise in the co-op, particularly within countercultural communities. As Cox points out, the co-ops faced many of the same problems as the communes, when ideology scraped against practicality. "The counterculture was all about experiencing life in ways that freed people from the oppressive chains of convention. How do you run a business when freedom and personal expression are the chief goals? The answer, of course, is that you cannot—unless you confine the opportunities for such liberating pursuits to areas that have no bearing on the bottom line" (12).

26. Brightman, *Sweet Chaos*, 261.

27. See Paul Gilroy, *The Black Atlantic: Modernity and Double Consciousness* (Cambridge: Harvard University Press, 1993), 101.

28. See *Anthem of the Sun*, Warner Bros. Records 1749, 1968.

29. Brightman, *Sweet Chaos*, 51.

30. "The Nitty-Gritty Sound," *Newsweek*, December 19, 1966, 102; cited in Bernard Gendron, *Between Monmartre and the Mudd Club: Popular Music and the Avant-Garde* (Chicago: University of Chicago Press, 2002), 204.

31. Gendron, *Between Montmartre*, 207.

32. Richard Goldstein, "Real Jazz Should Blow the Mind," *New York Times*, August 20, 1967, 13.

33. Harrison, *The Dead Book*, 171.

34. For further biographical information about Huxley's use of mescaline and hallucinogens, see Nicholas Murray, *Aldous Huxley: A Biography* (New York: St. Martin's Press, 2002), and for further critique of the relation between hallucinogen use and the shaping of countercultural spirituality, see John Horgan, *Rational Mysticism: Dispatches from the Border between Science and Spirituality* (New York: Houghton Mifflin, 2003).

35. See Aldous Huxley, *The Doors of Perception, and Heaven and Hell* (New York: Harper and Row, 1963, c. 1956).

36. See Martin A. Lee and Bruce Shlain, *Acid Dreams: The Complete Social History of LSD* (New York: Grove Press, 1985). Lee and Shlain write that in the forties, the CIA experimented with various drugs, including marijuana, for the purposes of interrogation. By the fifties, LSD was included on the test list, used in what the CIA called "behavior control endeavors." A handful of laboratories, including their resident scientists and psychiatrists, were linked to this governmental research. In 1953, Allen Dulles, the newly appointed CIA director, authorized Operation MK-ULTRA, the CIA's mind control pro-

gram that used, among other things, hallucinogens in an effort to fight the Cold War. The doctors involved discovered additional possibilities in hallucinogens. From test results, they hypothesized that LSD could be a means to peace and spiritual enlightenment.

37. The counterculture indulged fantasies about "natural" Native American hallucinogenic drugs and their potential for the escape from modern materialistic America for which Alpert, Ginsberg, and Leary advocated. Of course, drugs such as peyote were used by Native Americans in rituals that were part of lifelong dedication to spiritual development. Nonetheless, the counterculture celebrated anthropologist Carlos Castaneda's first book, among others, almost as if it were a study guide to taking Native American hallucinogens. See Carlos Castaneda, *The Teachings of Don Juan: A Yaqui Way of Knowledge* (Berkeley and Los Angeles: University of California Press, 1968).

38. Brightman, *Sweet Chaos*, 177.

CHAPTER FIVE

1. Transcripts of the first three parts of "The Houseboat Summit" from February 1967 are located online. "Part One: Changes" is at http://www.vallejo.to/articles/summit_pt1.htm; "Part Two: To Drop Out or Not" is at http://www.vallejo.to/articles/summit_pt2.htm; and "Part Three: A Magic Geography" is at http://www.vallejo.to/articles/summit_pt3.htm (consulted August 10, 2007). The entire original transcript can be found in the *San Francisco Oracle*, March–April 1967.

2. See "The Varieties of Hip: Advertisements of the 1960s," in Frank's *The Conquest of Cool*, 132–67.

3. Watts's and Leary's discussion of "dropping out" that culminates in Leary's assertion that subcultures need no leadership is in "Part Three: A Magic Geography" of the Houseboat Summit under the specific theme of "The Energy to Create."

4. The quotations are from the online transcript of "Part Three: A Magic Geography" of the Houseboat Summit, in a section of discussion leading up to the four men painting a portrait of subcultural "Magic Geography."

5. See "Extreme Rebellion" in Heath and Potter's *Nation of Rebels*, 135–60.

6. Ashleigh Brilliant, *The Haight Ashbury Songbook: Songs of Love and Haight*, a twenty-five-cent pamphlet (self-published, 1967), Bancroft Archive Library at the University of California, Berkeley.

7. The *San Francisco Oracle*, the Haight-Ashbury's underground

newspaper, started in January 1967 and lasted until early 1968. Funded by Ron and Jay Thelin, and published and edited by Be-In organizer Allen Cohen, the newspaper's design and production took place in the Psychedelic Shop (most likely the first head shop in the country, owned by the Thelins). Lee and Shlain, in *Acid Dreams*, 148, point out that "when Ron and Jay Thelin opened the Psychedelic Shop near the corner of Haight and Ashbury in January 1966, they had a clear-cut purpose: spread the word about LSD. . . . The Thelin brothers were turned on to acid by Allen Cohen, who was then dealing some of Owsley's finest."

8. This information is listed on the website, authored by *San Francisco Oracle* editor Allen Cohen, entitled "Additional Notes on the S.F. Oracle: For the *Haight-Ashbury in The Sixties* CD-ROM. Part 1," located at http://www.rockument.com/WEBORA.html, consulted August 10, 2007.

9. Roszak, *Making of a Counter Culture*, 64.

10. Ibid., 141, 150.

11. See Herbert Marcuse, *One-Dimensional Man: Studies in the Ideology of Advanced Industrial Society* (Boston: Beacon Press, 1964).

12. Herbert Marcuse, *Eros and Civilization: A Philosophical Inquiry into Freud* (Boston: Beacon Press, 1966), xvii.

13. In her book *Utopia Limited: The Sixties and the Emergence of the Postmodern* (Durham, NC: Duke University Press, 2004), Marianne DeKoven has a detailed account and analysis of the role of Marcuse's work in a global cultural transition to postmodernism in the sixties. See chapter 1, "Modern to Postmodern in Herbert Marcuse," 26–56.

14. See David Allyn, *Make Love, Not War: The Sexual Revolution* (New York: Routledge, 2001). Allyn relays the following episode about Perls to illustrate the hypocrisy and destructive behavior his philosophy engendered without "a system of ethics" to give it social foundation: "Counterculture philosopher Alan Watts remembers: 'Once [Perls] saw a particularly beautiful girl sitting in the baths at Esalen. He looked at her for a long time, and then went over to her and said, 'You vant [sic] to suck my prick.' And by God, she did'" (201).

15. In his recent book *A Secret History of Consciousness* (Great Barrington, MA: Lindisfarne, 2003), Gary Valentine Lachman looks in detail at the origins of the "contemporary" new age movement. Among other things, he points out that one of the most likely "predecessors" of the actual phrase *new age* was the serious quasi-academic journal *New Age* published by the esoteric thinker, writer, and philosopher A. R. Orage in the early decades of the twentieth century.

16. For a further discussion of Laing's "politics of the self," see DeKoven, *Utopia Limited*, 200–209.

17. Roszak, *Making of a Counter Culture*, 134.

18. See Lachman, *Turn Off Your Mind*, 100.

19. Liza Williams, from an article in the *Oracle of Southern California*, March 1967, quoted in Hopkins, *The Hippie Papers*, 200. Located in the Bancroft Archive Library at the University of California, Berkeley.

20. For more details about the Big Sur retreat, see "Additional Notes on the S.F. Oracle: For the *Haight-Ashbury in The Sixties* CD-ROM. Part 2," located at http://www.rockument.com/WEBORA2 .html, consulted August 10, 2007.

21. For a more extensive history of Leary's role in the LSD revolution, see Lee and Shlain, *Acid Dreams*, 70–113. Describing Leary as a "great PR man," Lee and Shlain often compare Leary's propagandizing techniques to those employed by mainstream institutions and political strategists. For example: "While the Eastern vibes surrounding the acid sessions at Millbrook may have been benign, Leary's methodology was in some ways analogous to that of the CIA and the military, which also 'programmed' trips" (109).

22. Goldstein, *Reporting the Counterculture*, 82. Goldstein points out that the *Voice* encouraged his style of "rogue reporting" to serve "as a carrier of messages between the counterculture and the mass" (xv).

23. Warren Hinckle, "A Social History of the Hippies," originally reprinted from *Ramparts* (March 1967) and then in Howard, *The Sixties*, 207–32. Specific quotes from Timothy Leary are printed on pp. 224–25.

24. Allyn, *Make Love, Not War*, 41.

25. Ibid., 51.

26. Tuli Kupferberg, "The Coming Catastrophic Age of Leisure," in Berke, *Counter Culture*, 82.

27. Harrison, *The Dead Book*, 131.

28. Melton, "Everything Seemed Beautiful," 153.

29. Cohen, "Additional Notes," part 1.

30. Robert Crumb, quote from 1967, cited in *The Digger Papers*.

31. See Peck, *Uncovering the Sixties*, 46–47.

32. Jerry Farber, "The Student as Nigger," *LA Free Press*, March 3, 1967, 162.

33. Marco Vassi, "Relaxation, Awareness, and Breathing," reprinted from *The Stoned Apocalypse* (New York: Trident Press, 1972), in Howard, *The Sixties*, 233.

34. Bodroghkozy, *Groove Tube*, 13.

35. See Beth Bailey, "Sex as a Weapon: Underground Comix and the Paradox of Liberation," in Braunstein and Doyle, *Imagine Nation*, 305–24.

36. Roszak, *Making of a Counter Culture,* 141.

37. Valerie Wilmer, "Jimi Hendrix: An Experience," *Down Beat,* April 4, 1968, 19.

38. Sheila Whiteley, *The Space between the Notes: Rock and the Counter-Culture* (London: Routledge, 1992). See also Sheila Whiteley, "Progressive Rock and Psychedelic Coding in the Work of Jimi Hendrix," in *Reading Pop: Approaches to Textual Analysis in Popular Music,* ed. Richard Middleton (Oxford: Oxford University Press, 2000).

39. Robert Fink, "Elvis Everywhere: Musicology and Popular Music Studies at the Twilight of the Canon," *American Music* 16, no. 2 (1998): 143.

40. Slick, *Somebody to Love,* 225.

41. See McLuhan, *War and Peace.* The margins of most of the pages of the book include quotes from Joyce's *Finnegans Wake,* printed in various sizes and fonts.

42. Fast, *Houses of the Holy,* 18.

43. Pearlman, "Younger by Far," 6.

44. See Bellman, "Indian Resonances," 292–306.

45. See Hunter S. Thompson, *Fear and Loathing in Las Vegas: A Savage Journey to the Heart of the American Dream* (New York: Popular Library, 1971).

46. Cohen, "Additional Notes," part 3.

47. Allyn, *Make Love, Not War,* 12–15.

48. The Public Broadcasting System (PBS) aired a documentary titled "The Pill" on February 24, 2003, that gave an extensive history of the birth control pill and its sociological, economic, and political development and resounding impact in American culture, in particular. The PBS American Experience Online companion website to the documentary, which includes a time line of the major events in the pill's history, can be accessed at http://www.pbs.org/wgbh/amex/pill/index.html, consulted August 10, 2007.

49. Echols, *Shaky Ground,* 71–72.

50. In addition to a detailed description of how she "laid" Jim Morrison, Slick's *Somebody to Love* autobiography is filled with details about everything from her various lovers' penis sizes to ratings of their sexual skill. On the whole, such descriptions come across as little more than locker-room bragging. For example, in her story about recording *Surrealistic Pillow,* she suddenly notes, "During our stay at the Tropicana, I was not only getting to know the music business, I was also getting to 'know' my fellow band members" (113).

51. Echols, *Shaky Ground,* 34.

52. See Bodroghkozy, *Groove Tube;* and Frank, *The Conquest of Cool.*

53. Ian MacDonald, *Revolution in the Head: The Beatles' Records and the Sixties* (New York: Henry Holt, 1994), 210.

54. *Crawdaddy,* November 1968, 3, a reprint of an unidentified article from the *San Francisco Oracle.*

55. See Alan Mairson, "65760 Not Quite Utopia," *National Geographic,* August 2005, 114–18. In *Natasha's Dance: A Cultural History of Russia* (London: Allen Lane, Penguin, 2002), author Orlando Figes tells the story of how, in 1874, thousands of students left the universities in Moscow and Saint Petersburg to go to the country to start "laboring communes" with the peasantry. The students each had their own motivations for "going to the people," but Figes explains that, in general, they were impelled by a feeling of guilt for their own privilege and Russia's past of serfdom. One of the interesting points of comparison possible here is that the motivations of the counterculture in the American sixties were arguably quite different from those of the Russian populists. But as it turns out, the results were somewhat the same. Like the American communes in the sixties or the East West commune featured in *National Geographic,* there were breakdowns over work, food, resources, and sex in these Russian labor communes too.

CHAPTER SIX

1. Take, for example, Credence Clearwater Revival's two hit singles—"Proud Mary" and "Born on the Bayou." The second song lent its name to *Bayou Country,* the album that would hit number seven on the nationwide charts in early 1969. The album's popularity, and the prominence of the two songs in particular, was due, in large part, to how rooted the music and the band's persona were in the countercultural sensibility. Contrary to name and appearance, Credence Clearwater Revival had no tangible roots in the South, or Louisiana in particular. The band—born and bred in the basements of San Francisco Bay Area suburban homes and the auditoriums of El Cerrito public schools—played together for over ten years before the members emerged as stars from the San Francisco scene. The band honed a sound that included finger-picking guitar techniques, twangy instrumental tone colors, equally twangy vocal accents, and catchy lyrics sung from worn, raspy vocal chords that seemed to come direct from down-home, old-timey locals in the Bayou. Credence spoke the lingo: anything mainstream, materialist, government-sponsored, or remotely associated with the eight-hour workday was "the man"—a symbol that represented everything that the counterculture was not.

2. Brightman, *Sweet Chaos*, 169.

3. Ibid., 127.

4. Karlene Faith, *The Long Prison Journey of Leslie Van Houten: Life beyond the Cult* (Boston: Northeastern University Press, 2001), 54.

5. Charles Manson, quoted from interviews by John Gilmore and Ron Kenner in *The Garbage People* (Los Angeles: Omega Press, 1971), 33.

6. The web of connections in Manson's story is dense. The following is a brief description of some prominent players that entered the history early on in San Francisco. In 1967, Manson met Abigail Folger, the coffee heiress. At the time, Folger provided economic support to establish the Straight Theater near where Manson lived in the Haight. Two years later, she was taking classes at the Esalen Institute (where she might have run into Manson), and house-sitting for director Roman Polanski at Cielo Drive. On September 21, 1967, the rock group Magick Powerhouse of Oz played at the Straight Theater in celebration of the "equinox of the gods." The band's lead guitarist (and sitar player), Bobby Beausoleil, most likely met Manson around this time. Beausoleil later moved to Los Angeles and became a follower of Manson. On Manson's orders, he assisted in the murder of Hollywood executive Gary Hinman and was later convicted. Among other points of connection, Beausoleil and Manson shared a racist sensibility—Beausoleil would lead a chapter of the Aryan Brotherhood in his California prison. The above information about Manson's acquaintances come from Maury Terry, *The Ultimate Evil: An Investigation into America's Most Dangerous Satanic Cult* (Garden City, NY: Dolphin, 1987), 495–96, and Gilmore and Kenner, *The Garbage People*, 177.

7. Transcripts of the first three parts of "The Houseboat Summit" from February 1967 in Sausalito, CA—Part One: Changes; Part Two: To Drop Out or Not; Part Three: A Magic Geography—are located online at http://www.vallejo.to/articles/summit_ptl.htm. This quote comes from the above website and the entire original transcript can be found in *The San Francisco Oracle* 7 (March/April 1967).

8. Gilmore and Kenner, *The Garbage People*, 61.

9. Lachman, *Turn Off Your Mind*, 320. Lachman's history of the interactions of Manson, Wilson, other musicians, music industry people, and countercultural figures is extensive. In particular, see chapter 11, "Magical Satanic Mystery Tours" (279–334). Melcher had produced albums for the Byrds and Paul Revere and the Raiders, and, in 1968, he lived with actress Candice Bergen in the house on Cielo Drive. As Barney Hoskyns explains in *Waiting for the Sun*, Melcher did

not appear to be as susceptible to outside influence as Dennis Wilson. "The fact that Dennis claimed he felt the same 'weirdness and presence' on meeting the Maharishi that he'd felt when he first met Manson says a great deal about the thin sixties line between hippie spirituality and cultist brainwashing" (152).

10. See the interviews with Van Houten in Faith, *The Long Prison Journey*.

11. Gilmore and Kenner, *The Garbage People*, 64.

12. Although Manson never achieved his musical goals in the late sixties, it is clear that extreme cult behavior is still a marketable commodity. Manson released two albums from prison, *Manson Live at San Quentin* and *Lie*. And other musicians, including Axel Rose and the Lemonheads, have recorded his songs.

13. Brightman, *Sweet Chaos*, 128.

14. Ibid., 210.

15. Gitlin, *The Sixties*, 406–7.

16. See chapter 4, "Loathing and Learning in Las Vegas," in DeKoven, *Utopia Limited*, 86–113.

17. Cohen, "Additional Notes," part 3.

18. Cantwell, *When We Were Good*, 285–86.

19. Roszak, *Making of a Counter Culture*, 27.

20. With seething irony, jazz critic Frank Kofsky also saw that by 1968, those identified with the counterculture were now playing a role that the mainstream media had created for them. In his regular column in *Jazz and Pop* magazine called "The Scene," Kofsky critiqued the counterculture's excessiveness and trendiness by entitling his July 1968 column, "The Seen," by Phrank Cough-ski. "Long live pretentiousness passing itself off as profundity. Long live perpetual adolescence. Long live any and every form of bullshit, because bullshit is so much easier to manufacture." Frank Kofsky, or Phrank Cough-ski, "The Seen," *Jazz and Pop*, July 1968, 43.

21. Cohen, "Additional Notes," part 2.

22. Hinckle, "Social History of Hippies," 232.

23. Jerry Garcia, "Jerry Garcia, the Guru," 34–36.

24. Before Garcia, Los Angeles pop music experimentalist Frank Zappa remarked on the cultural disparity between Los Angeles and San Francisco. From a 1965 interview printed in *The Real Frank Zappa Book* (New York: Poseidon Press, 1989), Zappa sarcastically observed: "To the friscoids way of thinking, everything that came from THEIR town was *really important Art,* and anything from anyplace else (especially LA) was dogshit. . . . One of the reasons musicians moved to San Francisco was to be certified as part of *the Real Deal*" (68).

25. Goldstein, *Reporting the Counterculture,* 54.

26. Joan Didion, *The White Album* (New York: Farrar, Straus and Giroux, 1990), 87.

27. Mikhail Bakhtin, *Rabelais and His World,* trans. Helene Iswolsky (Bloomington: Indiana University Press, 1984), 10.

28. Charles Manson, quoted in Gilmore and Kenner, *The Garbage People,* 17.

29. Allen Cohen, "Additional Notes on the S.F. Oracle: For the *Haight-Ashbury in The Sixties* CD-ROM. Part 4," located at http://www.rockument.com/WEBORA4.html, consulted August 10, 2007.

30. Heath and Potter, *Nation of Rebels,* 80–81.

Bibliography

Abrahams, Edward. *The Lyrical Left and the Origins of Cultural Radicalism in America*. Charlottesville: University Press of Virginia, 1986.

Adams, Rebecca G. and Robert Sardiello, eds. *Deadhead Social Science: You Ain't Gonna Learn What You Don't Want to Know*. Walnut Creek, Oxford: AltaMira Press, 2000.

Adorno, Theodor W. *Aesthetic Theory*. Trans. Robert Hullot-Kentor. Eds. Gretel Adorno and Rolf Tiedemann. Minneapolis: University of Minnesota Press, 1997.

Albert, Judith Clavir and Stew Albert, eds. *The Sixties Papers*. New York: Praeger, 1985.

Aldgate, Anthony, James Chapman, and Arthur Marwick, eds. *Windows on the Sixties*. New York: I.B. Tauris, 2000.

Allyn, David. *Make Love, Not War. The Sexual Revolution: An Unfettered History*. New York: Routledge, 2001.

Anderson, Benedict. *Imagined Communities*. London: Verso, 1983, 1991.

Anderson, Perry. *The Origins of Postmodernity*. London: Verso, 1998.

Anderson, Terry. *The Sixties*. New York: Longman, 1999.

Attali, Jacques. *Noise: The Political Economy of Music*. Trans. Brian Massumi. Minneapolis: University of Minnesota Press, 1985.

Baker, Houston A., Jr. *Afro-American Poetics*. Madison: The University of Wisconsin Press, 1988.

Bakhtin, Mikhail. *The Dialogic Imagination*. Trans. Caryl Emerson and Michael Holquist. Austin: University of Texas Press, 1981.

Bakhtin, Mikhail. *Rabelais and His World*. Trans. Helene Iswolsky. Bloomington: Indiana University Press, 1984.

Baldwin, James. *The Fire Next Time*. New York: Dial, 1963.

Bangs, Lester. *Psychotic Reactions and Carburetor Dung*. New York: Vintage Books, 1987.

Bayles, Martha. *Hole in Our Soul: The Loss of Beauty and Meaning in American Popular Music*. New York: The Free Press, 1994.

Bellman, Jonathan, ed. *The Exotic in Western Music*. Boston: Northeastern University Press, 1998.

Berman, Marshall. *All That is Solid Melts into Air: The Experience of Modernity*. New York: Penguin Books, 1988.

Berman, Russell A. *Modern Culture and Critical Theory: Art, Politics, and the Legacy of the Frankfurt School*. Madison: The University of Wisconsin Press, 1989.

Bhabba, Homi. *The Location of Culture*. New York: Routledge, 1994.

Birringer, Johannes. *Theatre, Theory, Postmodernism*. Bloomington: Indiana University Press, 1991.

Bloom, Alexander, ed. *Long Time Gone: Sixties America Then and Now*. Oxford: Oxford University Press, 2001.

Bloom, Alexander and Wini Breines, eds. *Takin' it to the streets: A Sixties Reader*. New York: Oxford University Press, 1995.

Bloom, Allan. *The Closing of the American Mind*. New York: Simon and Schuster, 1987.

Bodroghkozy, Aniko. *Groove Tube: Sixties Television and the Youth Rebellion*. Durham, London: Duke University Press, 2001.

Borthwick, Stuart and Ron Moy. *Popular Music Genres*. New York: Routledge, 2004.

Branch, Taylor. *Parting the Waters: America in the King Years 1954–63*. New York: Simon and Schuster, 1988.

Branch, Taylor. *Pillar of Fire: America in the King Years 1963–65*. New York: Simon and Schuster, 1998.

Branch, Taylor. *At Canaan's Edge: America in the King Years 1965–68*. New York: Simon and Schuster, 2006.

Braunstein, Peter and Michael William Doyle, eds. *Imagine Nation: The American Counterculture of the 1960s and 70s*. New York, London: Routledge, 2002.

Breitman, George, ed. *Malcolm X Speaks: Selected Speeches and Statements*. New York: Grove Press, Inc., 1965.

Brightman, Carol. *Sweet Chaos: The Grateful Dead's American Adventure*. New York: Clarkson Potter/Publishers, 1998.

Brilliant, Ashleigh. *The Haight Ashbury Songbook: Songs of Love and Haight*. (25 cents pamphlet), 1967.

Brooks, David. *Bobos in Paradise: The New Upper Class and How They Got There*. New York: A Touchstone Book, 2000.

Bürger, Peter. *Theory of the Avant-Garde*. Trans. Michael Shaw. Minneapolis: University of Minnesota Press, 1984.

Burke, Joseph, ed. *Counter Culture: Bhudda Bhudda*. London: Peter Owen Limited/Fire Books Limited, 1969.

Burner, David. *Making Peace with the 60s*. Princeton: Princeton University Press, 1996.

Burroughs, William S. *Naked Lunch*. London: John Calder, 1964.

Campbell, Joseph. *The Hero With a Thousand Faces*. Princeton: Princeton University Press, 1949, 1968.

Cantwell, Robert. *When We Were Good: The Folk Revival*. Cambridge, London: Harvard University Press, 1996.

Carby, Hazel V. "It Jus Be's Dat Way Sometime": The Sexual Politics of Women's Blues," in Ellen Carol DuBois and Vicki L. Ruiz, eds., *Unequal Sisters: A Multi-Cultural Reader in U.S. Women's History*. New York and London: Routledge, 1990: 238–49.

Carson, Clayborne, David J. Garrow, Gerald Gill, Vincent Harding, and Darlene Clark Hine, eds. *The Eyes on the Prize Civil Rights Reader*. New York: Penguin Books, 1991.

Castaneda, Carlos. *The Teachings of Don Juan: A Yaqui way of knowledge*. Berkeley: The University of California Press, 1968.

Cavallo, Dominick. *A Fiction of the Past: The Sixties in American History*. New York: St. Martin's Press, 1999.

Cavan, Sherri. *Hippies of the Haight*. St. Louis: New Critics Press, Inc., 1972.

Christgau, Robert. *Any Ol' Way You Choose It: Rock and Other Pop Music, 1967–1973*. Baltimore: Penguin Books, 1975.

Christgau, Robert. *Grown Up All Wrong: 75 Great Rock and Pop Artists From Vaudeville to Techno*. Cambridge: Harvard University Press, 1998.

Clecak, Peter. *Radical Paradoxes: Dilemmas of the American Left: 1945–1970*. New York: Harper and Row Publishers, 1973.

Cohen, Allen. "Additional Notes on the S.F. Oracle: For the *Haight-Ashbury in The Sixties* CD-ROM. Parts 1–4." Located at http://www.rockument.com/WEBORA.html.

Cohen, Allen, ed. *The San Francisco Oracle* Nos. 1–12. San Francisco, September 1966–January 1968.

Collier, Peter and David Horowitz, eds. *Destructive Generation: Second Thoughts about the Sixties*. New York: Summit Books, 1989.

Cooper, David, ed. *To Free a Generation. The Dialectics of Liberation*. London: Collier Books, 1969.

Cortright, David. *Soldiers in Revolt: GI Resistance During the Vietnam War*. Chicago: Haymarket Books, 2005.

Countdown: a subterranean magazine. New York: A Signet Book, 1966–70.

Cox, Craig. *Storefront Revolution: Food Co-ops and the Counterculture*. New Brunswick, New Jersey: Rutgers University Press, 1994.

Crawdaddy 7–20 (1967–1968).

Crone, Richard. *Hippy Hi.* (self-published), 1967.

Crowley, Aleister. *The Confessions of Aleister Crowley.* London: Cape, 1969.

Crumb, Robert. *America.* San Francisco: Last Gasp, 1995.

Dalton, David. *Piece of My Heart: A portrait of Janis Joplin.* New York: A Da Capo Press, Inc., 1985.

Danto, Arthur C. *After the End of Art: Contemporary Art and the Pale of History.* Princeton: Princeton University Press, 1997.

Danto, Arthur C. *Beyond the Brillo Box: The Visual Arts in Post-Historical Perspective.* Berkeley: University of California Press, 1992.

de Certeau, Michel. *Heterologies: Discourse on the Other.* Trans. Brian Massumi. Minneapolis: University of Minneapolis Press, 1986.

DeKoven, Marianne. *Utopia Limited: The Sixties and the Emergence of the Postmodern.* Durham and London: Duke University Press, 2004.

Denning, Michael. *The Cultural Front: The Laboring of American Culture in the Twentieth Century.* London: Verso, 1997.

DeVeaux, Scott. *The Birth of BeBop: A Social and Musical History.* Berkeley: The University of California Press, 1997.

Didion, Joan. *Slouching Towards Bethlehem.* New York: Farrar, Straus, and Giroux, 1968.

Didion, Joan. *The White Album.* NY: Farrar, Straus and Giroux, 1990.

The Digger Papers (free pamphlet), 1968.

Dodd, David G. and Diana Spaulding, eds. *The Grateful Dead Reader.* Oxford: Oxford University Press, 2000.

Down Beat Magazine 33–36 (1966–1969).

Durham, Meenakshi Gigi and Douglas M. Kellner, eds. *Media and Cultural Studies: KeyWorks.* Oxford: Blackwell Publishing, 2001.

Dyson, Michael Eric. *I May Not Get There With You: The True Martin Luther King, Jr.* New York: A Touchstone Book, 2000.

Echols, Alice. *Scars of Sweet Paradise: The Life and Times of Janis Joplin.* New York: Metropolitan Books, Henry Holt and Company, 1999.

Echols, Alice. *Shaky Ground: The '60s and Its Aftershocks.* New York: Columbia University Press, 2002.

Eco, Umberto. *Travels in Hyperreality.* New York: Harcourt, Brace, and Jovanovich, 1990.

Ellison, Ralph. *Shadow and Act.* New York: Vintage International, 1964.

Ellwood, Robert S. *The Sixties Spiritual Awakening: American Religion Moving from Modern to Postmodern.* New Brunswick, NJ: Rutgers University Press, 1994.

Emerson, Ralph Waldo. *Emerson's Essays.* New York: Everyman's Library, 1906, 1971.

Faith, Karlene. *The Long Prison Journey of Leslie Van Houten: Life Beyond the Cult.* Boston: Northeastern University Press, 2001.

Fanon, Frantz. *Black Skin, White Masks.* Trans. Charles Lam Markmann. New York: Grove Press, Inc., 1967.

Fanon, Frantz. *The Wretched of the Earth.* Trans. Constance Farrington. New York: Grove Press, 1963.

Farber, David. *The Age of Great Dreams: America in the 1960s.* New York: Hill and Wang, 1994.

Farber, David, ed. *The Sixties: From Memory to History.* Chapel Hill: The University of North Carolina Press, 1994.

Fast, Susan. *In the Houses of the Holy: Led Zeppelin and the Power of Rock Music.* Oxford: Oxford University Press, 2001.

Fink, Robert. "Elvis Everywhere: Musicology and Popular Music Studies at the Twilight of the Canon," *American Music* 16/2 (1998): 135 79.

Fitzgerald, Frances. *Fire in the Lake: The Vietnamese and the Americans in Vietnam.* Boston: An Atlantic Monthly Press Book, 1972.

Forsdick, Charles. *Victor Segalen and the Aesthetics of Diversity: Journeys between Cultures.* Oxford: Oxford University Press, 2000.

Foster, Hal, ed. *The Anti-Aesthetic: Essays on Postmodern Culture.* Port Townsend, WA: Bay Press, 1983.

Frank, Thomas. *The Conquest of Cool: Business Culture, Counterculture, and the Rise of Hip Consumerism.* Chicago: The University of Chicago Press, 1997.

Franklin, H. Bruce. *M.I.A. or Mythmaking in America.* New York: Lawrence Hill Books, 1992.

Frith, Simon, Will Straw, and John Street, eds. *The Cambridge Companion to Pop and Rock.* Cambridge: Cambridge University Press, 2001.

Gaddis, John Lewis. *Strategies of Containment: A Critical Appraisal of Postwar American National Security.* Revised Expanded Edition. Oxford: Oxford University Press, 2005.

Garofalo, Reebee. *Rockin' Out: Popular Music in the USA.* Boston: Allyn and Bacon, 1997.

Gates, Henry Louis, Jr. *The Signifying Monkey: A Theory of African-American Literary Criticism* Oxford: Oxford University Press, 1988.

Gendron, Bernard. *Between Montmartre and the Mudd Club: Popular Music and the Avant-Garde.* Chicago: University of Chicago Press, 2002.

Gilman, Sander S. *Difference and Pathology: Stereotypes of Sexuality, Race, and Madness.* Ithaca and London: Cornell University Press, 1985.

Gilmore, John and Ron Kenner. *The Garbage People.* Los Angeles: Omega Press, 1971.

Gilroy, Paul. *The Black Atlantic: Modernity and Double Consciousness.* Cambridge: Harvard University Press, 1993.

Ginsberg, Allen, Timothy Leary, Gary Snyder, and Alan Watts. "The Houseboat Summit. Part One: Changes; Part Two: To Drop Out or Not; Part Three: A Magic Geography." Sausalito, CA: February 1967. Located online at http://www.vallejo.to/articles/summit_ptl.htm.

Ginsberg, Allen. *Howl and other Poems.* San Francisco: City Lights Books, 1956.

Gitlin, Todd. *The Sixties: Years of Hope, Days of Rage.* New York: Bantam Books, 1993.

Gleason, Ralph. *The Jefferson Airplane and the San Francisco Sound.* New York: Ballantine, 1969.

Goffman, Ken. *Counter Culture Through the Ages: From Abraham to Acid House.* New York: Villard, 2004.

Goldstein, Richard. *Reporting the Counterculture.* Boston: Unwin Hyman, 1989.

Golembiewski, Robert T., Charles S. Bullock, and Harrell R. Rodgers, Jr., eds. *The new politics: polarization or utopia?* New York: McGraw Hill, 1970.

Halberstam, David. *The Fifties.* New York: Fawcett Columbine, 1994.

Halberstam, David. *The Best and the Brightest.* New York: Random House, 1969. Reprint of 20th Anniversary edition by Ballantine Books, 1993.

Halberstam, David. *The Powers that Be.* Chicago: University of Illinois Press, 1975, 2000.

Harraway, Donna. *Simians, Cyborgs, and Women: The Reinvention of Nature.* New York: Routledge, 1991.

Harrison, Hank. *The Dead Book: A Social History of the Haight-Ashbury Experience.* San Francisco: The Archives Press, 1973.

Haskins, James and Kathleen Benson. *The 60s Reader.* New York: Viking Kestrel, 1988.

Hayward, Philip, ed. *Widening the Horizons: Exoticism in Post-War Popular Music.* London: Perfect Beat Publications, 2001.

Heath, Joseph and Andrew Potter. *Nation of Rebels: Why Counterculture became Consumer Culture.* New York: HarperBusiness, 2004.

Hebdige, Dick. *Subculture: The Meaning of Style.* London: Methuen, 1979.

Heller, Joseph. *Catch-22.* New York: Simon & Schuster, Inc., 1961.

Herman, Edward and Noam Chomsky. *Manufacturing Consent: The Political Economy of the Mass Media.* New York: Pantheon Books, 1988.

Herring, George C. *America's Longest War: The United States and Vietnam 1950–1975.* Fourth Edition. New York: Mcgraw-Hill, Inc., 2001.

Hesse, Hermann. *The Glass Bead Game.* London: Penguin Paperbacks, 1972.

Hesse, Hermann. *The Journey to the East.* Trans. Hilda Rosner. New York: The Noonday Press, Inc., 1957.

Hesse, Hermann. *Steppenwolf.* London: Penguin Paperbacks, 1965.

Hobbs, Stuart. *The End of the American Avant-Garde.* New York: New York University Press, 1997.

Hoffman, Abbie. *Woodstock Nation.* New York: Vintage Books, 1969.

Holm-Hudson, Kevin, ed. *Progressive Rock Reconsidered.* New York: Routledge, 2002.

Hopkins, Jerry, ed. *The Hippie Papers: Notes from the Underground Press.* New York: A Signet Book, 1968.

Hopkins, Jerry. *The Jimi Hendrix Experience.* New York: Arcade Publishing, 1983.

Horgan, John. *Rational Mysticism: Dispatches from the Border between Science and Spirituality.* New York: Houghton Mifflin, 2003.

Hoskyns, Barney. *Waiting for the Sun: Strange Days, Weird Scenes and the Sound of Los Angeles.* NY: St. Martin's Press, 1996.

Howard, Gerald, ed. *The Sixties: The Art, Attitudes, Politics, and Media of Our Most Explosive Decade.* New York: Marlowe & Company, 1982, 1995.

Huggan, Graham. *The Post-Colonial Exotic: Marketing the Margins.* London: Routledge, 2001.

Huxley, Aldous. *Brave New World.* New York: Perennial Library, Harper and Row, 1946, 1969.

Huxley, Aldous. *The Doors of Perception, and Heaven and Hell.* New York: Harper and Row, 1956, 1963.

Huxley, Aldous. *The Perennial Philosophy.* New York: Harper and Row, Publishers, 1944, 1970.

Huyssen, Andreas. *After the Great Divide: Modernism, Mass Culture, Postmodernism.* Bloomington: Indiana University Press, 1986.

Jacoby, Russell. *The End of Utopia: Politics and Culture in an Age of Apathy.* New York: Basic Books, 1999.

Jameson, Frederic. *Postmodernism, or, The Cultural Logic of Late Capitalism.* Durham: Duke University Press, 1991.

Jameson, Fredric. "Postmodernism, or the Cultural Logic of Late Capitalism." *New Left Review* 146 (1984): 53–92.

Jamison, Andrew and Ron Eyerman. *Seeds of the Sixties.* Berkeley: University of California Press, 1994.

Joyce, James. *Finnegans Wake*. New York: Penguin Books, 1939, 1968.

Joyce, James. *Ulysses*. Hans Walter Gabler, ed. New York: Vintage Books, 1986.

Jazz Journal 18–20 (1965–1967).

Jazz and Pop 6–10 (1967–1971).

Jerome, Fred. *The Einstein File: J. Edgar Hoover's Secret War against the World's Most Famous Scientist*. New York: St. Martin's Press, 2002.

Jones, LeRoi. *Blues People: The Negro Experience in White America and the Music that developed from it*. New York: Morrow Quill Paperbacks, 1963.

Kahin, G.M. *The Asian-African Conference*. New York: Cornell University Press, 1956.

Kaiser, Charles. *1968 in America: Music, Politics, Chaos, Counterculture, and the Shaping of a Generation*. New York: Grove Press, 1988.

Kanter, Rosabeth Moss. *Commitment and Community: Communes and Utopias in Sociological Perspective*. Cambridge: Harvard University Press, 1972.

Kerouac, Jack. *On the Road*. London: Andre Duetsch, 1957.

Kesey, Ken. *One Flew Over the Cuckoo's Nest*. New York: Viking, 1962.

King, Richard. *The Party of Eros: Radical Social Thought and the Realm of Freedom*. Chapel Hill: The University of North Carolina Press, 1972.

Kofsky, Frank. *Black Nationalism and the Revolution in Music*. New York: Pathfinder Press, Inc., 1970.

Kostelanetz, Richard, ed. *The Frank Zappa Companion: Four Decades of Commentary*. New York: Schirmer Books, 1997.

Lachman, Gary Valentine. *A Secret History of Consciousness*. MA: Lindisfarne Books, 2003.

Lachman, Gary Valentine. *turn off your mind: The Mystic Sixties and the Dark Side of the Age of Aquarius*. London: Sidgwick and Jackson, 2001.

Laing, R. D. *The Politics of Experience and the Bird of Paradise*. London: Penguin Books, 1967.

Leary, Timothy. "Love, Leary, LSD." *LA Free Press*. Jan. 13, 1967.

Leary, Timothy, Ralph Metzner, and Richard Alpert. *The Psychedelic Experience*. New York: University Books, 1964.

Lee, Martin A. and Bruce Shlain. *Acid Dreams: The Complete Social History of LSD: The CIA, The Sixties, and Beyond*. NY: Grove Press, 1985.

Lemann, Nicholas. *The Promised Land: The Great Migration and how it changed America*. New York: Vintage Books, 1991.

Lemke, Gayle, ed. *Bill Graham Presents the Art of the Fillmore: The Poster Series 1966–1971*. New York: Thunder's Mouth Press, 1999.

Levy, Peter B., ed. *American in the Sixties. Right, Left, and Center: A Documentary History*. London: Praeger, 1998.

Lewisohn, Mark. *The Beatles Recording Sessions: The Official Abbey Road Studio Session Notes 1962–1970*. New York: Harmony Books, 1988.

Lipsitz, George. *American Studies in a Moment of Danger*. Minneapolis: University of Minnesota Press, 2001.

Lipsitz, George. *The Possessive Investment in Whiteness: How White People Profit From Identity Politics*. Philadelphia: Temple University Press, 1998.

Locke, Ralph P. "Constructing the Oriental 'Other': Saint-Saens's *Samson et Dalila*," *Cambridge Opera Journal* 3: 3 (1994): 261–302.

Los Angeles Free Press, 1967.

Lyotard, Jean-Francois. *The Postmodern Condition: A Report on Knowledge*. Trans. Geoff Bennington and Brian Massumi. Minneapolis: University of Minnesota Press, 1984.

Macan, Edward. *Rocking the Classics: English Progressive Rock and the Counterculture*. New York: Oxford University Press, 1997.

MacDonald, Ian. *Revolution in the Head: The Beatles' Records and the Sixties*. New York: Henry Holt and Company, 1994.

Macedo, Stephen, ed. *Reassessing the Sixties: Debating the Political and Cultural Legacy*. New York: W.W. Norton & Company, 1997.

Mailer, Norman. *The Armies of the Night: History as a Novel, The Novel as History*. New York: A Signet Book, 1968.

Mairson, Alan. "65760 Not Quite Utopia," *National Geographic Magazine* (August 2005): 114–18.

Manuel, Peter. "Andalusian, Gypsy, and Class Identity in the Contemporary Flamenco Complex," *Ethnomusicology* 33: 1 (Winter 1989): 47–65.

Maraniss, David. *They Marched Into Sunlight: War and Peace in Vietnam and America, October 1967*. New York: Simon and Schuster Paperbacks, 2003.

Marchand, Philip. *Marshall McLuhan: The Medium is the Messenger*. New York: Ticknor & Fields, 1989.

Marcus, Greil. *Invisible Republic: Bob Dylan's Basement Tapes*. New York: Henry Holt and Company, 1998.

Marcus, Greil. *Mystery Train: Images of America in Rock 'n' Roll Music*. Fourth Edition. New York: Plume Printing, 1997.

Marcuse, Herbert. *Eros and Civilization: A Philosophical Inquiry into Freud*. Boston: Beacon Press, 1955, 1966.

Marcuse, Herbert. *One-Dimensional Man: Studies in the Ideology of Advanced Industrial Society*. Boston: Beacon Press, 1964.

Marsh, Dave. *Fortunate Son: Criticism and Journalism by America's Best-Known Rock Writer*. New York: Random House, 1985.

May, Elaine Tyler. *Homeward Bound: American Families in the Cold War Era*. New York: Basic Books, Inc., Publishers, 1988.

McAdams, Frank. *The American War Film: History and Hollywood*. London: Praeger, 2002.

McClary, Susan. *Georges Bizet: Carmen*. Cambridge: Cambridge University Press, 1992.

McClary, Susan. *Feminine Endings: Music, Gender, and Sexuality*. Minnesota: University of Minnesota Press, 1991.

McCord, William. *Voyages to Utopia: From Monastery to Commune, The Search for the Perfect Society in Modern Times*. New York: W. W. Norton and Company, 1989.

McLuhan, Marshall and Quentin Fiore. *The Medium is the Message: An Inventory of Effects*. New York: Bantam Books, 1967.

McLuhan, Marshall and Quentin Fiore. *War and Peace in the Global Village*. New York: Bantam Books, 1968.

McRobbie, Angela. *Postmodernism and Popular Culture*. London: Routledge, 1992.

Menocal, Maria Rosa. *The Ornament of the World: How Muslims, Jews, and Christians Created a Culture of Tolerance in Medieval Spain*. Boston: Back Bay Books, 2002.

Mellers, Wilfrid. *Twilight of the Gods: The Beatles in Retrospect*. London: Faber & Faber, 1973.

Meyer, Carter Jones and Diana Roger, eds. *Selling the Indian: Commercializing and Appropriating American Indian Cultures*. Tuscon: University of Arizona Press, 2001.

Meyer, Leonard B. *Music, the Arts, and Ideas: Patterns and Predictions in Twentieth-Century Culture*. Chicago: The University of Chicago Press, 1967.

Middleton, Richard, ed. *Reading Pop: Approaches to Textual Analysis in Popular Music*. Oxford: Oxford University Press, 2000.

Middleton, Richard. *Studying Popular Music*. Philadelphia: Open University Press, 1990.

Miller, Henry. *The Tropic of Cancer*. New York: Signet, 1953, 1995.

Miller, James. *Flowers in the Dustbin: The Rise of Rock and Roll, 1947–1977*. New York: Simon & Schuster, 1999.

Miller, John. *Egotopia: Narcissism and the New American Landscape*. Tuscaloosa: The University of Alabama Press, 1997.

Moore, Allan. *The Beatles: Sgt. Pepper's Lonely Hearts Club Band*. Cambridge: Cambridge University Press, 1997.

More, Thomas. *Utopia*. Trans. Clarence H. Miller. New Haven, London: Yale Nota Bene, 2001.

Moretti, Franco. *Modern Epic: The World System from Goethe to Garcia Marquez*. London: Verso, 1996.

Moretti, Franco. *Signs Taken for Wonders: Essays in the Sociology of Literary Forms.* London: Verso, 1988, 1997.

Morris, Mitchell. "Ecotopian Sounds: or, the Music of John Luther Adams and Strong Environmentalism," in Per F. Broman, Nora A. Engerbretsen, and Bo Alphonce, eds. *Crosscurrents and Counterpoints: Offerings in Honor of Bengt Hambraeus at 70,* (Goteborg, 1998): 129–41.

Murray, Nicholas. *Aldous Huxley: A Biography.* New York: St. Martin's Press, 2002.

Musgrove, Frank. *Ecstasy and Holiness: counter culture and the open society.* London: Methuen and Co. Ltd., 1974.

Needleman, Jacob. *The New Religions: The Meaning of the Spiritual Revolution and the Teachings of the East.* New York: Doubleday, 1970.

Noebel, David A. *The Marxist Minstrels: A Handbook on Communist Subversion of Music.* Tulsa: American Christian College Press, 1974.

Oaks, Robert F. *San Francisco's Fillmore District (Images of America).* San Francisco: Arcadia Publishing, 2005.

Olalquiaga, Celeste. *The Artificial Kingdom: A Treasury of Kitsch Experience.* New York: Pantheon Books, 1998.

The Oracle of Southern California, 1967.

Pawlick, Thomas F. *The End of Food: How the Food Industry is Destroying Our Food Supply—And What We Can Do About It.* Fort Lee, NJ: Baracade Books, Inc., 2006.

Peck, Abe. *Uncovering the Sixties: The Life and Times of the Underground Press.* New York: Pantheon Books, 1985.

Pfeil, Fred. *Another Tale to Tell: Politics and Narrative in Postmodern Culture.* London: Verso, 1990.

Pincus-Witten, Robert. *Postminimalism into Maximalism: American Art, 1966–1986.* Ann Arbor, Michigan: UMI Research Press, 1987.

Platinga, Leon. "Review of Leonard Meyer's *Music, the Arts, and Ideas.*" *Journal of Music Theory* 13, no. 1 (Spring 1969): 141–47.

Pratt, Ray. *Rhythm and Resistance: Explorations in the Political Uses of Popular Music.* New York: Praeger, 1990.

Prown, Jules David and Kenneth Haltman, eds. *American Artifacts: Essays in Material Culture.* East Lansing: Michigan State University Press, 2000.

Pynchon, Thomas. *The Crying of Lot 49.* New York: Lippincott, 1966.

Radano, Ronald and Philip V. Bohlman, eds. *Music and the Racial Imagination.* Chicago and London: The University of Chicago Press, 2000.

Rocco, John, ed. *Dead Reckonings: The Life and Times of the Grateful Dead.* New York: Schirmer Books, 1999.

Rockin' at the Red Dog: The Dawn of Psychedelic Rock. A Mary Works Production. DVD. Monterey Video, 2005.

Rossinow, Doug. *The Politics of Authenticity: Liberalism, Christianity, and the New Left*. New York: Columbia University Press, 1998.

Roszak, Theodore. *America the Wise: Longevity and the Culture of Compassion*. Boston: Houghton Mifflin, 1998.

Roszak, Theodore. *The Making of a Counter Culture: Reflections on the Technocratic Society and Its Youthful Opposition*. New York: Anchor Books, 1969.

Said, Edward. *Culture and Imperialism*. New York: Knopf, 1994.

Said, Edward. *Orientalism*. New York: Vintage Books, 1979.

Sales, Grover. *Jazz: America's Classical Music*. New York: Prentice Hall Press, 1984.

Selvin, Joel. *Monterey Pop: June 16–18, 1967*. San Francisco: Chronicle Books, 1992.

Selvin, Joel. *The Musical History Tour: A Guide to over 200 of the Bay Area's Most Memorable Music Sites*. San Francisco: Chronicle Books, 1996.

Selvin, Joel. *Summer of Love: The Inside Story of LSD, Rock & Roll, Free Love and High Times in the Wild West*. New York: Cooper Square Press, 1999.

Shankar, Ravi. *My Music, My Life*. New York: Simon and Schuster, 1968.

Shapiro, Harry. *Waiting for the Man: The Story of Drugs and Popular Music*. London: Quartet Books, 1988.

Sheehan, Neil. *A Bright Shining Lie: John Paul Vann and America in Vietnam*. New York: First Vintage Books Edition, 1989.

Shepard, Paul. *Man in the Landscape: A Historic View of the Esthetics of Nature*. Austin: Texas A & M University Press, 1967, 1991.

Sidran, Ben. *Black Talk*. New York: Holt, Rinehart and Winston, 1971.

Slick, Grace with Andrea Cagan. *Somebody to Love: A Rock and Roll Memoir*. NY: Warner Books, 1998.

Solie, Ruth A., ed. *Musicology and Difference: Gender and Sexuality in Music Scholarship*. Berkeley: University of California Press, 1993.

Sontag, Susan. *Against Interpretation*. New York: Farrar, Straus, and Giroux, 1966.

Spivak, Chakravorty. *A Critique of Postcolonial Reason: Toward a History of the Vanishing Present*. Cambridge: Harvard University Press, 1999.

Stanley, Ray. *The Hippie Cult Murders*. New York: A MacFadden-Bartell Book, 1970.

Steigerwald, David. *The Sixties and the End of Modern America*. New York: St. Martin's Press, 1995.

Stephens, Julie. *Anti-disciplinary protest: sixties radicalism and postmodernism.* Cambridge: Cambridge University Press, 1998.

Stine, Peter, ed. *The Sixties.* Detroit: Wayne State University Press, 1988.

Szatmary, David P. *Rockin' in Time: A Social History of Rock-and-Roll,* Fourth Edition. New Jersey: Prentice Hall, 2000.

Tang, Truong Nhu. *A Viet Cong Memoir: An Inside Account of the Vietnam War and Its Aftermath.* New York: First Vintage Books Edition, 1986.

Taylor, Eugene. *Shadow Culture: Psychology and Spirituality in America.* Washington D. C.: Counterpoint, 1999.

Terry, Maury. *The Ultimate Evil: An Investigation into America's Most Dangerous Satanic Cult.* Garden City, NY: A Dolphin Book, 1987.

Thompson, Hunter S. *Fear and Loathing in Las Vegas: A Savage Journey to the Heart of the American Dream.* New York: Popular Library, 1971.

Thompson, Hunter S. *The Hell's Angels: A Strange and Terrible Saga.* New York: Random House, 1967.

Thurman, Robert. *Inner Revolution: Life, Liberty, and the Pursuit of Real Happiness.* New York: Riverhead Books, 1998.

Tolkien, J.R.R. *Lord of the Rings.* New York: Houghton Mifflin Company, 1965, 1994.

Treitler, Leo. "On Historical Criticism." *Musical Quarterly* LIII, no. 2 (April 1967): 188–205.

Treitler, Leo. "The Present as History." *Perspectives of New Music* 7, no. 2 (Spring–Summer 1969): 1–58.

Unger, Debi and Irwin Unger. *The Times were a Changin': a sixties reader.* New York: Three Rivers Press, 1998.

Vonnegut, Kurt, Jr. *Slaughterhouse Five.* New York: Delacorte, 1969.

Walser, Robert. "Deep Jazz: Notes on Interiority, Race, and Criticism," in Joel Pfister and Nancy Schnog, eds., *Inventing the Psychological: Toward a Cultural History of Emotional Life in America.* New Haven: Yale University Press, 1997.

Walser, Robert. *Running with the Devil: Power, Gender, and Madness in Heavy Metal Music.* Hanover, London: Wesleyan University Press, 1993.

Ward, Brian. *Just my soul responding: Rhythm and Blues, black consciousness and race relations.* London: UCL Press, 1998.

Watts, Alan. *The Spirit of Zen.* London: John Murray, 1958.

Watts, Alan. *Psychotherapy East & West.* New York: Vintage Books, 1961, 1975.

Waxman, Steve. *Instruments of Desire: The Electric Guitar and the Shaping of Musical Experience.* Cambridge: Harvard University Press, 1999.

West, Elmer S., Jr., ed. *Extremism Left and Right*. Grand Rapids, MI: William B. Eerdmans Publishing Company, 1972.

Whiteley, Sheila. *The Space Between the Notes: Rock and the Counter-culture*. London: Routledge, 1992.

Whiteley, Sheila. *Women and Popular Music: Sexuality, Identity and Subjectivity*. New York: Routledge, 2000.

Williams, Raymond. *Keywords: A vocabulary of culture and society*. New York: Oxford University Press, 1985.

Wolfe, Tom. *The Electric Kool-Aid Acid Test*. New York: Bantam Books, 1968.

The World of Music 12:2 (1970).

Zappa, Frank. *The Real Frank Zappa Book*. New York: Poseidon Press, 1989.

Zinn, Howard. *The Twentieth Century: A People's History*. New York: Harper's Perennial, 1998.

Zinn, Howard. *The Zinn Reader: Writings on Disobedience and Democracy*. New York: Seven Stories Press, 1997.

Acknowledgments

Grateful acknowledgment to Ida Griffin for permission to include a reprint of the 1967 "Human Be-In" poster by her late husband, poster artist Rick Griffin; to Ashleigh Brilliant for permission to reprint the lyrics of his song, "How Delinquent Can You Be?" as well as the first verse and chorus of his song "The Intercourse Song"; and to Lisa Law for permission to use one of her black and white photographs of the Human Be-In on the cover and in the frontispiece of this book.

I have received a wealth of input and help from mentors, academic colleagues, students, and editors during the writing process. The devoted members of staff at the University of California Los Angeles music library, University of California Santa Barbara music library, and the University of California Berkeley Bancroft Archive Library helped me access much of the information incorporated into this book. My serious investigation of sixties culture began during graduate studies at UCLA. My professors there provided outstanding guidance—including Susan McClary, Robert Walser, Mitchell Morris, Tamara Levitz, Ian Krouse, and Robert Fink. Warm thanks go especially to Robert Fink, a talented and inspiring advisor who has continued to be a mentor on this project. Bob's influence is present throughout the book, not in the mistakes (which are all mine), but echoing in the historical and cultural analysis. English and Women's Studies Professor Alice Echols, now at the University of Southern California, and Frederick Crews, professor emeritus of English at University of California Berkeley, both took time to read parts of the book manuscript during the writing process. Their expertise is appreciated. Interaction and exchange with my students over the past few years, especially in the sixties courses at Antioch University Los Angeles, helped immeasurably—and continues to provide fertile ground for investigation—in analyzing and refining ideas that are explored in this book. At the University of Michigan Press, it has been my luck to have worked with a group of sharp editors and assistants as well as to have received useful and thorough suggestions from two anonymous readers. Many thanks to Marcia LaBrenz, Christy Byks-Jazayeri, and, particularly, to Chris Hebert, for taking on my proposal and manuscript and working through the revisions with his keen sense of wording and language.

During this process, I have repeatedly benefited from the insights of my dear friend and colleague, Professor Maiko Kawabata. Several members of my family have endured, and hopefully enjoyed, the stages of transforming this project into a book. Thanks to my cousin, Professor Jon Zimmerman, for always being available with advice. To my father, Seth, for his ongoing encouragement to persist. He models in every way what it can be to make an effort. To my husband Mathew, for accompanying me on this journey, providing unconditional support, much needed laughter, and thoughtful exchange. To our baby boy Kairo, for helping me hear the Grateful Dead in a new way. And finally to my mother, Louise, who balances intelligence, humor, emotional strength, and serious reflection with grace and refinement. An extraordinary editor, she has been a sounding board for so many of the ideas explored in this book, reading through the manuscript dozens of times over the years and shepherding it through transformations and revisions to reach its present state.

Index

biographical information on, 14–15, 135
and countercultural sensibility, 130, 134, 160, 172
at Houseboat Summit, 11–12, 124–26, 145
and LSD, 14–15, 119, 134–36, 138
"tune in, turn on, drop out," 7, 124, 145, 153, 171
Love (band), 68–69
Love Pageant Rally, 59, 157

Maharishi Mahesh Yogi, 161, 194n63, 205n9
Malcolm X, 22, 31
Mamas and the Papas, 161, 168
Manson, Charles, 21, 157, 173, 189n20, 205n12
biographical information on, 158–63, 204n6, 204–5n9
and distortion of countercultural sensibility, 168–70, 174, 205n12
Marcus, Greil, 35–36
Marcuse, Herbert, 21, 130–32
Eros and Civilization, 131
Marin, city and county of, 28, 122–23
Grateful Dead in, 57, 113, 122
Houseboat Summit in, 124
Marsh, Dave, 36, 191n39
Masculine, 41, 112, 147, 150
and utilitarian association, 109, 111–12
McLuhan, Marshall, 49–50, 143
Medieval (Medievalism), 104–5
Miller, Henry, 21, 132–33
Monterey Pop Festival (1967), 15–16, 42, 57, 98, 100–101, 157, 160, 162, 167
Motown, 41–42, 59, 156

Native American, 24, 58, 100, 199n37
on Be-In poster, 7–10
New Age, 15, 132, 158, 200n15
New Left, 31, 50, 76, 89, 130, 164
and women, 149–50
Newton, Huey, 30–33. *See also* Black Panthers

Oracle, The, 11, 109, 124, 129–30, 134–35, 167, 197n21. *See also* Cohen, Allen
Orientalism, 61, 73–74, 87
Owsley, Augustus III, 15, 184n38, 200n7

Paul Butterfield Blues Band, 37, 39–40, 78, 96
Perls, Fritz, 131–32, 200n14
Poland, Jefferson. *See* Sexual Freedom League
Political protest, 1, 6, 11, 12, 29, 31, 36, 150
against Vietnam War, 76, 78–79, 187n6, 193n50
Psychedelic Shop, the, 130, 137, 166–67, 200n7

Quicksilver Messenger Service, 15, 24, 39

Racism, 28, 34, 54, 164–65
Radicals, 2, 31, 54, 76, 79, 99, 187n6
Feminists, 150
1930s Left, 107–8, 196n17
Radio, AM and FM, 41, 55, 59, 66–67, 79–80, 102–3, 114, 188n13
KMPX and Tom Donahue, 59, 81
KPFA, 77
Redding, Otis, 27, 29, 42–44, 156

Watts, Alan, 11–12, 124–25, 130, 133, 134, 171. *See also* Buddhism
Who, The, 16, 41
Williams, Raymond, 94
Women, 140–42, 147–51. *See also* Blues queens; Feminine; Joplin, Janis; Slick, Grace
  and double standard, 140, 149, 151
  in *Fear and Loathing in Las Vegas*, 148, 165
  and girl groups, 41
  nature, as symbol of, 109–12
  as sexual objects, 128, 139–40, 148–49, 171
Women's Rights Movement, 150, 178n5
Woodstock Festival, 157, 162

Zappa, Frank, 205n24

Text design by Mary H. Sexton
Typesetting by Delmastype, Ann Arbor, Michigan

Text font: Stone Serif
In 1987, Sumner Stone completed his designs for the
Stone type family, which consists of three subfamilies,
Serif, Sans, and Informal. ITC Stone Serif is a modern
look at "transitional" fonts—a nod to those which, in the
evolution of type design, occupy an intermediate position
between old style and modern.
—courtesy www.adobe.com

Display font: Franklin Gothic Condensed
One of the most popular sans serif types ever produced,
Franklin Gothic was designed by Morris Fuller Benton in
1902 for American Type Founders. In 1991, David Berlow
completed the family for ITC by creating compressed and
condensed weights.
—courtesy www.adobe.com